The Segregation Era, 1863–1954

The Segregation Era
1863-1954

• A MODERN READER

EDITED BY

ALLEN WEINSTEIN AND FRANK OTTO GATELL

NEW YORK

OXFORD UNIVERSITY PRESS

LONDON 1970 TORONTO

Table of Contents

v

Introduction

"The first war was 'bout freedom and the war right after it was equalization." So spoke an aged Negro, reminiscing during the 1930's for folklorist B. A. Botkin about slavery, the Civil War, and its brief Reconstruction aftermath. Even as the centennial decade of the first war drifts into history, the second war continues, stark and unabated. A new phase of the conflict began with the Civil Rights and Black Revolution upheavals of the previous decade and a half.

For close to a century, the American Negro combatants in the struggle for "equalization" remained largely on the defensive, protecting their lives and their culture and a small ragbag of political and economic gains against the fire of white hostility and the ice of white indifference. This first, post-slavery phase, which we call "the segregation era," began crumbling in 1954, when the Supreme Court struck down the legal underpinnings of segregation in public schools (and elsewhere) in the *Brown* vs. *Board of Education* decision. Although the foundations of black militancy, both peaceful and violent, are integral parts of the Negro's past, the action of the Supreme Court in 1954 and subsequent decisions invalidating many other patterns of *legalized* segregation in the United States prepared the ground for the massive frontal assault upon racism that remains the primary fact of our national existence today and the leading challenge to its preservation.

The task of translating emancipation into the judicial beginnings of equality took nine decades, ninety years of Negro striving and suffering. The full history of this black Odyssey remains to be written, but in the telling it should be remembered, in James Baldwin's words, that "the oppressed and the oppressor are bound together within the same society; they accept the same criteria, they share the same beliefs, they both alike depend on the same reality."

No simple nor single interpretative overview can speak for the varied and tangled richness of the black experience from the Civil War to the post-World II Black Revolution. The different strands of this history came together at many points, Reconstruction for example, yet at other times they clashed dramatically, as when W.E.B. Du Bois battled Booker T. Washington for leadership of their neglected people. In addition to chronicling and analyzing these and other arresting episodes, historians have also treated the equally important and persistent dilemmas faced at every point in their lives by ordinary black men and women over the last hundred years.

The cultivation and the nurture of black history in America has not been the preserve of any one group of scholars. Its current flowering resulted from the pioneering and preserving efforts of many writers, black and white. Among the former, especially those laboring during the unrewarding but vital "lean years," were Carter G. Woodson, founder of the *Journal of Negro History*, A. A. Taylor, pioneer Reconstruction revisionist, Horace M. Bond, E. Franklin Frazier, a sociologist, and the historian-sociologist-genius W. E. B. Du Bois; and, in a more recent generation, such men as John Hope Franklin and Rayford W. Logan. These scholars, and numerous other black historians, labored in the past often without sympathy or recognition from many of their white colleagues. Their achievements take on more significance because of that fact, but none of them sought the questionable role of oracle.

Within the scholarly community, though on the other side of the color line, can be found such outstanding white historians of black history as C. Vann Woodward, August Meier, Kenneth Stampp, James McPherson, Stanley Elkins, Herbert Aptheker, Philip Foner, the anthropologist Melville Herskovitz, and the Swedish economist Gunnar Myrdal. Their work, in conjunction with the work of the black authors cited above, has provided the indispensable foundation for the rise of an intellectually viable and culturally stimulating black history. As the impact of the Black Studies movement on the teaching and writing of American history makes itself increasingly felt, and as black students and historians explore their historical roots professionally, they will find that many men of good will and sharp mind have trod before them in an area that most of academia hardly knew existed.

Why study black history? For blacks the answer is self-evident, but what aboue the nine out of ten white Americans? C. Vann Woodward of Yale University has observed that "American history, the white man's version, could profit from an infusion of Soul," and he adds that "now is a time to do honor to heroes [in Black history]." Woodward, perhaps more than any other white historian, has practiced his preachings admirably. Yet at the same time he warns against the danger of a narrow ethocentrism in black history: "the historian will keep in mind that the stage of history was never peopled exclusively by heroes, villains and oppressed innocents, that scamps and time-servers and antiheroes have always played their parts" among all groups. Recognizing this obvious truth reminds us of the need to study adequately both the Negro's experience as a black man and his experience as an American. In other words, black history deals with the Negro's relation to the broader national experience as well as his inner ethnic group history.

The essays that follow represent a sampling of the most important historical treatments of the post-emancipation black experience. They examine the major problems faced by American Negroes since the Civil War and describe some of their major lines of response. One controlling aspect is that posed by the dilemma of agricultural peonage and the resulting black migration into the cities, where even harsher varieties of economic and social deprivation awaited a rapidly growing Negro proletariat. Also, the efforts of black men to maintain and extend their tenuous possession of voting rights find expression in these pages along with the violent reactions of whites over the past century to any sustained form of black assertiveness. Contradictions between American ideals of equality and the realities of race subordination and Negrophobia are portrayed graphically in selections on lynching, race riots, and the implementation of the caste system. These factors made it inevitable that in the fact of political exclusion and social stigmatization American blacks would fall back primarily upon their own resources, upon their own cultural achievements and possibilities, in order to avoid going insane, collectively, in a hostile, white world they had never made.

The quest for inner strength, though but partially successful, nevertheless provided a bridge for the next stages of black history, the renewal of the search by black Americans for real freedom. The latter is the obvious common theme running through all the essays presented here, the unifying element which has persisted through time, through persecution and accommodation, through pride and protest, from the "Segregation Era" described in this volume into the Black Revolution of our own day.

I: THE CIVIL WAR AND THE BLACKS,
1863–1865

The Fight for Freedom

• The mythology of American slavery included the widely held proposition that black men did not wish to be free. The apparent "docility" of many slaves, their numerous adaptations to the coercive realities of bondage, and the wishful thinking of their masters all conspired to nurture this myth. The Civil War experience undermined fatally the belief in innate black docility, but new understanding came neither quickly nor easily for most whites. The Negro had to struggle first for the right to fight. Those who joined the battle, the many thousands of ex-slaves and the smaller number of pre-war free Negroes, continued to shoulder the burden of white race prejudice. Discrimination, as the following selection by Benjamin Quarles shows, dogged the Negro soldier's every step. Accepted finally as part of the Union Army after the Emancipation Proclamation, his rewards included lower pay, inferior equipment, and official pussyfooting over his status. Incredibly, under these circumstances, the black regiments somehow maintained high morale and eventually proved themselves in battle.

"Do you think I'll make a soldier?" is the opening line of a popular Negro spiritual. The singer who voices the inquiry has no doubt that he'll make a soldier; he only raises the question as to whether his listener thinks so too. The nearly 180,000 blacks who donned the Union blue had no misgivings about their ability to make efficient soldiers. "What are you, anyhow?" was the question asked in an insulting tone to one of Colonel Thomas W. Higginson's men. The soldier drew himself erect, "When God made me, I wasn't much, but I's a man now."

The Negro who joined the army was not likely to "crack up," even though he faced problems not met by the white soldier. The

From Benjamin Quarles, *The Negro in the Civil War* (Boston: Little, Brown and Company, 1953), pp. 199–213, 215–20. New York: Russell & Russell, 1968. Reprinted by permission.

3

Negro recruit had steeled himself from the beginning to meet these difficulties, even though many of them were not inconsiderable. Perhaps it did not matter much if his regiment was listed under "United States Colored Troops" by an order from the Adjutant General's office dated March 11, 1864, which stated that thenceforth all black regiments be designated by numbers and include the word "colored." Perhaps it did not matter much if the War Department, with Lincoln's approval, issued on March 9, 1863, a "United States Infantry Tactics for the Use of Colored Troops."

A much sorer spot, however, was the matter of pay. Negroes in the army received $10 a month, of which $3 was paid in clothing; white soldiers received $13, plus clothing—a difference of $6 a month. The pay of the Negro was based on a decision of the solicitor of the War Department, William Whiting, who on June 4, 1863, ruled that Negro soldiers were to be paid under the provisions of the Militia Act of July 17, 1862, which stipulated that persons of African descent could be used for military service, for which they would be entitled to $10 a month, $3 of which might be in clothing. This act did not have in mind Negroes actually bearing arms, and it referred only to those Negroes who had recently been freed from bondage. Nonetheless until Congress acted, Negro soldiers were to be paid, said Whiting, as military laborers, under the act of July 17, 1862.

John A. Andrew, governor of Massachusetts, was greatly troubled over the solicitor's ruling since he had promised the men of the Fifty-fourth and Fifty-fifth equality in every respect with the other state regiments. Andrew hastened to Washington and talked to Lincoln, Stanton, Secretary of the Treasury Chase and Secretary of State Seward. He urged the President to get an opinion from the attorney general. Lincoln did so. Supporting Andrew, Bate's reply stated that the $10 a month pay was meant solely for those Negroes who had been slaves.

Lincoln did nothing—elections were approaching. Stanton moved slowly too, doubtless because he feared that equal pay might interfere with the recruitment of white soldiers. When asked by John Mercer Langston what was the duty of colored men in view of the lower wage, Stanton took refuge in the clouds:

> The duty of the colored man is to defend his country, whenever, wherever and in whatever form, is the same with that of the white men. It does not depend on, nor is it affected by, what the country pays. The true way to secure her rewards and win her confidence is not to stipulate for them, but to deserve them.

Disappointed over his failure at Washington, Andrew returned to the state house and sent a recommendation to the legislature that corrective action be taken. In quick response the Massachusetts lawmakers passed an act on November 16 to make up the deficiencies in the monthly pay of the Fifty-fourth and Fifty-fifth. Andrew then mailed to the two regiments duplicates of his address to the legislature and copies of the legislative enactment equalizing pay.

A week later the governor received an answer from the Fifty-fourth declining to accept any money from Massachusetts. Notwithstanding the generous action of the legislature, wrote Colonel Hallowell, the men of the Fifty-fourth wanted it known that they had enlisted as other soldiers from the state, and that they would rather continue to serve without pay until their enlistments ran out, rather than accept from the national government less than the amount paid to other soldiers.

This stand did not come as a complete surprise. Three times previously had the Fifty-fourth been mustered in for pay; three times had they declined, refusing the money until they could get justice with it. And while they were appreciative of the deficiency enactment of the state legislature, they were not willing, as Theodore Tilton put it, "that the Federal Government should throw mud upon them, even though Massachusetts stands ready to wipe it off."

The action of the Fifty-fourth in refusing to accept less than a soldier's pay stirred the country. In the halls of Congress the hot debates flared up anew after February 2, 1864, when Senator Wilson of Massachusetts introduced a joint resolution to equalize pay. After endless argument, Congress passed an act on June 15, 1864, which provided retroactively that as of January 1, 1864, colored soldiers were to receive the same uniform, clothing, arms, equipments, camp equipage, rations, medical and hospital attendance, pay, and emoluments, other than bounty, as other soldiers. . . ." The law further provided that if the Negro soldier had been free on April 19, 1861, he would be paid the difference, from the time of his enlistment to January 1, 1864, between what he had received and the full pay allowed by law during the same period to white soldiers.

Most Negro soldiers who had enlisted prior to January 1, 1864, found it easy to qualify for this back pay since "the fact of freedom is to be determined by the statement of the soldier, under oath," as ordered by the War Department in a communication on August 1, 1864, to all officers commanding Negro troops. Officers were not required to go behind the oaths, and few ex-slave soldiers would have any compunctions in swearing that they "owed no man unrequited labor on or before the 19th day of April, 1861."

The Massachusetts regiments had a red-letter day when Paymaster Lockwood arrived at Folly Island in late September. It required $170,000 to pay the Fifty-fourth for its eighteen months of unsalaried service. The pay average was about $200 per volunteer. The men were overjoyed. "Songs burst out everywhere," wrote Captain Emilio. "The fiddle and other music long neglected enlivens the tents night and day."

The Fifty-fifth likewise had a gala celebration upon receiving the arrears in pay. "The boys are in great glee," wrote bronzed and bearded Sergeant James Ruffin of Company F to his sister-in-law, Josephine Ruffin. "We had a glorious celebration, there was a procession, then a mass meeting when speeches of various gentlemen were made, and readings of resolutions to be published in the papers. In the evening we had a Grand Supper. All passed off very creditable." The soldiers paid off all their loans to the officers and their indebtedness to the sutlers, wrote Burt G. Wilder, an officer in the Fifty-fifth, and sent home over $60,000 by Adams Express. . . .

Another hazard run by the Negro volunteer was that of inferior arms and equipment. The ordnance department often sent materials that were either obsolete or faultily constructed—bayonets, for example, that did not fit muskets. Brigadier General Ullman expressed his distress, in a letter to Henry Wilson early in December 1863, at having to send his Negro soldiers into battle with "arms almost entirely unserviceable." Lorenzo Thomas, after an inspection of the eight companies of a colored regiment stationed on Ship Island, Mississippi, advised Stanton on April 7, 1864, that the men be furnished with Springfield muskets:

> This Regiment, like most of this class of soldiers, have the old flintlock muskets, altered to percussion, which have been in use for a long time. The muskets of this Regiment were condemned once, and have been condemned by an Inspector a second time.

Negro regiments also faced the performing of an excessive amount of fatigue duty. Aside from the seven colored regiments which were specifically organized for assignment on labor details, Negro troops were usually given garrison duty rather than field service. The garrisoning of forts and arsenals, month in and month out, became dull, monotonous and demoralizing. A Negro soldier might become dispirited, feeling that he was being singled out as a common laborer to perform such tasks as building bridges, draining marshes, filling sand-bags, unloading vessels, throwing up entrenchments and drawing can-non to the front and mounting them. The War Department, perhaps unwittingly, strengthened this attitude that fatigue duty was the natural lot of the black enlisted man by issuing in April 1863 Special Order No. 13, addressed to the commanders of Negro troops in the Valley of the Mississippi:

> One of the duties to be required of Regiments of African descent, will be to secure abandoned Cotton, and have it conveyed to the Levee for shipment to the Quartermaster at Memphis, Tennessee.

Greatest of the grievances of the black volunteer was the dread of the fate that might be his if he fell into the hands of the enemy. A Negro in martial regalia "offended the Southern view of 'the eternal fitness of things.' " Hence Confederate military and civilian officials never referred to blacks in blue as soldiers—they were designated "slaves in arms," or "slaves in armed rebellion." This was a natural attitude for a slaveholding society. As a Virginia daily explained: "The very foundation of slavery would be fatally wounded if we were insane enough to treat black men as the equal of white, and insurgent slaves as equivalent to our brave white soldiers."

On the last day in April 1863, the Confederate Congress, in line with a proclamation made by President Davis four months previously and in accordance with his subsequent recommendations, passed a law decreeing that Negroes who were "taken in arms against the Confeder-ate States," or who gave aid and comfort to its enemies, should be captured in the South be dealt with according to the laws of the state in which they were seized. This punishment was the equivalent of a death sentence since the law in every one of the seceded states would have branded such Negroes as incendiaries and insurrection-ists.

Disliking an-eye-for-an-eye policy, Lincoln at first had thought of limiting the employment of Negro military laborers to places suffi-ciently removed from the war fronts as to prevent their being cap-tured. In early January he discussed such a course with Secretaries Stanton and Welles.

But increasingly public opinion in the North cried out for repay-ment in kind. "They have proposed in Richmond to sell our cooks &c into slavery," wired Assistant Secretary of the Navy G. V. Fox to Admiral S. F. Du Pont. "If they do, I think we can retaliate." Bowing to the storm, Lincoln issued an order on July 30, 1863, that for every Union soldier killed in violation of the laws of war, a Rebel soldier would be put to death, and that for every Union soldier enslaved or sold into slavery, a Rebel soldier would be placed at hard labor on the public works.

As the war progressed and the number of Negro regiments multiplied, the South modified its stated policy as to captured blacks. Not many were sold into slavery—that practice was rare. In a few instances Negroes were killed rather than captured, notably at Fort Pillow, on the east bank of the Mississippi, some forty miles above Memphis, where on April 12, 1864, a Rebel force swept into the garrison, and of the 262 Negro soldiers stationed there, 229 were killed, wounded in escape or buried alive. Major General Nathan Bedford Forrest, the able and ruthless Confederate commander, was not squeamish about bloodletting: "War means fighting, and fighting means killing", was a favorite maxim of his. Doubtless, too, there were instances in which Negro troops were slain after they were captured. "I hope I may never see a Negro Soldier," wrote a Mississippi boy to his mother, "or I cannot be a Christian Soldier."

The South consistently contended that slaves captured in arms should be returned to their masters, but in actual practice, Negro soldiers, ex-slave and freeborn, although not formally regarded as prisoners of war, were treated about as humanely as white prisoners. Perhaps Negro captives were discriminated against as to daily rations, shelter and prison duties, but there was no such officially stated policy. If captured Negroes were sometimes put to work building Rebel fortifications, this circumstance was not wholly disadvantageous. Such prisoner-laborers would be reasonably sure of getting enough to eat, and would not be penned up in such a notorious prison slaughterhouse as Andersonville where the death rate of Union soldiers averaged eight and one half per hour. . . .

The colored volunteer was aware of the hardships that he faced by virtue of having a black skin, but these discouragements did not prevent him from striving to become a good soldier. Fortunately the caliber of officers in Negro regiments was on the whole conducive to making a soldier. A regiment that was well trained and disciplined and whose morale was good was one in which the officers had gained the confidence of the men in the ranks and won their devotion.

The commissioned officers in Negro units were almost always white men—fewer than one hundred Negroes were commissioned during the war—and this scarcity of black officers was vigorously condemned by colored spokesmen, especially since those who led troops into battle did well under fire. But the whites who commanded Negro regiments were, as a group, officers of above average character and efficiency. True, there were white officers like the coarse and brutal Lieutenant Colonel Augustus Benedict who had to be reduced from an officer after horsewhipping two members of a regimental band, the Fourth Regiment Corps d'Afrique, at Fort Jackson, Louisiana, on December 8, 1863, and thereby precipitating a camp mutiny in which 125 soldiers fired their guns off. But although Negro troops had to suffer their share of officers with a sadistic love of cruelty, an Augustus Benedict was the exception rather than the rule. . . .

In order to screen the officer candidates, the Bureau established in May 1863 a Board of Examiners for the Command of Colored Troops. With Brigadier General Silas Casey as permanent president, the Board of Examiners was made up of two colonels, one lieutenant colonel, one surgeon and one lieutenant, the last-named being a recorder or secretary. Before giving the candidate a written examination, the board first assured itself that he was loyal to the Union, had a good moral character and was physically sound. If a candidate met these tests he was given an examination in infantry tactics, army regulations and "capacity to command." A successful applicant was recommended to the War Department for a commission according to his merits. In the two years of its existence the board examined approximately 3000 candidates, 1700 of whom they recommended for commissions from colonel down to second lieutenant. . . .

Good officers helped in making good soldiers, but the greatest asset of the Negro volunteer was his own spirit and outlook. He was prepared to keep his chin up despite the enemy on the battle front and a skeptical public opinion on the home front. His morale was up because he had convincing reasons for enlisting. He felt that he was striking a body blow at slavery: H. Ford Douglass who prior to the organizing of colored regiments, managed to join a white unit, the Ninety-fifth Regiment of Illinois Volunteers, was anxious to serve so that, as he phrased it, he might "be better prepared to play his part in the great drama of the Negro's redemption." The black soldier felt that he had a personal stake in the war: "I in dis army still, Cunnel," doggedly said Abram Fuller of the First South Carolina Volunteers, as he was handed his discharge papers for physical disability on November 21, 1863. "To save the country from ruin," was the announced reason that induced the enlistment of Christian A. Fleetwood, Sergeant Major of the Fourth United States Colored Troops, and one of the fourteen Negro recipients of the Congressional Medal for heroic conduct on the field of battle.

Many of the Negro volunteers were able to adjust easily to army life because they had been military laborers. As teamsters, cooks and servants, they had been in the front lines of the armies of both the blue and the gray. Hence they were not raw recruits; they knew what to expect. It was unlikely that they would ever join the ranks of the deserters.

The army, moreover, had something to offer many Negroes, especially former slaves. The black volunteer was often better fed and clothed than ever before in his life, and hence he spent little time in "griping" over camp inconveniences and discomforts; he did not say much if the shoddy clothing turned to rags, if the soles fell off his shoes, if the rations were delayed and if the gritty hardtack required soaking in boiling coffee until it became malleable enought to fry in pork grease.

The white soldier not engaged in combat tended to become restless and fidgety under the monotonous daily routine, doing the same thing over day after day from morning gun at sunrise until taps at ten-thirty. But the one-time slave had come from an even more simple and monotonous plantation round. Hence he was exhilarated by army life with its din and bustle—its marchings and countermarchings, its blowing of bugles, beating of drums and playing of fifes. Negro volunteers other than those in fatigue regiments had little incentive to count the number of days to the end of enlistment. . . .

The Negro recruits were likely to have good morale because they took pride in being elevated to the rank of soldier. Hence, they kept their campgrounds neat and clean; spit-and-polish staff officers making inspection delighted in the orderly appearance of the barracks, and in the punctilious pains of the black recruits to do the militarily correct thing. For dress parade, Negro soldiers reported with arms burnished, belts polished, shoes blacked and clothes bushed. . . .

And, finally, because the Negro recruit believed in the Union cause and felt proud of his trust in wearing the blue, he was thoroughly loyal. He felt no inclination to be traitorous, to "go over" to the enemy, or even to listen to the defeatist talk of malcontents. On guard duty he never betrayed a countersign, if an exception could be made of that overzealous sentinel who challenged a party with the words: "Who comes dar? Halt, an' gib de countersign, *Charleston.*"

By his motivation and by his aptitude for soldiering the Negro volunteer was ready for the trial by battle—ready, as he soon proved, to pay "the last full measure of devotion." . . .

Port Hudson in the spring of 1863 was the last remaining Rebel fortification on the Lower Mississippi. The river above and below was controlled by Union gunboats, but unconquered Port Hudson still stood to point a threatening, death-charged finger at any Yankee vessel that ran by its batteries, day or night. If Port Hudson fell, Vicksburg, two hundred miles up the river, would fall, thus "redeeming" the Mississippi and cutting the Confederacy in two. General N. P. Banks, commanding in the Department of the Gulf, was ordered to reduce Port Hudson in co-operation with General Grant's operations against Vicksburg.

Assaulting Port Hudson was no holiday task. Built by slave labor, that formidable work presented a strong profile along its entire length of line stretching over three miles. Its face to the Mississippi River was an eighty foot bluff. Its semicircle of abatis—felled trees with the branches sharpened and turned toward the enemy—was buttressed by a series of rifle pits and outworks. Its parapets averaged twenty feet in thickness, and below the parapets was a fifteen-foot ditch. The Port mounted twenty siege guns and thirty pieces of field artillery, and its rear grounds afforded first-rate facilities for the prompt shifting of troops from one point to another. On May 25 the Confederates retired into this stronghold, having been compelled to contract their outer lines. The time had come.

On the early morning of May 27, the air already sultry and the heat oppressive, the Union artillery opened up a brisk cannonade against Port Hudson, preparatory to the assault. "About half an hour by the sun this morning," reported Rebel officer, W. R. Miller, "the enemy opened up an infernal fire on our lines." The Union strategy was to subject the stronghold to four hours of bombardment and then to rush in simultaneously all along the line.

On the extreme right facing two forts, Banks had placed the Native Guards. Numbering 1080, they formed into four lines. At ten o'clock the bugle sounded, followed by the sharp command, "Charge!" The response of the troops was described by the well-known contemporary poet, George H. Boker:

> "Now," the flag-sergeant cried,
> "Though death and hell betide,
> Let the whole nation see
> If we are fit to be
> Free in this land; or bound

Down, like the whining hound—
Bound with red stripes of pain
In our old chains again!"
Oh! what a shout there went
From the black regiment!

Unaffected by all the talk of the Negro's lack of soldierly qualities, which they had heard since the first hour of their enlistments, the two black regiments moved forward in quick time and with spirit and dash, entering the woods in their immediate front. The terrain over the half mile from their camp to the works of the enemy was pockmarked with gullies and ravines, strewn with felled trees, and interlaced with entangled brushwood like an obstacle race.

The Rebels were ready for the stormers. "We are laying in our rifle-pits, awaiting the hated foe," wrote John A. Kennedy of Company H, First Alabama, in his diary. "If they come in sight they will catch it, shure as two and two makes four."

As the assaulting soldiers emerged from the wooded area and started their charge up to the works in full face of the batteries, the Rebels opened up with everything—grape, canister, shell and musketry. Sheets of flame flashed along the forts as the Negro soldiers reeled from the direct fire upon them from the front and an enfilading, raking cross fire along their length, spewn from a six-gun battery on the left and a redoubt of six pieces of artillery on the right.

Men spun and fell before the deadly hail, their last cries hushed and unheard in the roaring thunder of the enemy artillery. Their comrades, many of whom had never smelled powder before, charged into the storm of bullets, moving with fixed purpose toward the string of Rebel batteries lined up against the high bluff.

"Steady men, steady," said Captain André Cailloux of Company E, First Native Guards, his dark skin actually a bit ashen from the sulphurous smoke. A prominent Catholic layman of wealth and attainment who liked to boast that he was "the blackest man in America," Cailloux had received his civil and military education in Paris. The idol of his men, he moved along the line speaking words of encouragement, now in French and now in English. His company, the color company, was an especial target for Rebel sharpshooters. Cailloux's left arm was shattered, but he refused to leave the field. Just as he reached the flooded ditch, he shouted, "Follow me," his last words. A second later a shell hit him and he fell with his body facing forwards to the foe.

His followers were halted by the ditch, eight feet deep and twenty feet wide. Their losses already severe, there was no alternative except to retire. They had expected to engage the Rebels but had met the backflow of the river. As they withdrew, they were severely cut up.

The shattered columns wheeled to the rear and re-formed. A second time on the double quick they rushed square up to the edge of the ditch, some fifty yards from the enemy guns. Easy targets, they could scarcely hope to cross or ford the gully. "Yet," wrote eyewitness John A. Foster, colonel of the One Hundred Seventy-fifth New York Volunteers, "they made several efforts to swim and cross it, preparatory to an assault on the enemy's works, and this, too, in fair view of the enemy, and at short musket range." A score of volunteers from Companies E and G, Third Native Guards, recklessly plunged into the water, holding their rifles and cartridge boxes above their heads. They would never answer roll call again.

At the field hospital many of the black soldiers whose wounds were slight, asked that their cuts and bruises be dressed as soon as possible, so that they might rejoin their comrades. One soldier returning to the front limping painfully was halted and asked where he was going. His explanation was revealing: "I am shot bad in de leg, and dey want me to go to the hospital, but I guess I can give 'em a little more yet." The surgeon in charge over the two regiments, J. T. Paine, a busy man on that day of carnage, wrote that he had "seen all kinds of soldiers, yet I have never seen any who, for courage and unflinching bravery, surpass our colored."

Yet the second assault, like the first, was repulsed. Almost incredibly, during these two operations the center and the left wings of the Union forces had failed to mount their offensives. Their four-hour delay in attacking meant that from ten in the morning until two in the afternoon, the right had borne the complete burden of the battle and thus had received the undivided attention of the Rebel guns. However, even under the combined attack of the three wings, it would not have been easy to take an elaborate and skillfully planned work like Port Hudson. Hurling against it masses of men, no matter how gallant, was not a good answer. Indeed, the combined land assaults probably did less damage to the Confederates than did the Union fleet of six vessels—the sloop of war *Hartford* and the gunboat *Albatross* above the stronghold, and the sloops of war *Monongahela* and *Richmond*, the gunboat *Genesee* and the ironclad *Essex* below—whose total of eighty-six guns rained shot and shell into the Rebel fortification.

But Brigadier General William F. Dwight needed one final illustration before he would learn the lesson. He sent word by an aide: "Tell Colonel Nelson that I shall consider that he has accomplished nothing unless he takes those guns."

For the third time the Negro regiments dressed into line, their ranks now thinned. Again they charged and again they were greeted with volleys of musketry. Falling treetops, severed by Rebel shells, crashed down on the advancing blacks. On they went, vainly attempting to ignore the tempest of rifle bullets and the iron shower of grape and round shot.

Anselmas Planciancois was bearing the flag in front of the enemy's works when the top of his head was lifted off by a six-pounder. As he fell, still clutching the banner, a struggle ensued between the two color-corporals, each wishing to have the honor of bearing the blood-bespattered flag. The issue was settled only after one had been seriously injured in the set-to. The victorious bearer did not enjoy his triumph long—he was soon picked off. Indeed, the honor of that flag cost the lives of six men.

With a final desperate charge the black soldiers rushed forward and again reached a point only fifty yards from the Rebel batteries. So vigorous was their forward thrust, that a newspaper reporter covering the battle, expressed a belief that "if only ordinarily supported by artillery and reserve, no one can convince us that they would not have opened a passage through the enemy's works." But the Rebel defenders emptied their rifles, cannon and mortars upon the heads of their colored adversaries. Severe fighting continued on the right part of the line until four o'clock in the afternoon, but Port Hudson was not to be taken that day. Finally came the inevitable order to retreat, and the Negro troops "marched off as if on parade."

As a military operation the assault was entirely unsuccessful. Yet the behavior of the black regiments was one bright spot. Their conduct had been under especial scrutiny since Port Hudson was the first real battle in which Negro soldiers were engaged. Had they flinched under fire, the future of the Negro soldier would have been jeopardized. But they had not flinched. "No body of troops—Western, Eastern or rebel—have fought better in the war," editorialized the New York *Times* on June 13, 1863. General Banks in his report to H. W. Halleck reflected the attitude of all officers who commanded on the right:

> The position occupied by these troops was one of importance, and called for the utmost steadiness and bravery. . . . It gives me pleasure to report that they answered every expectation. No

troops could be more determined or more daring. . . . The history of this day proves conclusively that the Government will find in this class of troops effective supporters and defenders.

The casualties sustained by the colored regiments gave evidence of their role. They suffered 37 killed, 155 wounded and 116 missing. Comprising one twelfth of the Union troops engaged, they bore one-eighth of the loss in numbers killed, one tenth in wounded and three fourths in missing.

The Promise of Land

• *The free Negro had always been the odd man in American society before the Civil War—the odd man out. But war and emancipation changed the free Negro "problem" from one that involved a despised though manageable minority to one that concerned nearly one-fifth of the country's population. A new system had to be devised overnight to accommodate the millions of freedmen and to deal with problems created by two centuries of slavery. Those sympathetic to the blacks recognized that without a real measure of economic independence, emancipation alone would offer little concrete help to the ex-slave in adjusting to freedom. The freed black knew the land best, and in his possession of land lay the promise of a secure future. When Union troops captured the Sea Islands off the coast of South Carolina, early in the war, rich cotton-growing lands and their black cultivators became the focus of a major social experiment. Abolitionist administrators, teachers, and clergymen urged the federal government to honor its responsibility for assisting the freedmen and carve homesteads out of confiscated rebel estates. Professor Willie Lee Rose here describes the plans of Sea Island freedmen and their abolitionist patrons, pointing out the distance that lay between these hopes and their partial fulfillment. Her study, entitled* Rehearsal for Reconstruction, *illuminates the tragic prologue to the Reconstruction drama, which paralleled in many ways the failure of the Sea Islands experiment.*

Parson French had selected his text. On a fine October Sunday, just outside a little church near the center of Port Royal Island, he was speaking to a throng of freedmen, Negro soldiers, and their missionary

From Willie Lee Rose, *Rehearsal for Reconstruction: The Port Royal Experiment* (Indianapolis: Bobbs-Merrill Company, 1964), pp. 272–96 (footnotes omitted). Copyright © 1964, by The Bobbs-Merrill Company, Inc. Reprinted by permission of the publishers.

16

friends. Fond as French was of the rich imagery of the Old Testament, no subject in all the ancient books could have had quite the appeal for the evangelist as the words of Moses to the Children of Israel: "Behold the Lord they God hath set the land before thee; go up and possess it, as the Lord God of they fathers hath said unto thee; fear not, neither be discouraged."

A few weeks before, in his instructions of September 16, 1863, to the Direct Tax Commissioners of South Carolina, President Lincoln had outlined the plans of the government for the disposition of the 60,000 acres of land that the commission had bid in for the United States at the sale of the preceding March. At an auction scheduled for early in 1864, the property was to be offered at public sale in lots not exceeding 320 acres, with the important exception of certain lands retained for naval, military, educational, and charitable purposes. Within the last category came the special provision reserving for "heads of families of the African race" certain specifically named plantations, which were to be subdivided into small twenty-acre lots and sold at a preferred rate of $1.25 per acre. The intention of the government had been understood in the islands for some time, and the commissioners . . . had been surveying the lands and erecting small houses on the lots designed for freedmen. Now that the word was official, the missionaries lost no time in telling the people of their advantages.

The Negroes who met to hear the news on Port Royal Island opened their services with the ringing spiritual:

> *Children of a Heavenly King,*
> *As we journey, let us sing, . . .*

After Mr. French delivered a stirring sermon about Moses and the promised land, General Saxton explained the President's instructions and also explained to the colored people why they ought to own a little land to secure their future. In the Western tradition of "squatter rights," the freedmen agreed upon plans for claiming the land, framed a few rules for their future government, and pledged allegiance to the United States. Sergeant Prince Rivers, Colonel Higginson's able and tireless recruiting officer, seized the occasion to make a speech in favor of enlistment, emphasizing the especially generous provision for soldiers to own land. He made the most of the manly and independent feelings of a freedman who became a soldier for the Union and ended by exhorting the "cowards" who would not join the army to be at least fair with the old men and women in the competition that would inevitably ensue for the best land. Afterward, the Negroes were invited to inspect a rude little model house that was brought out for the occasion. Approximately 16 by 20 feet, the cabin was made of poles and planks ingeniously put together without benefit of nails. The cost of the prospective landowners who would erect the cabins on their tiny freeholds was $25.

On November 3 Saxton formally issued his instructions in a circular published in the *Free South*, telling the people to deposit their money, together with an accurate description of the land they wanted to own, at his headquarters. Captain Hooper would take charge, and "at the sale, *if possible*, bid in the land for the person who has filed the claim. . . ." . . .

General Saxton and Parson French had launched themselves upon a doubtful course of circumventing the President's instructions. Disappointed that only "alternate quarter sections" of the Port Royal lands were set aside for Negro settlement, Governor Saxton was encouraging the freedmen to build their cabins upon the public lands of their own choice in the hope of establishing a subsequent clear claim. While appearing to *implement* the instructions, he was, in fact, seizing the initiative in the tax commissioners' own bailiwick. The commissioners understood at once.

The President's instructions of September, 1863, had encompassed the plans of the majority of the commission, and they clearly did not envision a wholesale surrender of the rich island districts to "charitable purposes" at $1.25 per acre. The plantations specifically indicated for Negro sales under the instructions comprised only 16,000 of the 60,000 acres open for sale. In the eyes of most observers keenly interested in the future of the Negroes, the plan was unfair and inadequate to the needs of the freedmen. Saxton's ambiguous instructions assume, in the light of subsequent developments, all the earmarks of deliberate obfuscation in a worthy cause. If the freedmen happily and innocently struck their claims hither and yon over the islands, was there not a good chance that the commissioners would be obliged to have the instructions changed to suit the status quo? Would not *all* the lands in this way eventually fall to the black people who had so justly earned them through years of unrequited toil?

Such seems to have been the reasoning implicit in Saxton's instructions of November 3, in which he voiced his hopeful opinion that if a Negro struck his claim and was prepared to pay "the government price" he "should have an acknowledged right to purchase."

Commissioner Brisbane was upset. There was nothing to do with "pre-emption" in his instructions. At a conference in Washington during the summer, he had reached an agreement with the Commissioner of Internal Revenue that the rich Sea Islands could not be disposed of on the same basis as the virgin lands of the West. A general pre-emption plan was not appropriate for the "improved" agricultural lands of the South. According to the instructions of September 16, "charitable purposes" constituted a mere embellishment to the main point, raising revenue. The implication is plain enough that there was no expectation that *all* the Port Royal freedmen would be provided with land at $1.25 per acre. The commissioners had authority to issue "certificates" to the small lots to such heads of Negro families as applied, "preferring such as by their good conduct, meritorious services or exemplary character, will be examples of moral propriety and industry" to their race. The idea of elimination of some applicants was implicit. In a hasty letter to Washington, Commissioner Brisbane and Commissioner William Wording protested that the mass meetings Saxton and French were promoting were stirring up a troublesome spirit. They accused the pair, accurately enough, of giving the people the notion that "squatter sovereignty" in the land would be acknowledged.

The commissioners had their hands full, for Saxton had become an extremely difficult man to criticize directly. The general, though perhaps not a profound or original thinker, was a man who appeared to be even more guileless than he actually was. A doubt of his sincere devotion to the welfare of his islanders could never be entertained seriously in any quarter. As is the universal practice in such cases, the general's advisers bore the brunt of criticism whenever Saxton's policies were questioned. The worst the commissioners dared to assert against the general was that he was "ambitious in his sphere" and "very much" under the influence of Chaplain French. . . . But French and Saxton did not constitute the full extent of the commissioners' problem. Of the two newspapers published on the islands, the *Free South* was by far the abler journal. James G. Thompson, the editor, had given up his job as a plantation superintendent to conduct the small weekly, which concerned itself primarily with freedmen's affairs and the microscopic politics of Port Royal. Thompson supported the plan of General Saxton, who was at once his good friend and his brother-in-law; as a talented journalist, armed with a stinging and clever style, Thompson was a formidable enemy of the tax commission. . . .

The worst problem for the commissioners, however, was an internal division between Brisbane and W. E. Wording on the one hand and Commissioner Abram D. Smith on the other. Smith had made common cause with Saxton and French to obtain pre-emptions for the freedmen; he joined them in the desire to see *all* the land thrown open to the Negroes at the preferred rate of $1.25 per acre. Much to the ire of his fellow commissioners, Smith had graced the Saxton-French mass meetings with his official presence. . . .

In truth, everybody wanted the leading part in conducting the freedmen to the promised land, and Commissioners Wording and Brisbane would not readily admit that Commissioner Smith, or Governor Saxton and Chaplain French, for that matter, were better Calebs and Joshuas than they were. The essential problem was that the disputing parties had differing perspectives on the new Canaan. Each saw a vision, and each party regarded the other as impractical—and visionary. On one point they were in absolute agreement: The steps taken at Port Royal would provide a pattern for the future agricultural reconstruction of the South. The breaking-up of the great estates was an essential feature. Both parties were contending for a far wider application of their theories than the Sea Islands alone.

The majority of the tax commissioners envisioned a mixed settlement of Negroes and whites covering the islands with farms of widely varying sizes. They believed that the ownership of small acreages of from five to twenty acres would provide the freedmen with sufficient independence to release them from the threat of peonage to the prospective white Northern owners who would presumably purchase the larger farms contiguous to the "alternate quarter sections" of Negro settlements. This would, they believed, enhance the value of the Negro farms and also convey certain other benefits. The larger owners would be able to organize agricultural activities on their land and to provide employment for landless Negroes and those with limited acreages. Although the commissioners did not line it out, assuming that Sea-Island cotton would continue to be the primary staple was to grant their plan a number of salient points. Community use of the marsh meadows, woodlands, livestock, and farm equipment would be a distinct advantage to numbers of freedmen who might otherwise be unable to undertake the independent operations on a farm consisting of a single plot of arable land. . . .

It may be further stressed that under the plan of the commission Negroes who had managed to accumulate the capital were entirely free to compete at the general auction, if they could fix upon a farm of a size within their means; some farms slated for public sale were as small as forty and eighty acres. Negroes were also free to pool their funds and buy their own plantations. This had been done successfully in some instances as early as the original sale of March, 1863. Yet another means whereby the freedmen could gain land on generous terms was through the special provision that soldiers could purchase with only one quarter of the price as down payment and three years to pay.

The commissioners had been busy for months working out their blueprint for the future of the Sea Island district. According to their plan, education for all was to be provided through the income from leasing reserved "School Farms." . . . Many observers before and since have thought it more than passing strange that the best deep-water port on the South Atlantic coastline should be of no account commercially, and Brisbane was sure that after the war a great future in trade was waiting. . . .

There was certainly an aura of unreality in Brisbane's plans, set forth in neat charts of cities yet unborn, replete with town greens and college campuses. The element, however, that was most open to the charge of impracticality was the provision for a completely new survey of the whole region. The new lines cut across the islands at ruthless right angles, completely disregarding the ancient plantation markers, the winding creeks and inlets, and the time-honored task divisions in the great cotton fields. . . .

The main point at issue, however, was the conviction of the Governor, Commissioner Smith, French, and numbers of other missionaries that the commission had not made sufficient provision for Negro landownership. While the commissioners looked to revenue as well as "charitable purposes," their opponents wanted all the Port Royal lands for the freedmen, not as a special benefit but as a natural right. The specter of the profiteering landlord again loomed large in their minds.

While still underplaying the internal differences among the authorities, Saxton continued to promote meetings among the people, encouraging them to select lands and educating them on the advantages of owning property. This knowledge was by no means intuitive. . . . The constricted life under slavery and the great isolation of the islands had encouraged an attachment to home that the urbane Northerners were slow to understand but could not fail to recognize.

Saxton had his most impressive audience on New Year's Day of 1864. A bitter east wind rose with the dawn, and the overcast skies provided an inauspicious setting for the great celebration the Governor had organized to commemorate the first anniversary of emancipation. But the weather could not expunge the spirit of revolutionary hope and enthusiasm of the day. In accepting a presentation sword from the freed people, Saxton made a speech that conveyed his personal vision of their future. He recalled the "destitution and ignorance" of two years before and complimented the swift progress of the people, which had exceeded his "most sanguine expectations." He urged them forward on the "career of improvement." In a grand peroration he depicted an agrarian idyl where the people would live together in peace and happiness; it was the typical abolitionist dream of a free peasantry:

> . . . Ere two . . . [more] years be added to the great record of the past, we may see these islands covered with neat cottages, each the centre of a happy home, little farms well tilled, school houses built and teachers hired to instruct your children. These islands are as fertile as any upon which the sun shines, the rivers and bays swarming with the finest fish: the necessaries and luxuries of life are produced here in rare abundance and excellence.

For the rest, the great cotton staple would provide "an endless source of wealth" to the people. Whether the cold and shivering freedmen also envisioned this we do not know, but they must surely have sensed that the revolution was in full swing by the general tenor of the events of the day. Above the speakers' stand the names of John Brown and Toussaint l'Ouverture were emblazoned alongside those of Washington, Lincoln, and Robert Gould Shaw. Lest the significance be lost upon his audience, Colonel Charles Van Wyck spoke to the theme of "servile insurrection," which *he* would no more stop, he said, than any other act of the Almighty that might be inflicted upon the rebels. In a highly dubious compliment to the orderly and sensible people who had come to celebrate the day, he flung out, "If unchaining the fiend will work our deliverance, then let the fiend be unchained."

Many of the island notables spoke on the occasion, but one familiar face was not seen. Chaplain French was in Washington, and nobody could have been more concerned about the outcome of his visit than General Saxton. Under the conviction that no amount of persuasion could induce the tax commission, as it was constituted, to approve pre-emption rights for the freedmen, the Chaplain had gone to Washington to bring his persuasive personality again to bear upon the Secretary of the Treasury. . . . Whether French "tricked" Chase, as was later charged, is impossible to say. His subsequent behavior does indicate an unseemly haste to carry out the completely revised plans that he brought triumphantly back to Beaufort in early January. But his conscience never showed a sign of malaise. . . .

By terms of the new instructions of December 31, 1863, all the lands owned by the government on the islands not reserved for military or educational purposes were thrown open to pre-emption at the rate of $1.25 per acre. Only two-fifths of the price was due upon pre-emption, and the remainder, at the receipt of the deed. The pre-emptor could be "any loyal person" of twenty-one years of age or more who had since the time of the Federal occupation resided for six months within the Department or was in residence at the time of the issuance of the instructions. Such loyal persons could pre-empt twenty- or forty-acre tracts. In this provision lay the genesis of the famous postward expectation of the freed slaves that the government would provide them with forty acres of land. Under the second clause, soldiers and sailors could pre-empt twenty acres if single and forty if married, under precisely the same arrangements as for other "loyal persons."

General Saxton went to work promptly and, armed now with full authority, he urged the Negroes to take up their lands, instructing the superintendents to assist them. The general and the chaplain cleverly refused to allow the commissioners themselves to see the new instructions until after the departure of the vessel that had brought French back to Port Royal. The commissioners could not protest something they did not know about, and as a consequence pre-emption was well on its way to being made a reality before Brisbane and Wording found out the extent of the new instructions. Only Commissioner Smith was in on the secret.

A typical meeting was held on St. Helena on the seventeenth of January. The Brick Church was filled to overflowing with freedmen and missionaries who came to hear Saxton, French, and Judge Smith explain, as James Thompson phrased it, "those measures whose operation will reorganize the whole system of Southern Society." After the religious exercises, French read the instructions of the President, and nearly everyone of any consequence had an opportunity to make a speech. . . .

Within a few days the commissioners were literally swamped with pre-emption claims from all over the islands, most of them patiently worked out by the superintendents and carefully marked with the "x" of the pre-emptor. Sometimes, the shaky penciled signature of the claimant proclaimed the proud state of new literacy, but either way the little slips of paper represented the happy anticipation of the Negro farmer to own a bit of the "home place." Today packet after packet of these musty little papers may be found among the records of the tax commission, brittle and dry as the broken hopes to which they are the mute witnesses. For the pre-emption plan failed.

It was not the first or the last time that the interests of the freedmen were sacrificed in the conflicts of men who meant to help. General Saxton had stolen a march on the commission by acting promptly, but Brisbane and Wording were not without defenses. On January 15, after a strategic five-day delay, the new instructions were revealed to the commission; but even before the instructions were presented, Commissioner Smith had introduced a resolution obliging them to carry out President Lincoln's wishes.

Brisbane and Smith naturally voted it down and then began an infuriating campaign of passive resistance. They simply sat on their hands—after firing off a letter to Washington presenting their side of the argument and asking for further explanations. The advertisement for the public land sale continued to appear in the papers at the same time the pre-emption claims were pouring into the commissioners' headquarters at the Rhett house. Brisbane ignored them and would accept no money.

But he must have *read* at least a few of the pre-emptions. For among the claimants he found a significant number filed by white men in the Department, who were in point of law as free to pre-empt as the freedmen. The Reverend Dr. Solomon Peck, for instance, had taken up 160 acres by manipulating the possibilities of his numerous family to the best advantage. The John Hunn family at "Seaside" had also laid claim to a large amount of property, including the great plantation house of Edgar Fripp. While there was no massive onslaught upon the public lands by abolitionists-in-residence, there was plainly enough action to stiffen, if not to justify, Brisbane's claim that the more intelligent and greedy white people of the Department were gobbling up the lands at the expense of the freedmen.

In a rigorous analysis of the June 7, 1862, law and of the ways in which the December pre-emption instructions conflicted with it, Judge Brisbane's legal mind showed to good effect. . . . The new instructions were, in actuality, poorly rooted in law, and perhaps in the long view of history and the postwar legal history of the land question, it is well that the Negro land claims did not rest upon so weak a foundation. But at the time many people regarded Brisbane's triumph as one of legalism and wickedness.

Another salient point in Brisbane's belief was his prediction that the Negroes would be thrown into utter confusion and hopeless conflict over the pre-emptions. Supporters of the commission appear to have blown this out of proportion, for on Port Royal Island, and generally in areas where the freedmen could pre-empt their own home plantations, there was little trouble. Matters did not proceed so smoothly, however, on the eastern end of St. Helena Island, where the large holdings of Edward Philbrick's Boston concern made it impossible for the Negroes to pre-empt the "home place." . . .

While stubbornly refusing to acknowledge the pre-emptions, Brisbane and Wording were building up their own brief. All the while, they were subjected to the most steady public pressure. Seemingly, nearly everyone in the Department interested in the freedmen opposed their course. A meeting of Beaufort citizens who wished to prod them into action called out a stubborn statement from Brisbane that it was "utterly impossible" to give out information on how pre-emptions could be made. . . .

In early February the news came that Chase had reversed himself, had withdrawn the December pre-emption instructions, and wanted the public sale to go forward. Now the Negroes could only apply for the limited amount of land set aside for "charitable purposes." It was a triumph for paternalism. It is difficult to determine which of the many arguments Brisbane and Wording advanced was decisive. Their charges against the greedy white people and the wracking confusion among the freed people undoubtedly carried weight. More fundamental, perhaps, was the dubious legal standing of the pre-emption plan. Sorting and weighing the charges and countercharges emanating weekly from the Port Royal Islands must have provided Chase with a severe headache. . . .

It is just possible that the political implications of yet another personality factor may have been more important than all the legal arguments the commissioners made against the pre-emption plan. For the conflicts on the board were not limited purely to matters of land policy and the future economic security of the freedmen. While Brisbane and Wording may have been, as was freely charged, more solicitous of the United States Treasury than of the freedmen's security, they at least had no outstanding personal vices to discredit their influence. Even the missionaries who supported him knew that *their* man on the commission was a heavy drinker. It was too bad, as Judge Smith was pronounced a "judicious" man when sober. Superintendent H. G. Judd, who actively pushed Smith's plan, said ironically, "if you catch him before ten, you will find him sober and clear; but then he doesn't get up till quarter of ten." Brisbane and Wording had been peppering Chase and Commissioner of Internal Revenue Joseph J. Lewis for several months with complaints of Smith's frequent intoxication. . . . An abstemious man, Salmon P. Chase did not suffer drunkards gladly. Smith's fall from official favor coincides roughly with retraction of the pre-emption instructions.

As early as February 4 Brisbane was assuring a prospective land investor in Lynn, Massachusetts, that it was now quite safe to buy lands in South Carolina and that the pre-emptions were not being allowed. He predicted comfortably that the Negroes would work for the Northern buyers once they recovered from the ill effects "of some professed friends of the blacks discouraging them from working for the whites."

Father French, as his fellow evangels called him, had enough faith to live by, and he was resourceful. He gently and mournfully protested to Chase that "The willows bend again under the weight of broken harps. The voice of joy and thanksgiving has given place to mourning." Chase had made a mistake that he would understand some day, and French said he could forgo the Secretary's confidence *"in time, so I have it through all eternity." He* had one little request. Could not the pre-emptions made under the December instructions, and before their retraction, be acknowledged? Even thus he could have won the game, for as Thompson pointed out in the *Free South* (a fact Chase probably did not know), "Before the order of suspension reached the commissioners, more than a thousand persons had secured [by pre-emption] the right to purchase, at $1.25 per acre, from twenty to eighty acres each; and to-day the United States has not eighty contiguous acres of tillable land to offer at public sale." But no soothing word came from the federal treasury.

French had signed his despondent note to Chase "Yours for the *truth* and *justice* even to the *bottom of the crucible.*" But his air of patient resignation was not quite real. Now he took up the cudgels in earnest and followed a course some regarded as "jesuitical," dangerous, and even treasonable. At every church service, even at funerals, he seized the occasion to tell the freedmen of their wrongs. He exhorted them to take the land they needed and stay there, defending it if need be, even with their hoe handles. He told them to give the prospective buyers as much trouble as possible in dispossessing them and urged them "to plant for themselves instead of others." Pointing to the white purchasers of the year before, Philbrick in particular, French declared that they were "getting rich" on black labor and that the Negroes "were no richer at the end of the year than they were at the beginning."

Neither side had really accepted defeat, and the struggle broke into the open on February 18 as the crowds of buyers, pre-emptors, freedmen, and missionaries gathered before the Rhett house for the land auction. Brisbane and Smith locked horns, as the question recurred again and again whether a given plot of land was pre-empted or not. Brisbane always said it was not and Smith always said it was; little land changed hands. . . .

When the sale was resumed the following week, the indefatigable Brisbane wore Smith down, and the latter retired from the conflict "in disgust." The lands then sold at prices that created considerable astonishment in the Department. The tax commission was pleased to report that the lands had on an average sold for more than $11 an acre and added smugly in their account to revenue Commissioner Joseph Lewis, "You will readily see therefore what an imposition upon the government it would have been to have had these lands pre-empted at $1.25 an acre." . . .

There were ample signs of impending trouble. A group of superintendents returning to St. Helena from the sale of February 26 were met near Land's End by a crowd of freed people, who surrounded them clamoring for information and "complaining that their land—that they had pre-empted—had been sold away from them, and declaring that they wouldn't work for the purchase. They protested they would have paid as much for the land as anyone. The people of Redwood Point, Laura Towne reported, also had refused to work for the new owner, and would not permit their pre-emption money to be returned. All around were increasing signs that the freedmen were becoming fully awake to their economic needs.

The actions of the Negroes on Wassa Island and on the Marion Chaplin plantation indicated a road around the pre-emption suspension that French and Saxton had not seen or had been too stubborn to accept. On these places the people had pooled their funds and brought their own lands, intending to work them in common. If the superintendents had taken lively action after the suspension was known this might have been done on a larger scale; but their clinging to a forlorn hope had deprived the Negroes of leadership and had left the black people with a sense of frustration and bitterness toward the government that was deeper than it had been since the Federal occupation. Few white men were now exempt from their profound distrust. There had perhaps been a grain of truth in William Gannett's idea that only suffering would arouse the people, and 1864 was a bad year.

An unusually severe season of disease in the winter had lowered morale, and the senseless government recruiting policy of the spring had depressed the freedmen even more. It is a profound commentary on the integrity and consistency of Federal policy during the war that on the land question the freedmen were regarded paternalistically and given an opportunity to buy small "charitable" allocations of land, while they were at the same time ruthlessly exploited for military service in a manner far from paternal. Nevertheless, the plan of the tax commissioners, limited and faulty as it was, did represent a minor commitment to the idea that the government had some responsibility toward launching the newly-released slaves on the road toward economic independence. It also represented some constructive thinking about postwar economic and social problems, which had already been allowed to drift too long. But the shuffling, struggling contradictions and delay had embittered the people, who regarded the betrayal of their hopes to inherit the land as the last straw. A deep and sullen anger developed which the Northerners understood but did not view with sufficient sympathy. Small wonder it was that smallpox, the ancient plague, was by March known as the "Government lump."

Even after the sales of the spring of 1864, however, vast acreages still remained in government hands, and the question of the right of the freedmen to possess them at minimum cost would remain alive for a long time. The profound social question of the place of the freedmen in the post-bellum economic structure would be increasingly agitated.

II: RECONSTRUCTION,
1865–1877

A New World of Freedom

• *Joel Williamson describes in the following selection the varied reactions of ex-slaves and ex-masters in South Carolina to emancipation. Discarding the older notion that the freedmen behaved mainly as thoughtless political playthings manipulated by self-serving whites, Williamson seeks to understand the inner reactions of blacks to freedom, as well as their overt behavior. He is less concerned in this selection with Negro involvement in South Carolina public life than with the overwhelmingly positive response of blacks to emancipation. Despite the severe handicaps that slavery had imposed on the bondsman, the South Carolina black community nevertheless demonstrated abundant evidence that it could assume the rights and responsibilities of citizenship. The freed slaves swiftly made significant adjustments to their new status. It remained to be seen whether whites, in South Carolina, the South, and in Washington, could become similarly flexible in their attitudes and responses.*

Freedom was a nominal legacy of the war, yet telling the slave that he was free did not make him so. Ultimately, the Negro had to establish his freedom by some deliberate, conscious act entirely his own, or he would remain a slave in fact, if not in name. Emancipation simply gave him that choice. With near unanimity, Negroes in South Carolina chose liberty.

In the spring of 1865, the news of emancipation and the close of the war filtered slowly into the hinterland of South Carolina. In mid-May, the commanding general of the Department of the South, Q. A. Gillmore, issued a proclamation declaring that governmental policy would soon be made known. "It is deemed sufficient, meanwhile," he said, "to announce that the people of the black race are free citizens

From Joel Williamson, *After Slavery: The Negro in South Carolina During Reconstruction* (Chapel Hill: University of North Carolina Press, 1965), pp. 32–42, 44–47, 49–54, 63 (footnotes omitted). Reprinted by permission of the publisher.

31

of the United States, that it is the fixed intention of a wise and bene-
ficent government to protect them in the enjoyment of their freedom
and the fruits of their industry. . . ." Upon hearing of the order, a
few masters formally released their slaves. Francis W. Pickens, for instance, the secession governor of the state and an extensive planter on
the Savannah River in Edgefield District, heard of the order on May
23, and on the same day he called his slaves together, acknowledged
their emancipation, and contracted to pay them for their labor during
the remainder of the year. Most slaveholders were not so forehanded,
releasing their slaves only after occupation forces arrived from the
coastal area late in May and subsequently. Even after the occupation
was completed, a few masters, particularly among those living in the
uplands in the extreme western portion of the state, stubbornly refused to recognize the new status of their Negro laborers. Under these
circumstances, many Negroes became certain of their emancipation
only by traveling to the lower districts with the men who still acted
as their masters. A resident of Pendleton, visiting Columbia late in
June with a neighbor and the neighbor's slave, noted with alarm that
Toney, the slave, had "shown symptoms of demoralization since his
arrival here." Apparently observing the presence of Union troops in
the city and the formal recognition of emancipation generally accorded
to the Negroes there, Toney "got somewhat excited and talked of
making a 'bargin' when he returned to Pendleton." "No Negro is
improved by a visit to Columbia," the Carolinian concluded, "& a
visit to Charleston is his certain destruction."

By whatever means the Negro learned of emancipation, the most
obvious method of affirming his freedom was simply to desert the site
of his slavery and the presence of his master. Patience Johnson, an
ex-slave on a Laurens District plantation, must have expressed the
sentiment of many freedmen when she answered a request by her
mistress that she remain in her usual place and work for wages. "No,
Miss," she declined, "I must go, if I stay here I'll never know I am
free."

Contrary to tradition, however, the typical slave upon hearing of
emancipation did not shout with delight, throw his hat into the air,
gather the few possessions he claimed, and run pellmell for Charleston.
The great majority received the news quietly and began to make deliberate preparations to terminate their slavery definitely by some
overt act. Representative of the reaction of the freedmen in the lower
and middle districts was that of the Negroes on the Elmore plantation

near Columbia. On May 24, as the secret channels of slave communication crackled with rumors of emancipation, an impatient field hand named Caleb ran away. On May 27, Union forces occupied Columbia. "We told the negroes they were free on the 30th"; noted young Grace Elmore, "they waited patiently and respectably." Nevertheless, the freedmen initiated arrangements for separation. "Philis, Jane and Nelly volunteered to finish Albert's shirts before they left and to give good warning before they left," Grace reported, while Jack, the driver, "will stay till the crops are done." Not all of the freedmen were as explicit in stating their plans. "Old Mary, the nurse, took the news quietly on Sat evening; said that none could be happy without prayer, and Monday by day light she took herself off, leaving the poor baby without a nurse."

In the upcountry, the same pattern prevailed. In Spartanburg District, David Golightly Harris first heard of Gillmore's emancipation order on June 5, but made no mention of the news to his slaves. On the same day, however, and apparently before Harris himself had heard of the order, York, one of his field hands, "disappeared." The remainder said "nothing on the subject" and continued to "work as usual." Desertion on neighboring plantations became increasingly frequent, and, in early July, another of Harris' slaves, Old Will, disappeared, "to try to enjoy the freedom the Yankey's have promised the negroes." By late July, it was rumored that some masters in the neighborhood were recognizing formally the freedom of their laborers. Finally, in mid-August, occupation forces stationed in Spartanburg ordered masters to explicitly inform the Negroes of their freedom. On August 15, most did so. When Harris made the announcement to his slaves, only one, Ann, left immediately, while "the others wisely concluded they would remain until New Years [sic] day."

Desertion was a common means by which the ex-slave asserted his freedom; yet variations in the time and spirit of the desertion yield interesting insights into the Negro's attitudes toward his new status. Generally, freedmen who as slaves had labored as domestics, mechanics, and in the extractive industries departed at the first reasonably convenient opportunity. In doing so, they typically exhibited some degree of malice toward their recent owners. On the other hand, those who had labored in the fields generally finished the year in their accustomed places, and when they left seldom departed with expressions of ill will toward their late masters.

It is astonishing that among the servant or domestic class (where slave labor was reputedly least arduous and relations with the master most intimate and satisfactory), defection was almost complete. Correspondence and diaries of the period are replete with instances in which the master or mistress declared "all of our servants have departed." . . .

The frequency with which domestics deserted their masters discredits the myth of the "faithful old family servant" (the ex-slave) loyally cleaving to his master through the pinching years of Reconstruction. Most of the "faithful new" were literally old, or else very young, or infirm, or encumbered by family arrangements which made desertion impossible. . . .

Doubtless, some servants did remain with their late masters from motives of genuine loyalty and contentment. A Charlestonian wrote in September, 1866, that his "old" coachman and the coachman's wife held steadfast in their devotion to him all during the war and afterward. Such instances were rare, however, and became increasingly so as Reconstruction progressed. . . .

In spite of obvious and often painful realities, the myth of the "faithful old family servant" persisted both North and South and even grew in the years following Reconstruction. . . . But in the South the myth had a rather more tragic aspect. Living in a world they never made, life for Southerners was somehow eased by this small fiction which evoked a pleasurable image of the better world they had aspired to build. This was possibly what a lady of Charleston was saying in 1873 when she wrote to a friend upon the death of an elderly woman servant who had been her slave. "I feel a link has been broken, an occasion lamented," she sadly declared, "a really burial of what can never take place again." And it could not, if, indeed, it ever had.

Mechanics and laborers outside of agriculture (in lumbering, mining, turpentine, and other industries) were as quick as domestics to leave their masters. Even where they did not desert their late owners, there was often a disposition to do so. In July, 1865, E. J. Parker, engaged in the turpentine business in the deep piney woods of Williamsburg District, despaired of inducing his former slaves to continue laboring for him even for wages. . . .

The liberty of freedmen engaged in agriculture to leave their former masters was restricted by the insistence of the occupation forces and the Freedmen's Bureau that plantation owners and laborers contract to harvest and divide the 1865 crop before parting. Many who did not contract found it convenient, nevertheless, to complete the agricultural season. But even as they worked they eagerly anticipated the New Year and the Christmas holidays that preceded it as a kind of second emancipation. . . .

The inclination of domestics, mechanics, and laborers in the extractive industries and on relatively small plantations to leave their masters at the first reasonable opportunity while agriculturalists on the larger plantations remained suggests that desertion correlated very closely with the degree of proximity that had existed between the slave and his owner and, further, that the freedman was much more interested in leaving behind the personal reminders of slavery than he was the physical.

In South Carolina, the mass movement among the Negro population was not the "aimless," endless, far-flung wandering so often described. Freedmen most often left their homes to separate themselves distinctly from slavery, but their destination was nearly always fixed by economic design or necessity. Most migrants resettled themselves within a matter of days or weeks and within a few miles of the place which, as slaves, they had called home. "In almost every yard," wrote Emma Holmes in June, 1865, "servants are leaving but going to wait on other people for food merely, sometimes with the promise of clothing." Many former domestics went into the fields to labor, and, conversely, a few agricultural laborers entered household service. . . .

Having proved their freedom by leaving their former masters, many Negroes, apparently, were soon willing to return to them. By late September, two out of the three servants who had deserted James Hemphill's Chester household had returned. . . . A large number of agricultural laborers also returned to their native plantations after a short stay abroad. . . .

While migrants were motivated by combinations of many desires, much of their behavior is explained by their love of the homeplace—the "old range" as they themselves rather warmly termed it. White contemporaries, perhaps obsessed with the idea that theirs was a white man's land, never fully appreciated the fact that Negroes, too, were strongly devoted to the soil upon which they had been born and labored. . . . Thus, ironically, the Negro frequently moved to get away from his late master, but he almost always moved to settle in the very locale where he had served in bondage. . . .

In the first weeks of emancipation, many (perhaps most) freedmen interpreted their liberty as a temporary release from labor. . . .

Yet, the mass of Negroes did not equate freedom with permanent idleness. In fact, they wanted to work, but only for themselves and at their own discretion. Almost universally, they showed an aversion to cultivating the great staple—cotton, and a willingness to grow food crops sufficient for themselves and their families. . . .

When arrangements were satisfactory, the great mass of Negroes exhibited an eagerness to labor. Indeed, enforced idleness made the Negro agrarian uneasy. "We wants to git away to work on our own hook," explained a migrant waiting on a Charleston wharf for a steamer to return him to his home plantation. "It's not a good time at all here. We does nothing but suffer from smoke and ketch cold. We want to begin de planting business." By the early spring of 1866, most Negro farmers had done precisely that.

Apparently, Negroes labored less arduously in freedom than they had in slavery. To many whites, the slowdown seemed a stoppage. During the hot, dry summer of 1865, when the woods were in danger of bursting into flames, a planter near Grahamville complained to the Bureau officer that "my negroes in the fariest weather refuse to go out to work at all, to save my place from danger of fire." A flagrant show of ingratitude, he thought, "as this was their old home, to which they said they were anxious to move, it seems now to avoid work altogether." However, he admitted, "they did do some work." . . .

Of course, there were freedmen who lost the habit of labor during the transition from slavery to freedom. These tended to collect in the larger cities, on abandoned plantations, and, occasionally, on the farm of some larcenous poor white. . . . In time, however, the military and the Bureau were successful in clearing idlers from the population centers. More frightening to the whites than urban idlers were those in the country. . . .

Idleness of this hardened sort soon dwindled to negligible proportions. Much of the continued malingering was apparently a manifestation of the Negro's dissatisfaction with his rewards under the new system, a sort of unorganized slowdown by which he fought his employer or prospective employer. Idleness, of course, had been a normal part of slavery, and it was no less evident among the whites than Negroes. Sundays, Christmas, and New Year's Day were customarily holidays from labor for both races and remained so. Further, agrarian communities normally recognized the laying-by season in the early summer and the end of the harvest season in the fall and winter as periods of reduced labor, celebrations, and idleness. It is not surprising that the Negro in freedom continued to recognize them as such, and to relish them all the more.

Desertion, migration, and idleness were temporary as mass phenomena among the Negro population in postwar South Carolina. Much more lasting was the universal tendency among freedmen to identify their freedom with liberty to ignore the infinite minor regulations that had been imposed upon them as slaves. They assumed new forms of dress, kept dogs and guns, hunted, and they traveled about without passes. Many refused to yield the sidewalks to the white gentry, omitted the slave-period obeisances, and rode horses or mules or in carriages in the presence of white pedestrians. They conversed in public and in secret with any number of other Negroes and entered into associations for a variety of purposes.

The master class, exasperated and outraged by the assertiveness of the freedmen, was particularly alert in noting and meticulously recording this metamorphosis of their erstwhile bondsmen. In Camden, early in April, 1865, Emma Holmes, attending services in the Methodist Church where the Negroes sat in the galleries, was incensed at the Negro women who wore "round hats, gloves and even lace veils, the men alone looking respectable." A white resident returning to Charleston in June of the same year was appalled by "Negroes shoving white person[s] . . . [off] the walk. Negro women dressed in the most outré style, all with veils and parasols for which they have an especial fancy. Riding on horseback with negro soldiers and in carriages." At the same time, a planter on the lower Cooper River complained that the Negroes would not stay out of Charleston, where they "claim they are free," and the women are frequently seen "with blue & pink veils, etc." The same planter was mortified while hunting in the swamps with a group of white gentlemen to encounter suddenly a number of Negro men engaged in the same entertainment, armed with shotguns and following the hounds like ebony images of their white superiors.

To the freedman, his new liberty conveyed the right to assemble in public, to speak, and to celebrate—the cause most often and extravagantly celebrated being freedom itself. Celebrations occurred frequently, on plantations, in villages and towns, and pre-eminently in Charleston. The Negro community in Charleston was large, wealthy, well informed, and organized. Zion Church, having been established by the Presbyterians before the war primarily for the accommodation of their Negro members and having a seating capacity of two thousand, logically became the focal point of organized activity among the Negroes and their Northern friends. . . .

Other Negro communities were not long in following the example of Charleston. The editor of the *New York Times* praised the stand of the Negroes of Columbia in refusing to abandon plans to celebrate Independence Day in 1865 despite the protests of the whites. "They may not get the vote or court rights in this way," asserted the editor, "but there are a hundred petty regulations of the slave period which they can break to exert their influence. It is good that the white become accustomed to negro meetings." . . . Throughout Reconstruction, the Negroes made New Year's Day and Independence Day their special holidays and devoted them to the celebration of emancipation and union, concepts which were inseparably intertwined in their minds. On these days, even in the smallest villages, the Negro community usually staged some sort of jubilee.

These celebrations were significant as assertions of freedom, but they were also important in other ways. They obviously gave the Negro population a feeling of unity and an awareness of the power that unity bestowed. Further, they pushed forth leaders from among their own numbers who, in time, would translate that power into political realities.

Yet, while many Negroes manifested cordial feelings toward the whites, others exhibited insolence and insubordination. As the war drew to a close, and before emancipation became a certainty, such displays often served as a device by which Negroes tested their freedom. . . .

A very few Negroes believed that freedom warranted the exercise of vengeance upon the whites—that theft, arson, and violence even to the extremity of homicide were justifiable retributions for their bondage. This sentiment was particularly apparent in areas subjected to Union raids and it persisted through the summer and fall of 1865. After Sherman had passed through Camden, a serious case of arson was narrowly averted, and "many other attempts at setting fire were discovered either just in time, or after some damage had been done —both in Camden and the surrounding country—keeping everyone in a constant state of anxiety and alarm." In several communities, disturbances reached the proportions of insurrections. . . .

Notwithstanding the charges of the whites that Negro soldiers often instigated such disorders, the occupation rapidly established comparative peace. It is true, nevertheless, that the Negro population was most restless in those areas occupied by Negro troops—an area which included the lowcountry from Georgetown to Savannah and, roughly, the southern half of the state from the sea to the mountains. . . .

It is difficult to distinguish fact from fiction in the disordered first weeks that followed the war; but the rumor circuit buzzed with tales of whites murdered by Negroes, usually their ex-slaves. Emma E. Holmes reported that William Prioleau returned to his lowcountry plantation after the Union forces had passed and spent the night, "but never woke again. His throat was cut from ear to ear." Another planter reported killed was William Allen, "who was chopped to pieces in his barn," as Emma graphically related. . . .

The great mass of Negroes in South Carolina at the end of the Civil War hoped and expected that freedom meant that each would soon be settled upon his own plot of earth. Indeed, to the Negro agrarian freedom without land was incomprehensible. . . .

"Forty acres and a mule," that delightful bit of myopic mythology so often ascribed to the newly freed in the Reconstruction Period, at least in South Carolina during the spring and summer of 1865, represented far more than the chimercial ratings of ignorant darkies, irresponsible soldiers, and radical politicians. On the contrary, it symbolized rather precisely the policy to which the government had already given and was giving mass application in the Sea Islands. . . .

With perhaps one out of every ten Negro families in South Carolina settled upon their own land by the late summer of 1865, and with the apparent intention of the government, through the Bureau, to guarantee the security of their tenure and to accommodate others, it is not surprising that the landless freedmen should have thought their chances of winning the same boon were excellent. Moreover, where Negroes settled, they revealed an inflexible determination to hold their ground. "We own this land now," the freedmen of one lowcountry plantation impressed upon their late master when he returned from the war; "put it out of your head that it will ever be yours again." For a time, most owners believed that this was, indeed, a verity.

Thus, even in the early days of freedom, former slaves with amazing unanimity revealed—by mass desertion, migration, idleness, by the breaching of the infinite minor regulations of slavery, by a new candor in relationships with whites, and by their ambition to acquire land—a determination to put an end to their slavery. It is true that the Negro's freedom was still severely circumscribed a year after emancipation, and his experience during the whole term of Reconstruction could hardly be described as a success story. Yet, the Negro did not, upon emancipation, immediately jump a quick half-step forward and halt. In the favorable atmosphere generated by his political ascendency during Reconstruction, freedom for the Negro in South Carolina was a growing thing, flowering in areas political historians have often neglected. The growth was, in part, the result of cultivation by alien hands; but it was also the result of forces operating within the organism itself. The gains won during these early years enabled the Negro community to continue to move forward in vital areas of human endeavor in the post-Reconstruction period while, ironically, its political freedom was rapidly dwindling to virtual extinction. In this sense, far from being the disaster so often described, Reconstruction was for the Negroes of South Carolina a period of unequaled progress.

White Reconstruction

• *For a century, white America either distorted or ignored the Negro's true role in Reconstruction. Following on the heels of a war launched to preserve the Union but which ended with emancipation of four million slaves, Reconstruction possessed the potential for realizing much of the American democratic dream. Unfortunately, the reality never began to approach this potential. After a short survey of Reconstruction historiography, John Hope Franklin analyzes some of the period's myths, the reasons for its failure, and the actual subservient status of the Negro during an era of American history that his enemies claim he dominated. Reconstruction was neither radical nor black, but in the end, the freedman, his role severely limited, received much of the blame for the failure of Reconstruction's experiments. The opportunity to use the emerging Negro leadership class as a spearhead for the general advancement of the black community was lost.*

For more than a generation, there has been an increasing disposition, on the part of historians, to take another look at the Negro's role during the Reconstruction era. Indeed, it was as far back as 1910 that William E. B. Du Bois took issue with the early students of the period who had concluded, almost casually, that the Negro was a dupe, used by sinister whites for their own selfish ends, and that Negroes themselves had contributed substantially to the failure of Reconstruction. With a view to reaching all or most of the serious students of the period, Du Bois published an article in the *American Historical Review* in which he said,

> Granted . . . that the negroes were to some extent venal but to a much larger extent ignorant and deceived, the question is: did

From John Hope Franklin, "Reconstruction and the Negro," in Harold M. Hyman (ed.), *New Frontiers of the American Reconstruction* (Urbana: University of Illinois Press, 1966), pp. 59–76 (footnotes omitted). Reprinted by permission of the publisher and the author.

they show any signs of a disposition to learn better things? The theory of democratic governments is not that the will of the people is always right, but rather that normal human beings of average intelligence will, if given a chance, learn the right and best course by bitter experience. This is precisely what negro voters showed indubitable signs of doing. First, they strove for schools to abolish ignorance, and second, a large and growing number of them revolted against the carnival of extravagance and stealing that marred the beginning of Reconstruction, and joined with the best elements to institute reform. . . .

There is reason to doubt that Du Bois reached any considerable number of historians of the Reconstruction or, if he did, that he had any appreciable effect on the manner in which they viewed the critical years following the Civil War. The view that Reconstruction was a "tragic era" in which honest government disappeared from the South while Carpetbaggers and Scalawags manipulated Negro voters and functionaries for their own benefit continued to hold sway. The rise of the Ku Klux Klan in the years following World War I was a vivid reminder that the hooded knights had "saved" the South once and now they would save the entire nation from the evil forces that were always ready to take advantage of a situation.

In this atmosphere of deepening despair among Negroes, a young Negro historian, Alrutheus A. Taylor, sought to repair some of the damage. In several monographs and articles on South Carolina, Virginia, and Tennessee, he made a valiant attempt to rehabilitate the Negro during Reconstruction. While the situation differed markedly from state to state, Taylor was convinced that, in general, Negroes had not fared well at the hands of the white historians of the Reconstruction. In his study of Virginia he said:

> The Negroes of Virginia . . . cannot be charged with the mistakes in the reconstruction of the State. White men, the majority of whom were Virginians themselves, were the office-holders in Virginia during the reconstruction. The number of Negroes elected to office never became sufficient to determine any definite policy of the government except in a few cases of exercising a balance of power between militant factions. Those Negroes who attained office, moreover, were generally persons of intelligence or common sense and they gave a good account of themselves.

If Taylor's impact was limited, if not negligible, it was not only because of the rather pedestrian and ineffective style in which his sound scholarship was couched, but also because there was no disposition on the part of the professional and lay public to consider a revision of the point of view that had become firmly entrenched by the time Taylor was writing. Much more influential than Taylor's works was the popularization of the now-classic view of the Negro during Reconstruction by Claude Bowers, whose best-selling *Tragic Era: The Revolution After Lincoln* was published in 1929. After viewing the coalition developing between northern whites and Negroes, Bowers asserted, "Left to themselves, the negroes would have turned for leadership to the native whites, who understood them best. This was the danger. Imperative, then, that they should be taught to hate—and teachers of hate were plentiful." Bowers then proceeded to embroider the theme that Negro rule was widespread, Negro suffrage tragic, and Negro perfidy rampant.

Du Bois, who had first challenged the established view, was no more willing to accept that view in later years than he had been in 1910. Therefore, in 1935 he brought out his *Black Reconstruction,* with the significant subtitle: *An Essay Toward a History of the Part Which Black Folk Played in the Attempt to Reconstruct Democracy in America, 1860–1880.* Despite the rather halfhearted and unsuccessful attempt by Du Bois to fit the Reconstruction era into a prefabricated mold of Marxist dialectics, he did succeed in convincing many of his readers that the old view of the Negro's part in Reconstruction was shot through with inconsistencies, distortions, misrepresentations, and downright falsifications. Full of passion and bitterness that was the product of many years of what he regarded as his futile efforts in the civil rights movement, Du Bois' reading of the Reconstruction era challenged virtually every conclusion that had been reached by the earlier students of the period.

Du Bois was convinced that Negroes had been betrayed by the federal government and by many of the so-called reformers, and he argued this point throughout his lengthy work. He saw in Andrew Johnson unspeakable prejudice and in Ulysses S. Grant a tragic weakness combined with a lack of understanding of the presidency that bordered on irresponsibility. He saw in the murder and violence perpetrated by the Klan the supreme expression of barbarism and the tragic destruction of an incipient wholesome relationship between the black and white lower classes. Finally, he concludes: "The attempt to make black men American citizens was in a certain sense all a failure, but a splendid failure. It did not fail where it was expected to fail. It was Athanasius contra mundum, with back to the wall, outnumbered ten to one, with all the world against him. And only in his hands and heart the consciousness of a great and just cause; fighting the battle of all the oppressed and despised humanity of every race and color, against the massed hirelings of Religion, Science, Education, Law, and brute forces."

This is neither the time nor the place to review the work of Du Bois. . . . It is enough to say that after the publication of *Black Reconstruction* it would never again be possible to look at the period without raising serious doubts about earlier views of the Negro's role or without at least looking seriously at the bold positions taken by Du Bois. If Du Bois did nothing more—and he verily did much more—he made it possible for later reexaminations of the period to be viewed with greater tolerance and credibility. Thus, when Horace Mann Bond began in 1938 to revise the classic treatment of the Negro in Alabama Reconstruction that had been provided by Walter Lynwood Fleming, his work was widely regarded as a significant contribution to the history of the period. He provided convincing proof that neither the Negroes nor their allies were the heroes or villains of Alabama Reconstruction. The important ones to watch were a combination of native whites and northern businessmen who dominated the affairs of the state for the entire period.

After 1940 the studies of the Negro in Reconstruction began to appear more frequently. In that year Samuel D. Smith brought out his study of the Negro in Congress. A few years later Vernon L. Wharton published a penetrating study of the Negro in Mississippi. Within a few years C. Vann Woodward, Rayford W. Logan, George Bentley, Leslie Fishel, Otis Singletary, and Robert Durden published works bearing on various aspects of the Negro's role during Reconstruction. In more recent years the efforts have continued, and the recent work by LaWanda and John Cox, *Politics, Principle, and Prejudice,* and the volume by James McPherson in 1964, *The Struggle for Equality,* are outstanding in their handling of the role of the Negro in the political and social problems confronting the nation after the Civil War.

It would, of course, be folly to suggest that we now have an adequate picture of the Negro during Reconstruction. We still know *all too little* about the relationship between Negroes, Carpetbaggers, and Scalawags. The picture of the Negro in Congress is far from complete. What kind of party men were they; were they race men or merely the representatives of their congressional districts? No one has yet given us a full account of the Negro in the early days of peace: what the role was of the Negro conventions in 1865 and 1866, how many actually were in a position to assume leadership roles, and what they wanted from the state and federal governments. We need to know a great deal more than we now know about Negro *officeholders* at the *state and local* levels and the reactions of Negroes to the growing indifference of the federal government to their needs and their plights as well as their aspirations. In other words, we have *just begun* to see the results of the extensive reexamination of the role of the Negro during Reconstruction, and it would not be too much to say that at least some of the recent works could themselves bear critical reexamination.

Despite the fact that the student of Reconstruction can hardly be satisfied with what is now known about the Negro's role, he already has sufficient knowledge to conclude that some modification of the old view is fully justified. It would be well, therefore, to take notice of some of the new ways of looking at the problem and to examine their implications for the study of the general problem of Reconstruction.

As historians have viewed the early weeks and months following the close of the Civil War, they have had a good deal to say about the desperate plight of the freedmen. It is, of course, difficult to exaggerate this situation, and there has been much emphasis on the freedman's lack of competence to care for himself in a condition of freedom. Indeed, these has been much emphasis on the freedman who, in consequence of his ignorance and inexperience, was the ready prey of any and all who might seek to exploit him. There was more than a semblance of truth in this as it applied to the vast majority of Negroes. This view does not, however, give sufficient consideration to the not inconsiderable number of Negroes who, by training and experience, were quite prepared in 1865 to take care of themselves and even to assume some leadership roles.

In 1860 there were some 488,000 free Negroes in the United States, of whom 261,000—slightly more than one-half—lived in the slave states. Although the teaching of slaves and free Negroes to read and write was strictly forbidden by law in the slave states, thousands of slaves and free Negroes actually became literate. There were clandestine schools for Negroes in many communities in the South. In 1850, according to the census returns, there were 68 free Negroes attending school in Charleston, 53 in Mobile, 1,008 in New Orleans, and 1,453 in Baltimore. In numerous instances slaveholders taught their human chattel to read and write. Laws forbidding the teaching of slaves were for people on the other plantations; masters did whatever they pleased regarding their own slaves. And if they saw fit, they taught their slaves to read and write. Frederick Douglass received his first instruction from his mistress. Isaiah T. Montgomery of Mississippi received sufficient training to become the confidential accountant for his master, the brother of Jefferson Davis.

Meanwhile, Negroes were attending schools in many parts of the North. In 1850 there were more than 2,000 Negroes in Philadelphia; New York and Boston reported more than 1,400 each, while cities such as Providence, Brooklyn, New Haven, and Cincinnati each had several hundred Negroes in school. In some communities, such as Boston after 1855, they attended desegregated schools, while in other communities segregated education was the rule. In any case, the number of literate Negroes was steadily increasing.

It might actually be possible to compile some rather impressive figures on Negro literacy, especially when one recalls that many Negroes were educated abroad and when one adds to this number those who began their education in schools established by religious and philanthropic agencies during the war years. The point, however, is not to emphasize the general increase in literacy among Negroes—important as that may be—but to underscore the fact that by the end of the Civil War thousands of Negroes in the North and South were able to read and write. A further point is that in their various organizations—religious and benevolent—Negroes had opportunities to use their education and acquire experience in the management of their affairs.

One of the best proofs we have of the level of literacy and education of a considerable group of Negroes by 1865 is in their organizational activities. Within the first year following the close of the war Negroes in the North and South met in conventions to consider their common problems. These are the months that many historians have described as months of wandering and drifting on the part of the freedmen. Many of them did drift—from place to place—to "test" their freedom. Others, however, did not drift. Instead, they met in convention at Alexandria, Norfolk, Raleigh, Savannah, Charleston, Vicksburg, Nashville, and Cleveland to give attention to the problems they faced. The deliberations were orderly and dignified, and they were carefully recorded.

It is not too much to say that some of the representations made by these all-Negro conventions in 1865 are eloquent, and they give evidence not only of ample training but of a degree of understanding of the function of government that must have surprised many observers. For example, in their letter to President Andrew Johnson in May, 1865, a group of North Carolina Negroes said:

> Some of us are soldiers and have had the privilege of fighting for our country in this war. Since we have become Freemen, and been permitted the honor of being soldiers, we begin to feel that we are men, and are anxious to show our countrymen that we can and will fit ourselves for the creditable discharge of the duties of citizenship. We want the privilege of voting. It seems to us that men who are willing on the field of danger to carry the muskets of Republics in the days of peace ought to be permitted to carry its ballots; and certainly we cannot understand the justice of denying the elective franchise to men who have been fighting for the country, while it is freely given to men who have just returned from four years fighting against it.

These are the words of literate people, perfectly capable of thinking through their problems and perfectly aware of their betrayal by their own government.

During these years, thanks to the increasing educational opportunities provided by the Freedmen's Bureau and other agencies and thanks to their own organizational activities, many Negroes were rapidly assimilating the training and experience they needed to become participants in the affairs of their government. They therefore saw nothing unusual about their desire to enjoy the franchise, and more and more of them indicated such a desire. Inevitably many whites, especially those in the former Confederate states, raised questions about their qualifications and asserted that they lacked education and experience. This was the first time that such questions had been seriously raised since the ratification of the federal Constitution. Some Negroes thought these questions irrelevant, while others were certain that they could qualify if a reasonable test were fairly administered. Surely, all Negroes knew that race rather than education or experience was the major consideration in the suffrage question. All over the country there was some resistance to the enfranchisement of Negroes regardless of their educational qualifications, while in the South Negroes knew that they did not have the slightest chance of becoming enfranchised as long as the former Confederates were in power.

With no opportunity to participate in the political decisions regarding their own future, Negroes—even those who were college and university graduates—were unable to intervene effectively at any point. They were compelled, therefore, to accept decisions made for them by their former masters and the other whites who were eligible to serve their states under the Lincoln and Johnson plans of Reconstruction. Not only were Negroes without any voice in the decisions about their future, but they were also without any protection against the mistreatment or injustices to which they were subjected by the decision-makers. They *could and did* protest the enactment of harsh black codes by the state legislatures, but their protests were scarcely heard in the state capitals or even in Washington.

The absence of protection for the former slaves in the crucial first years following the end of the Civil War is one of the very remarkable phenomena of the early Reconstruction era. Even if one should argue —unsuccessfully, I believe—that the former masters continued to have the best interests of their former slaves in mind, there were the millions of whites, indeed the vast majority of southern whites, who had not been slaveholders. Many of them had much antipathy not only for the institution of slavery but for slaves as well. Whatever the attitude of former slaveholders or of nonslaveholders, the freedmen were left exposed to them and at their mercy. This was, of course, because of the rapid demobilization of the Union Army and the preoccupation of the military leaders with that process.

From the time that the Secretary of War issued the demobilization order on April 28, 1865, the troops were to be mustered out at the staggering rate of 300,000 per month. It was simply impossible to process that many men with the machinery in existence, but a vigorous effect was made to comply with the order. Within six months after the war's end more than 800,000 of the 1,034,064 officers and men in the United States Army had been demobilized. By the end of 1865 the government had 150,000 troops for all purposes, including garrisoning frontier posts and fighting the Indians, as well as supervising postwar operations in the South. Thus, by the end of December, 1865, North and South Carolina had 352 officers and 7,056 enlisted men. In the entire Division of the Gulf the number of white troops had been reduced to 10,000 men. There were vast stretches of territory in the former Confederacy where no Union soldier appeared after the late spring of 1865.

By the close of the Civil War some 186,000 Negroes had seen service in the Army of the United States. They were not demobilized at quite the rate of white soldiers. They had no businesses and professions and jobs to which to return. There was no reason for them to make an immediate return to civilian life. If anyone could be spared from civilian life, it was the Negro serviceman. Some former Confederates would claim, of course, that the Negro troops were being detained for the specific purpose of humiliating the prostrate South. There is not a shed of evidence to support this claim. Surely most of the Negro troops themselves had no interest in committing acts of recrimination, and the official reports on their conduct support this view, local complaints to the contrary notwithstanding. One of the commanding officers in Arkansas said that his regiment of Negro soldiers was so preoccupied with learning to read and write that they had time for little else. Indeed, not all whites complained of Negro troops. To offset the complaints against Negro troops in southern Georgia, all the principal citizens of Jasper, Florida, petitioned for the return of a company of colored troops which had been ordered from there. The point here is that in 1865 and 1866 there was not a sufficient number of United States troops, white or black, to provide even a semblance of protection for the 4,000,000 freedmen. The only protection they had was at the hands of the former Confederates, who hardly recognized any rights of Negroes that they were bound to respect.

When Congress took over the program of Reconstruction in 1867, the military supervision that had been reinstituted as the new governments were established was not only of short duration, but was, on the whole, ineffective. As soon as the new governments showed signs of stability the troops were withdrawn. In November, 1869, there were only 1,112 federal soldiers in Virginia, including those at Fortress Monroe. In Mississippi, at the same time, there were 716 officers and men scattered over the state. Since state militias could not be established without the permission of the federal government, the Reconstruction governments—and the Negroes—were with little or not protection from the antigovernment Ku Klux Klan and other guerrillas that sprang up all over the South. The situation became so desperate that Congress finally gave permission in 1869 for North Carolina, South Carolina, Florida, Alabama, Louisiana, and Arkansas to organize state militias. Some of the other states proceeded to organize militias without congressional authorization.

It was not always easy to enlist a sufficient number of white men to fill the militia quotas, and under the new dispensation Negroes were eligible anyway. To many white observers, the number of Negro militiamen seemed excessive, and the inference was drawn, as it was drawn in 1865, that the presence of such large numbers of armed Negroes was for the purpose of humiliating the whites. Because of the growing hostility to these armed groups and because of the increasing strength of the enemies of the Reconstruction governments, the state militias contributed, in a sense, to the downfall of the governments they were supposed to protect. It cannot be argued, however, that armed men, whether white or black, or whether federal or state, were of such numbers as to constitute a military occupation of the South. And without such occupation, the Negroes of the former Confederate states became the special targets and the victims of the groups who were determined to overthrow congressional Reconstruction.

Viewed in this light, Negroes became the easy prey of the hooded Klansmen and others of their ilk. The federal troops, if they were present at all, were insufficient in numbers to have any significant effect. President Grant, moreover, was most reluctant to dispatch troops to troubled areas and did so only when the situation became bloody and desperate. The state militias, with their large Negro contingents, merely fired the antagonism of those opposed to the Reconstruction governments and set them off on a reign of bloody terror that was unworthy of a civilized community. In the congressional hearings on the Klan terror in 1871, one Negro woman who occupied land that the whites wanted gave this testimony:

> They whipped me from the crown of my head to the soles of my feet. I was just raw. The blood oozed out through my frock all around the waist, clean through. . . . After I got away from them that night I ran to my house. My house was torn down. I went in and felt where my bed was. . . . I went to the other corner of the house and felt for my little children and I could not see them. . . . Their father lay out to the middle of the night, and my children lay out there too.

The period of congressional Reconstruction has been described by some as Negro rule, and the new governments in the South have been described as Black and Tan governments. The clear implication is that Negroes dominated the governments of the former Confederacy or that at least their role and their vote were crucial. Today, few, if any, serious students of the period would countenance any such description. It should be added, somewhat hastily, however, that many politicians and laymen who today attack civil rights and voting legislation do so on the ground that it would deliver the South to the Negro, whose role would be reminiscent of the Reconstruction era. While such a claim is both specious and fallacious, there persists the view, even among some serious students, that the Negro's influence during congressional Reconstruction was considerable and even decisive.

The only states in which Negroes were in the government in any considerable number were South Carolina, Mississippi, and Louisiana. In the first South Carolina legislature Negroes outnumbered whites eighty-seven to forty, but they controlled at no time any other branch of the state government. In Louisiana, they numbered forty-two out of eighty-four members of the lower house, although it should be remarked that the number is not precisely known because of the racial admixture of so many of the members. In Mississippi there were forty Negroes out of a total of 115 members in the first Reconstruction legislature. It is not necessary to review here the racial composition of the legislatures of the several states or of the other branches of the governments. One can state categorically that Negroes did not rule anywhere in the South.

This is not to say that there were not any individual Negroes who were without responsibility and influence. Here one must recall that much of the Negro leadership was both literate and experienced. In the several southern states not only were there Negroes who emerged as leaders but also the black Carpetbaggers, so-called, who returned to their southern homes after many years of absence. Some who moved South had never lived there before. In South Carolina Francis L. Cardozo, who became secretary of state and later the state treasurer, was educated at the University of Glasgow and at London, while J. J. Wright, who became a member of the state supreme court, had been educated at the University of Pennsylvania and was a member of the Pennsylvania bar. In Alabama James T. Rapier, who became a member of Congress, had been sent to Canada by his white father to be educated. Jonathan Gibbs, who became secretary of state in Florida, was a graduate of Dartmouth and had been a Presbyterian minister for several years before the beginning of the Civil War.

Obviously, these were exceptional men. After all, it would be unusual to find among the white members of these governments graduates of Glasgow, London, or Harvard. Most of the white *and* Negro leaders were self-made men, who, through perseverance, native ability, and sometimes a little bit of luck, made their way up to positions of influence and importance. Obviously also, there were some men in both races who made their way to power through chicanery, duplicity and fraud. Once in power they used their positions, as one might expect, to advance their own interests, frequently at the expense of the welfare of the larger community.

One principal reason why there was not and could not have been any such thing as Negro rule is not merely because the Negroes had insufficient political power but also because the coalition to which they belonged was both loose and ineffective. One group in the so-called coalition, the Scalawags, belonged to it not because they shared the Negro's ideals or aspirations but because they were qualified under the strict requirements laid down by the Congress. The other group, the Carpetbaggers, contained people whose views differed from each other almost as much as their general view differed from the former Con-federates. Some were investors who were politically neutral, some were Union soldiers who just liked the South, some were clever politi-cians, some were teachers in Negro schools, and indeed some were Negroes. It is inconceivable that these many groups could have agreed on a political or social program, and in the absence of substantial agreement the Negro wielded little influence and received few benefits.

In the constitutional conventions and in the subsequent govern-ments in each of the states, the groups making up the coalition were at odds with each other over such fundamental questions as the nature and amount of power to be vested in the state government, the matter of public education, and what, if anything, should be done to guaran-tee the rights of Negroes. Many of the native whites went over to the opposition when it appeared that the governments were moving to-ward equal rights for Negroes. Many northerners became lukewarm when the new governments threatened to impose restrictions on capital investments. Others from the North, the idealists, became disgusted with the manner in which the governments came under the influence of the venal business interests of all groups. Small wonder, under the circumstances, that they were unable to agree on the outlines of programs of welfare, social reform, and public educa-tion—conveniently segregated almost everywhere.

The Reconstruction governments in the South have been described by almost all historians as radical. While the description is almost permanently fixed, it does not appear to be very accurate. If some of the governments were corrupt and extravagant—and not all of them were—they were very much like state governments in other parts of the country at the time; indeed the federal government was not with-out its crooks and knaves. If some of them pressed for welfare legisla-tion and public education, they were seeking to close the gap that had separated them for a generation from the progressive states of the Northeast. If they moved toward universal suffrage, they were following the lead of states in the North and some countries abroad.

The only possible radical aspect was that, at the insistence of the federal government, Negroes had to be included in the new concept of universal education. But when one considers the growing number of Negroes who were acquiring education and experience, many of them could meet the standards that had not been required or expected of any other group in the history of American suffrage.

There is something quite tragic about the picture of the Negro as he entered upon his first century of freedom. In the beginning he was denied equal rights as a citizen on the ground that he was not qualified, and there was a disposition to deny him the opportunity to become qualified on the ground that he was unfit for citizenship and equality. But there is also something quite tragic about the picture of the United States as it entered its second century of independence. In the beginning it had captured the imagination of peoples around the world with its ringing declaration that all men were created equal. By the time that it had reached the respectable if not venerable age of one hundred years, it was reconsidering its earlier declaration, and neither the Fourteenth nor the Fifteenth amendments were sufficient to extend equal rights to all its citizens. It was the Negro, released from 250 years of human bondage, who brought about this reconsideration; but it was also the Negro who challenged, even dared, the country to deny its earlier pronouncements. If Reconstruction did nothing else, it called attention to the inescapable fact that the United States would have to move forward on the basis of equality, even if it included the Negro, or it would be compelled to retrogress to a point where its distinctiveness would no longer be valid. This has been the torment of the last hundred years, and it began with the Negro during Reconstruction.

III: DECLINE AND FALL,

1877–1900

An Old World of Bondage

• Once white southerners regained full political power in their states in the 1870's, even the few outward trappings of black power disappeared or began to recede. Northerners increasingly contented themselves with self-congratulation over ending slavery and restoring the Union, while ignoring or deprecating the economic and political problems of the freedmen. Conservative white "Redeemers" in the South drew closer to their northern counterparts, while rebuilding a strong Democratic party in the region; and as the Grant Era drew to a close, the "Negro Question" seemed safely pigeonholed as a matter for local authorities to handle. Southern blacks and a tiny band of northern white sympathizers knew quite well what "Redemption" meant for the Negro; peonage in freedom replaced peonage in slavery for most blacks. Desperately, thousands sought means to escape the subordination which whites at home and in Washington had designed for them. Rayford Logan describes the Exodus of 1879 and other movements and plans for Negro escape from bondage. He notes the decisive and negative contribution of federal inactivity, its refusal to continue even the limited programs of Reconstruction, in triggering unhappy Diasporas such as the Exodus.

The economic basis of second-class citizenship for Negroes was rooted deep in slavery. On the eve of the Civil War almost nine out of ten Negroes were slaves. The vast majority of these 3,953,760 slaves were field hands and domestic servants. A small number were carpenters, coopers, tailors, shoemakers, bootmakers, cabinet makers, plasterers, seamstresses. Others were employed in salt works, iron and lead

Abridged from Rayford W. Logan, *The Betrayal of the Negro* (The Macmillan Company, 1965), pp. 125–46 (footnotes omitted). Copyright © 1965 by Rayford W. Logan. Reprinted by permission of The Macmillan Company and the author.

mines, on railroad construction, on river boats and on docks. Some worked in textile mills, especially in Florida, Mississippi, Alabama, Georgia, South Carolina and Louisiana. The exigencies of the war, which increased the number of Negroes engaged in non-agricultural pursuits, particularly in iron works, coal mines and salt works, clearly demonstrated that "Negro labor, properly directed, was adaptable to diversified agriculture and to a varied industrial program." But at the end of the war most Southern Negroes were without capital, without the rudiments of education and without experience in work except as agricultural field hands and as domestic servants.

Contrary to the Marxist interpretations of Reconstruction, there was little sense of solidarity between white and black workers in the South. Prior to the war, most of the non-slaveholding and landless whites held slavery responsible for their own distress. White urban workers particularly resented the hiring of Negro slave artisans. It was in fact the plight of the poor whites that had led forward-looking Southerners like William Gregg to favor industrialism. They had accomplished little, however, except perhaps to increase the gulf between free black workers and white workers and to prepare the way for the almost exclusive employment of whites in the post-war industries.

The 488,000 free Negroes encountered many difficulties in their attempts to gain a livelihood. More than forty per cent of them lived in the South where they, like the non-slaveholding and landless whites, had to compete with slave labor. In addition, many Southern states circumscribed the mobility of Negroes even within the state and prohibited them from engaging in certain occupations. Despite all these handicaps, some of them became skilled artisans. They worked in fifty different occupations in Charleston and in more than seventy in North Carolina. In the slave state of Maryland, some 2,000 free Negroes of Baltimore engaged in nearly one hundred occupations, including paperhanging, engraving, quarrying, photography and tailoring. New Orleans had colored jewelers, architects and lithographers. "Almost every community had its free Negro carpenters, barbers, cabinet makers, and brickmasons; many had shopkeepers, salesmen, and clerks, even where it was a violation of the law." . . .

A few free Negroes had acquired property in larger amounts than is generally known. In New York City they owned more than $1,000,-000 worth of property, in Cincinnati more than $500,000 and comparable amounts in such cities as Philadelphia, Baltimore, Washington and Boston. Negro holdings in Providence were estimated at between $35,000 and $50,000 in 1839. Even more surprising is the amount of property possessed by free Negroes in the South. In Virginia they owned more than 60,000 acres of farm land and city real estate valued at $463,000; in North Carolina, more than $1,000,000 in real and personal property. Free Negroes in New Orleans paid taxes on property variously estimated at from $9,000,000 to $15,000,000. A few individual Negroes were wealthy. James Forten of Philadelphia had accumulated a fortune of more than $100,000 and Thomy Lafon of New Orleans, $500,000. A few Southern Negroes even held slaves.

It is thus inaccurate to assert, as do some orators, that the Negro started from scratch in 1865. Most free Negroes, none the less, in both North and South eked out a precarious existence. Moreover, the war had in many cases increased the bitterness against Negroes. Many Southern poor whites expressed bitter resentment against a "rich man's war and a poor man's fight." In some parts of the North, whites were equally bitter against the "nigger war." The most extreme manifestation of this attitude in the North erupted in the "Draft Riots" in New York City, July, 1863. For four days the city was in the hands of a mob against which the police were powerless. The mob demolished draft headquarters, chased and beat Negroes, hanged them from trees and lampposts. Much of this violence stemmed not only from aversion to fighting a war in which the whites had little interest but also, perhaps more so, from the competition of Negroes for jobs.

The economic basis for second-class citizenship for Negroes is found also in the failure of the federal government to accept responsibility for a long-range, comprehensive and intelligent policy of economic habilitation of the emancipated Negroes. Some fifty private organizations wrote a memorable chapter in the history of American philanthropy by providing substantial relief and inaugurating educational programs for the freedmen in the South. But, obviously, the job was too stupendous for private philanthropy. Either private capital or governmental action therefore had to provide the freedmen with economic opportunities to undergird their new political and civil rights. Southern capital could not provide the jobs. Northern capital, especially in the years immediately after the war, found more profitable investments in the East and West than in the South. The Black Codes of the Southern states, 1865-1866, showed clearly the determination to deny the freedmen equal economic opportunity. During the critical period immediately after the war, federal action alone could provide the freedmen with the economic opportunities without which their new political and civil liberties would have little foundation.

The nature and extent of the aid that the federal government should give to freedmen and the South in general precipitated in 1863 one of the earliest debates in American history on what is today called the "welfare state." Proponents of governmental aid insisted that private charity was insufficient to alleviate the woeful plight of the freedmen and that these latter could not measurably alleviate it through their own efforts. Opponents declared that governmental aid would be "revolutionary," that it would create a large number of bureaucrats and pave the way for corruption in government. They also contended that governmental aid would curtail the freedmen's initiative and self-reliance. After two years of debate Congress on March 3, 1865, finally approved a bill without a record vote and Lincoln immediately signed it. It was clearly designed as a war measure, for the Bureau of Refugees, Freedmen and Abandoned Lands was placed under the secretary of war and it was to continue for only one year after the end of the war. The secretary of war was to issue necessary provisions, clothing and fuel and, under the direction of the president, the commissioner in charge could set aside for the freedmen and refugees tracts of land of not more than forty acres to be leased to tenants. The lessees were to be protected in the use of the land for three years at a low rental and at the end of the term they could purchase the land at an appraised value. . . .

Most Southerners violently opposed the Freedmen's Bureau. They contended that it threatened to intervene between employer and worker. They further accused it of promoting political ambitions on the part of the colored population and of spreading the belief among the freedmen that they would be given forty acres and a mule. Because of strong Southern opposition and lack of vigorous Northern support, the main work of the Bureau continued only until 1869. Of course, it made mistakes, as did, for example, some of the relief and rehabilitation agencies in European countries devastated by World War II. But on balance, the Freedmen's Bureau helped the South to get back on its feet. Between 1865 and 1869 the Bureau issued more than 20,000,000 rations, approximately 5,000,000 to whites and 15,000,000 to Negroes. The medical department operated more than forty hospitals and treated some 450,000 cases of illness. The Bureau distributed a small portion of abandoned and confiscated lands to freedmen. It sought to protect them from violence and outrage, from serfdom, and to defend their right to hold property and to enforce contracts. Its most notable work was in the field of education. The limited operations after 1869 ceased in 1872, five years before the withdrawal of the last federal troops from Louisiana and South Carolina. As Du Bois wrote in 1903, a permanent Freedmen's Bureau, with adequate funds, might have provided "a great school of prospective citizenship, and solved in a way we have not yet solved the most perplexing and persistent of the Negro problems."

Until a few years ago it was popular to make fun of the "naive" belief encouraged by some agents of the Freedmen's Bureau that the freedmen were going to be given forty acres and a mule by the federal government. The levity decreased somewhat when the Great Depression of the 1930's revealed the plight of white sharecroppers who outnumbered colored by two to one. Perhaps because federal assistance then included more whites than Negroes, there was less opposition to various agricultural programs, especially after large planters and bankers discovered that they would receive directly and indirectly a great share of the largesse. More recently, the bitter attacks upon these New Deal projects and "socialistic" programs have begun again to influence American historiography. In the meanwhile, however, some historians have stopped sneering and laughing at the "forty acres and mule" joke. Some of them consider the failure of the federal government to expand and continue the insufficient program of land distribution through the Freedmen's Bureau the greatest blunder of Reconstruction. . . .

Although the Black Codes were repealed by the Reconstruction legislatures, the freedmen encountered great difficulty in acquiring land for the simple reason that few of them possessed the means of doing so. Some came into possession of land in various ways—through the assistance of the federal government, through a kindly planter who turned over land to them or an impoverished or indolent planter who allowed them to pay the back taxes and thus acquire title. In Florida they secured homesteads covering 160,000 acres within a year after emancipation. By 1874 Georgia Negroes owned more than 350,000 acres of land. It is not clear how many had been held by free Negroes prior to the war. Negroes in Virginia acquired perhaps some 80,000 acres of land in the late sixties and early seventies. In 1890, 120,738 Negroes owned farm homes, all of which except 12,253 were unencumbered. By 1900 the number had risen to 192,993, but the number of encumbered had risen from 12,253 to 54,017. The vast majority of these farm owners lived in the South. If it may be assumed that those who owned farm homes also owned their farms, they had made commendable progress. But their number was small, for almost 7,000,000 Negroes lived in the South which included, according to the Census, Delaware, Maryland, West Virginia and the District of Columbia.

These farm owners constituted only one-fourth of Negroes living on farms. The other three-fourths were tenants who were greatly exploited, especially by the crop-lien system. They were compelled to obtain advances from the country merchants for meal, bacon, molasses, cloth and tobacco as well as for tools, farm implements, fertilizer and work animals. The mark-up for the difference between cash and credit frequently amounted to from 40% to 100%. Since the value of the crops was sometimes less than the advances, the tenant started the new year in debt. Since, moreover, the books were kept by the merchants and many of the debtors could not read, the chances for cheating were usually not allowed to slip. It has been estimated that in some portions of the South nine-tenths of the farmers fell into debt. Many poor whites found escape in the textile mills. Some Negroes sought escape in flight.

As early as the beginning of the eighteenth century colonization of Negroes outside the United States had been advocated as a partial solution to slavery and the presence of unwanted free Negroes. In 1816 the American Colonization Society was formed for the purpose of settling Negroes in Africa. But perhaps not more than 25,000 had left the United States for Africa, Haiti and elsewhere by the end of the Civil War. Plans for colonizing in Liberia and other places were revived after the war, but the most important proposals for the migration if Negroes envisaged other parts of the United States. The federal government refused to aid any of the plans for migration. This refusal constitutes the third basis for the second-class citizenship of the Southern black farmers and farm workers who numbered almost one-half of all black workers.

The first proposals for federal aid to migration during the post-Reconstruction period resulted from the "Exodus" of 1879. It is no mere coincidence that the exodus began less than two years after the withdrawal of the last of the federal troops from the South. The seventeen hundred pages of testimony presented to a senatorial investigating committee naturally contain conflicting evidence. On the one hand, it was contended that the Southern white man was the Negro's best friend; that most Negroes were contented and prosperous; that only a small minority were disgruntled and that they had been stirred up by white agitators from the North. Some Negroes, whom recent authors have called "collaborationists," supported these assertions. It was argued further that Republicans were luring Negroes to the North in order to assure Republican victories and that transportation companies were enticing Negroes to leave home in order to increase their profits.

There were, however, real grievances. The crop-lien system probably kept more Negroes than whites in debt. Educational opportunities for Negroes were even more inadequate than those for whites. New industries relegated black workers to the lowest paid jobs. "Bulldozing" and other forms of violence prevented Negroes from voting and from becoming "uppity." They were frequently jailed for petty offenses. Most whites treated them with contempt or with a patronizing paternalism. Frederick Douglass gave a detailed summary of the Negroes' grievances in an address at Saratoga Springs before the American Social Science Association on September 12, 1879. . . . Crimes for which a white man went free brought severe punishment to a black man. "Wealthy and respectable" white men gave encouragement to midnight raids upon the defenseless. Even the old slave driver's whip had reappeared, "and the inhuman spectacle of the chain-gang is beginning to be seen." The fleeing Negroes had declared that the government of every Southern state was in the hands of the "old slave oligarchy," and they feared that "both departments" of the federal government would soon be in the same hands. "They believe that when the Government, State and National, shall be in the control of the old masters of the South, they will find means for reducing the freedmen to a condition analogous to slavery. They despair of any change for the better, declaring that everything is waxing worse for the Negro, and that his only means of safety is to leave the South." If only half this statement was true, Douglass added, the explanation for the exodus was abundantly clear.

But Douglass urged Negroes to stay in the South. As a staunch Republican, he proclaimed his faith in President Hayes's determination to assert his constitutional powers for the protection of Negroes in the South. He was on firmer ground when he pointed out that encouragement of the flight amounted to "an abandonment of the great and paramount principle of protection to person and property in every State of the Union." If it were conceded that the Federal government could not provide this protection in the South, what would be the final stopping-place for the Negro? Where would he go if some sand-lot orator in Kansas or California stirred up a mob as one was doing against the Chinese in California? Negroes should also stay in the South, because they had "a monopoly of the labor market" there, and because they had adopted "the careless and improvident habits of the South" which they could not quickly discard in the North. Douglass even doubted that many of these Southern Negroes could stand the more rigorous Northern climate. In what was perhaps the first evocation of the possible dire effects of radical doctrines from Russia, Douglass concluded: "The cry of 'Land and Liberty,' the watchword of the Nihilistic party in Russia, has a music sweet to the ear of all oppressed peoples, and well it shall be for the landholders of the South if they shall learn wisdom in time and adopt such a course of just treatment towards the landless laborers of the South in the future as shall make this popular watchword uncontagious and unknown among their laborers, and further stampede to the North wholly unknown, indescribable and impossible."

Richard T. Greener, first colored graduate of Harvard College (1870), member of the faculty of the University of South Carolina during Reconstruction and Dean of the Law School at Howard University (1879-1882) and later United States consul at Bombay and Vladivostok, appeared on the same program in opposition to Douglass. His principal argument held that the western lands were waiting for settlement, and were being rapidly filled up by Swedes, Norwegians, Mennonites, Icelanders and Poles. Six hundred thousand acres of public land had been taken up since June 30, 1878. Irish Catholics and Jews were raising money to help migration from cities to the West. He proposed therefore that Negroes should raise $200,-000, organize a National Executive Committee and have agents to buy land, procure cheap transportation and disseminate accurate information. This proposal for self-help was made necessary by the failure of Congress to assist the migrants.

On January 16, 1879, Senator Windom, Republican from Minnesota, had introduced a resolution for the appointment of a committee of seven senators to examine the expediency and practicability of encouraging the partial migration of Negroes to various states and territories of the United States. This resolution was the first gesture after the abolishment of the Freedmen's Bureau to provide federal aid for the welfare of the freedmen. It antedated the Blair bill and the Lodge bill by eleven years. But Windom was unable to obtain approval for a resolution that provided merely for the appointment of an investigating committee. Once more, it is evident that federal aid to economic welfare encountered more serious opposition than did federal aid to education or protection of the right to vote.

The debates on Windom's resolution have been overlooked even more that those on the Blair and Lodge bills. On February 7, 1879, the Republican senator from Minnesota insisted that constitutional amendments and acts of Congress had alike failed to enforce rights "solemnly" guaranteed to the freedmen. The "Southern question" still presented the most difficult problem in American politics. None of the methods that the federal government had adopted to protect the freedmen had proved effective. The Southern white man, he categorically asserted, would "tolerate no conditions but those of domination on one side and subserviency on the other. Centuries of negro slavery have rendered the white men of the South far less competent to deal with colored citizenship than they have the negro to exercise it." Windom was particularly concerned about those sections of the South in which Negroes were in the majority and where under the constitution and laws they would probably control the local government. The senator put his finger on one sore spot already mentioned, namely, that when Negroes elected Negroes to office, some white men were out of jobs. Since the federal government would no longer use force to protect Negroes in the right to vote, and since otherwise that right could not be exercised especially in regions where Negroes were in the majority, the only solution was migration. Migration to Liberia was impracticable for the simple reason that the natural increase of the colored population in the United States would be many times greater than the number that could possibly be transported to Africa. Such migration would also be tantamount to banning them from their own country.

Windom stated his conviction that there were several states where Negroes would be warmly welcomed and their rights protected. While he did not identify those states, he did mention specifically portions of the territories of Arizona, New Mexico and especially the Indian Territory where they would be similarly received. He did not mention, however, Idaho, Montana, North Dakota, South Dakota, Utah or Wyoming, territories much closer to Minnesota. Even if it became necessary to organize a new territory for the Negroes, he continued, no constitutional difficulty would ensue since it was not proposed to exclude any persons from the newly organized territory. Windom was not too precise on this point. He appears to have meant that if it were generally known that homesteads of from forty to eighty acres were for Negroes and that territorial officers would be mainly colored, then white settlers would voluntarily stay away. His proposal did not involve compulsory migration or federal support of the migrants. But his resolution did provide that the committee might report by bill or otherwise what was the most effective way of encouraging the migration. It was in this speech that Windom made the perspicacious observation that "the black man does not excite antagonism because he is black, but because he is a *citizen,* and as such may control an election." He estimated that the migration of only a quarter of a million from the overcrowded districts of the South would accomplish the aims he had in view. No senator continued the discussion.

When Windom on February 24 moved that the Senate consider his resolution he was immediately challenged by the Democrat, Saulsbury of Delaware. Saulsbury had objected in 1862 to the recognition of Haiti because it would lead to the eventual presence of a Haitian minister in the gallery reserved for diplomats. He declared in 1879 that Windom's resolution would incur expense and would do no good. Later, Saulsbury probably revealed his real objection when he charged: "It contains an implied accusation against certain States and certain congressional districts in this country that colored people are not allowed to vote." He wanted specific proof that the charge was accurate. Windom was willing to strike out the words that seemed to reflect this accusation. Since the morning hour had expired, the vice-president ruled that the Senate would proceed to unfinished business. Windom gave notice that he would press his resolution in the morning hour the next day. He was present on that day but he did not press his resolution.

He did not press it until December 15, 1879 when Voorhees, Democratic Senator from Indiana, alarmed by the migration of Negroes from North Carolina to Indiana, introduced a resolution for the appointment of a committee to investigate the causes of the migration. Windom on the next day offered an amendment that was substantially similar to his resolution of January 16 with the exception that it envisaged only territories as a refuge for the colored citizens of the South. Voorhees replied on December 18 that his purpose was to ascertain whether Negroes were leaving the South because of the injustice inflicted upon them or because of "a conspiracy on the part of disreputable people, both white and black, to disturb the condition of the black race at the South and make them discontented and unhappy and point to them greater advantages elsewhere which do not exist, thus spreading a delusion and a snare before them, and getting them to move about." He was certain that the good people of Indiana had no objections to "legitimate" settlers. But, in what must have been an appeal especially to West Coast Senators, he said that Indiana no more wanted Negroes brought in by "regiments, divisions and corps" than the people of California wanted Chinese landed upon them by organized societies. Indiana, moreover, had no wastelands for the freedmen to take up cheaply. It would be fruitful of evil if the "well-behaved and decent colored population" of Indiana had thrust upon them the migrants from North Carolina. If he were motivated by party considerations, he would urge that Negroes be encouraged to enter Indiana, for there would be five new Democratic voters to every new Negro settler. But Voorhees objected to Windom's amendment as being "premature." Let the Committee ascertain the facts without being instructed what to do after it had ascertained them. . . .

Windom's amendment was rejected, 18 yeas to 25 nays. Sixteen Republicans and two Democrats, both from the South, voted for the amendment. Hill's vote was perhaps a kind of defiant justification of his own position. Since Kellogg of Louisiana did not participate in the debate, it would be difficult to conjecture as to his reasons. Of the 25 negative votes, 12 were cast by senators from states that had seceded. Five were cast by Democratic senators from the border states of Kentucky, Delaware and Missouri that had been slaveholding states; two were from West Virginia, carved out of the former slaveholding state of Virginia. But six were from the Northern states of Illinois, Connecticut, Ohio, New Jersey, Oregon, and Indiana. These six votes could have swung the decision in favor of Windom's resolution, 24 to 19. . . .

While Congress was debating, investigating, reporting and doing nothing to aid migration, the movement from the South had assumed such proportions in the spring of 1879 that it has been labeled the "Exodus." Led by Henry Adams of Louisiana and Moses ("Pap") Singleton of Tennessee, some 40,000 Negroes virtually stampeded from Mississippi, Louisiana, Alabama and Georgia for the Midwest. The largest number fled to Kansas where, at first, they received a friendly welcome. The Topeka *Commonwealth* on April 7, 1879, pointed out that it was only fitting that Kansas which had fought to be a free state should become the home of ex-slaves. The governor welcomed one group to "the State made immortal by Old John Brown." But, as the number increased, the attitude changed especially since many of the migrants presented a woebegone spectacle. One author described them as follows:

> Hopeless, penniless and in rags, these poor people were thronging the wharves of St. Louis, crowding the steamers on the Mississippi River, hailing the passing steamers and imploring

them for a passage to the land of freedom, where the rights of citizens are respected and honest toil rewarded by compensations.

As a consequence, messengers were sent from Kansas to advise the Negroes not to migrate and, if they insisted on doing so, to provide themselves with necessary equipment. Some hotels and restaurants in Kansas refused the migrants accommodations. Singleton was so disappointed that he tried, unsuccessfully, to encourage Negroes to migrate to Liberia or Canada.

The destitution of the migrants was only partly offset by the efforts of the Freedmen's Relief Association. Reviving something of the fervor that had given much needed support to the "Free Soilers" in the days of "Bleeding Kansas," the Association raised some $25,000 in cash and $100,000 in clothing, bedding, household goods and other necessities. About one-sixth of the cash and one-fourth of the furnishings came from England. Thus assisted, and further aided by the Homestead Law, the migrants bought about 20,000 acres of land. Lack of funds, however, made it impossible for many of the farmers to buy equipment. Many of them found employment on railroads, in coal mines and in public works while the women took in washing, worked as house servants and kept apple stalls. There is no evidence available that the state contributed direct aid to the migrants, but it did build schools for children and maintained night classes for adults.

In addition to those who migrated to Kansas, some 4,000 moved to Iowa and Nebraska. Little is known about the fate of these migrants, but it is probable that it was similar to that of those who fled to Kansas. Until the Oklahoma Territory was thrown open to white settlement in 1889, a few Negroes were warmly received by the Indians. A traveler in Indian Territory in 1880 gave a very favorable account of their homes, farms, churches and schoolhouses.

It was thus clear that migration would not afford an effective avenue of escape for any considerable number of Negroes. The loss of Negro labor did, however, induce a reexamination of the treatment of black workers, especially in Mississippi. As early as May 6, 1879, a convention of leading white and colored citizens met in Vicksburg. It affirmed that the Constitution and laws of the United States had placed Negroes on a plane of absolute equality with the whites. The convention pledged its power and influence to protect the Negroes at the polls and recommended the abolition of the mischievous credit system. But the convention rejected a proposal of ex-Governor Foote to establish in every county a committee, composed of men who had the confidence of both whites and Negroes, to hear their complaints.

Ten years later, however, some Southerners favored the migration of Negroes from Southern states. This change of attitude was perhaps prompted by fear that Congress might pass a law providing for federal supervision of federal elections. President Harrison made such a proposal in his annual message of 1889. Senator M. C. Butler of South Carolina who had been one of the leaders in the Hamburg riot almost immediately introduced a bill, December 12, "to provide for the migration of persons of color from the Southern States." Morgan, an influential senator from Alabama who enjoyed friendly relations with many prominent Northerners, argued sarcastically that only a few statesmen wanted Negroes to remain massed in certain states with a view to taking control of the state governments. In support of the thesis that Negroes were incapable of absorbing the white man's culture, Morgan contended that the Portuguese experience in Africa after 400 years was conclusive. The failure of the Negroes of the Congo to organize a vast empire was further evidence of their incapacity for self-government, as was also the example of Haiti. Ingalls of Kansas opposed the bill because there was no reason to believe that the African could ever compete with the Anglo-Saxon in government, art, conquest or practical affairs. Butler did not believe in the "total, hopeless depravity of the Negro race," but he reasoned that, since the United States realized the necessity of separating Indians from whites, the necessity of removing Negroes from the United States should be equally obvious. Wade Hampton contended that every race, save the Caucasian, "is and ought to be regarded as alien in the United States." Vance of North Carolina pointed out that the Negro, though outnumbering the whites in many parts of the South, permitted himself to be intimidated and defrauded in the matter of suffrage. Hoar of Massachusetts retorted that no senator had ever conducted himself with more propriety, dignity and intelligence than had Bruce and that the colored members of the House were the equal of others in ability. He scoffed at the idea that Northerners should be silent on the problem of Negroes in the South only to have to listen to a proposal for even voluntary emigration to Africa. Blair suggested that, if 10,000 carefully selected white men were sent to Africa, the whole problem would be settled. Apparently not even Southern senators took Butler's bill seriously, for it did not come to a vote.

Less well known than the Exodus of 1879 is the attempt of a

colored man, Edwin P. McCabe, to create a Negro state out of the Oklahoma Territory. The Cherokee Strip was also considered as a possible new home for Negro migrants. McCabe, who had been state auditor of Kansas, is reported to have sent 300 colored families from North Carolina and 500 from South Carolina. Arrangements were said to have been made for 5,000 families to migrate to Oklahoma. But the federal government provided no aid to this project. Senators Ingalls and Plumb of Kansas supported the idea, as did several members of the House and General E. H. Funston. President Harrison granted McCabe an interview but took no steps to support his enterprise.

This movement failed not only because of the lack of federal support and private financial assistance but also because of the hostility of both Indians and whites. . . . It may be presumed that the Indians, who had welcomed a few Negroes in the 1870's, took alarm at the influx of a large number. *The New York Times* reported in 1891 that there were 22,000 Negroes in the Northeast Black Jack section. Perhaps the Indians were also aroused by white settlers who were determined to keep the territory for themselves. In any case, the Oklahoma Territory was no more prepared than Kansas, Iowa or Nebraska to absorb enough Negroes to relieve appreciably their miserable condition in the Southern states.

Plans for Southern Negroes to migrate to other parts of the United States or to emigrate continued to be formulated until the end of the century. The fact that many of these were projected in the 1890's suggests that the general deterioration of the Negro's status prompted them as it did earlier and later proposals. In 1894 the Knights of Labor proposed to send an organizer into the South to lecture on the advantages of colonization in the Congo Basin, Liberia and other parts of Africa. The Knights planned to petition Congress to make an appropriation to aid the project. There is no evidence that the petition was presented, probably because the Knights had almost disappeared from the ranks of organized labor. It is clear, however, that the Knights had abandoned the hope which had existed even until the late 1880's of organizing black workers in the South.

One of the few undertakings in the 1890's that resulted in actual migration was that organized by a colored man, variously known as H. Ellis and W. H. Ellis. Early in 1895, some 800 Negroes, largely recruited from Alabama towns by Ellis, attempted to settle near the village of Mapimi in the Mexican state of Durango. A severe winter, inadequate housing facilities and an outbreak of smallpox soon drove

most of the settlers back to the United States. On the recommendation of President Cleveland, the railroads that had transported the
migrants from the Texas border back to their homes were reim-
bursed, but there is no evidence that the government assisted the
distressed settlers.

One of the most interesting proposals was that in 1897 made by
the Americans who had executed a revolution in Hawaii that Negroes
be imported from Louisiana, Texas and Mississippi. This plan would
result in the displacement of Japanese laborers at the expiration of
their contracts. The Hawaiian government also planned to issue no
more six months' residence permits to Chinese. Evidence is lacking
that the plan materialized.

Brief mention of a few other proposals and actual migrations com-
pletes the picture, as it is known to date, of the evident yearning of
some Negroes to escape from the South. In 1877, 1894, and 1895,
three small ships chartered by private Negro enterprise, sailed for
Liberia. A proposal for a Negro state within the United States, advanced in 1883, received scant attention. Lillian K. Ray, a wealthy
English philanthropist, founded the town of Cedarlake, near Decatur,
Alabama, as an experiment to make Negroes an industrial population
distinct in themselves. Other all-Negro towns, especially in Mississippi, attracted Negroes from rural areas.

The Spanish American War required no such expansion of Northern industries as that which, during World War I and World War II,
finally led to the migration of hundreds of thousands of Negroes
from the South. Foreign immigrants, moreover, more than supplied the
need of Northern industries. Neither the North nor the sparsely
settled West afforded an escape for the approximately 9,000,000 Negroes of the South, about one-half of whom were engaged in agriculture.

Nor did the Populist Revolt provide an escape from thralldom.
The economic roots of the various organizations which since the
1870's had sought to improve the lot of farmers are well known.
They included primarily a decline in the price of farm products
without a corresponding decline in the cost of manufactured articles
and of transportation. The South suffered perhaps even more than
did the West, for the price of cotton fell more rapidly than did that
of either corn or wheat. In the period after the Civil War "Cotton
was King" even more than it had been prior to the war. Production
rose from five and a half million bales in 1880 to nine and a half at the
end of the century. Overproduction led to a drop in price from
twenty-nine cents in 1870 to seven cents in 1894. As in other farming

areas, farmers were compelled to borrow from banks at usurious rates of interest; unable to repay loans, they were forced in many instances to mortgage and frequently to lose their farms. Throughout the South nearly half the farms were tilled by renters whose exploitation by merchants through the mark-up or "pluck me" system has been already described. In brief, conditions in the South were surely no better and probably worse in the 1890's than they had been at the time of the Exodus of 1879. . . . [Even] success of the [Populist] Revolt would not necessarily have meant an improvement in agriculture in the South. After 1897, when the price of cotton began to rise, Negroes still were denied an equitable share in the rise. Free enterprise had not hurdled the "color line."

Folkways, Stateways, and Racism

• *It took longer to exclude the previously franchised blacks
from voting than it did to subordinate them economically,
but the former came almost as naturally as night follows day.
The delay arose mainly because southern white politicians
wished to play with the dwindling Negro vote to bolster their
particular party or faction. By the end of the century, however, even this controlled exercise of Negro suffrage had become offensive to most whites. The Southern Way became
incontestably the Way of White Supremacy. As a leading
southern historian, U. B. Phillips, later phrased it, white
southerners shared the belief that the South "must remain
a white man's country," in all ways and at all times. C.
Vann Woodward here traces the course of southern politics
at the end of the nineteenth century, and shows how the
race issue all but engulfed other political considerations,
giving the white South a costly unity that spelled degradation for its blacks and neglect of the region's economic
problems. That it also spelled subordination and poverty
for its Negro hating poor whites did not seem to matter.*

Before the South capitulated completely to the doctrines of the
extreme racists, three alternative philosophies of race relations were
put forward to compete for the region's adherence and support. One
of these, the conservative philosophy, attracted wide support and was
tried out in practice over a considerable period of time. The second
approach to the problem, that of the Southern radicals, received able
expression and won numerous adherents, but the lack of political
success on the part of the radical party of Populism limited the trial
by practice of that philosophy to rather inconclusive experiments.
The liberal philosophy of race relations, the third approach, received

able and forceful expression, but was promptly and almost totally rejected and never put to practice in that period. All three of these alternative philosophies rejected the doctrines of extreme racism and all three were indigenously and thoroughly Southern in origin. . . .

The conservative philosophy of race relations was not the only alternative to extreme racism and proscription offered to the South and tried out in practice by Southern white people. Another approach was that of the Southern radicals, as worked out and expressed by the Populists. The agrarian forerunners of the Populists—the Readjusters, Independents, and Greenbackers—also attempted to reach an understanding with the Negro, but they approached him through his Republican leaders to seek a pragmatic alliance of mutual political convenience. They rarely approached him directly and did not seek to convert him personally to their cause. The Populists eventually resorted in large measure to the same tactics. But first they went over the heads of the established leaders, largely Republican, and sought to convert the Negroes themselves, make them good Populists by conviction, fire them with the zeal they themselves felt for the common cause, integrate them thoroughly with the party, and give them a sense of belonging and tangible evidence that they did belong.

The Populists steered clear of the patronizing approach that both the radical Republicans and the conservative Democrats took toward the freedmen. They neither pictured themselves as the keepers of the liberal conscience and the Negro as the ward of the nation, as did the Republican radicals, nor did they assume the pose of *noblesse oblige* and regard the Negro as an object of paternalistic protection as did the Southern conservatives. The Populists fancied themselves as exponents of a new realism on race, free from the delusions of doctrinaire and sentimental liberalism on the one hand, and the illusions of romantic paternalism on the other. There was in the Populist approach to the Negro a limited type of equalitarianism quite different from that preached by the radical Republicans and wholly absent from the conservative approach. This was an equalitarianism of want and poverty, the kinship of a common grievance and a common oppressor. As a Texas Populist expressed the new equalitarianism, "They are in the ditch just like we are."

Dismissing irrational motives as of no great account, the Populists grounded their "realism" on the doctrine that "self-interest always controls"—the dubious postulate on which much economic and political thought of their day was based. As Tom Watson, foremost leader of Southern Populism, framed the credo: "Gratitude may fail; so may sympathy, and friendship, and generosity, and patriotism, but, in the long run, self-interest always controls." . . .

Deprecate emotional and irrational factors of prejudice as they did, the Populist strategists were perfectly aware that these factors were the most serious of all obstacles to their success in the South. It was even more difficult for them than for the conservatives to defy and circumvent race prejudice, since it ran highest and strongest among the very white elements to which the Populist appeal was especially addressed—the depressed lower economic classes. They were the classes from whose phobias and fanaticisms the conservatives offered to protect the Negro. To master these deep-rooted phobias and create a community of feeling and interest in which the two races could combine required greater political genius than the conservatives had to muster for their program. The wonder is not that the Populists eventually failed but that they made as much headway as they did against the overwhelming odds they faced.

The measures they took were sometimes drastic and, for the times, even heroic. At a time when Georgia led all the states in lynchings Watson announced that it was the object of his party to 'make lynch law odious to the people.' And in 1896 the Populist platform of Georgia contained a plank denouncing lynch law. In the campaign of 1892 a Negro Populist who had made sixty-three speeches for Watson was threatened with lynching and fled to him for protection. Two thousand armed white farmers, some of whom rode all night, responded to Watson's call for aid and remained on guard for two nights at his home to avert the threat of violence. . . .

To implement their promises the radicals went farther in the direction of racial integration than did the conservatives. "We have no disposition to ostracize the colored people," declared the president of the first Populist convention in Texas. "I am in favor of giving the colored man full representation. . . . He is a citizen just as much as we are, and the party that acts on that fact will gain the colored vote of the south." The convention cheered these sentiments and elected two Negroes to the state executive committee of the party. Other Southern states followed the example of Texas. Negroes were not put off with nominal duties and peripheral appointments, but were taken into the inmost councils of the party. They served with Southern whites as members of state, district, and county executive committees, campaign committees, and delegations to national conventions. Black and white campaigners spoke from the same platform to audiences of both races, and both had their places on official party tickets. Populist sheriffs saw to it that Negroes appeared for jury duty; and Populist editors sought out achievements of Negroes to praise in their columns.

In the opinion of Henry Demarest Lloyd, the Southern Populists gave "negroes of the South a political fellowship which they have never obtained, not even from their saviors, the Republicans." Certain it is that the Negroes responded with more enthusiasm and hope than to any other political movement since their disillusionment with radical Republicanism. It is altogether probable that during the brief Populist upheaval of the 'nineties Negroes and native whites achieved a greater comity of mind and harmony of political purpose than ever before or since in the South.

The obvious danger in this account of the race policies of Southern conservatives and radicals is one of giving an exaggerated impression of interracial harmony. There were Negrophobes among the radicals as well as among the conservatives, and there were hypocrites and dissemblers in both camps. The politician who flatters to attract votes is a familiar figure in all parties, and the discrepancy between platforms and performance is often as wide as the gap between theory and practice, or the contrast between ethical ideals and everyday conduct.

My only purpose has been to indicate that things have not always been the same in the South. In a time when the Negroes formed a much larger proportion of the population than they did later, when slavery was a live memory in the minds of both races, and when the memory of the hardships and bitterness of Reconstruction was still fresh, the race policies accepted and pursued in the South were sometimes milder than they became later. The policies of proscription, segregation, and disfranchisement that are often described as the immutable "folkways" of the South, impervious alike to legislative reform and armed intervention, are of a more recent origin. The effort to justify them as a consequence of Reconstruction and a necessity of the times is embarrassed by the fact that they did not originate in those times. And the belief that they are immutable and unchangeable is not supported by history.

The South's adoption of extreme racism was due not so much to a conversion as it was to a relaxation of the opposition. All the elements of fear, jealousy, proscription, hatred, and fanaticism had long been present, as they are present in various degrees of intensity in any society. What enabled them to rise to dominance was not so much

cleverness or ingenuity as it was a general weakening and discrediting of the numerous forces that had hitherto kept them in check.
. . .

The acquiescence of Northern liberalism in the Compromise of 1877 defined the beginning, but not the ultimate extent, of the liberal retreat on the race issue. The Compromise merely left the freedman to the custody of the conservative Redeemers upon their pledge that they would protect him in his constitutional rights. But as these pledges were forgotten or violated and the South veered toward proscription and extremism, Northern opinion shifted to the right, keeping pace with the South, conceding point after point, so that at no time were the sections very far apart on race policy. The failure of the liberals to resist this trend was due in part to political factors. Since reactionary politicians and their cause were identified with the bloody-shirt issue and the demagogic exploitation of sectional animosities, the liberals naturally felt themselves strongly drawn toward the cause of sectional reconciliation. And since the Negro was the symbol of sectional strife, the liberals joined in deprecating further agitation of his cause and in defending the Southern view of race in its less extreme forms. It was quite common in the 'eighties and 'nineties to find in the *Nation, Harper's Weekly,* the *North American Review,* or the *Atlantic Monthly* Northern liberals and former abolitionists mouthing the shibboleths of white supremacy regarding the Negro's innate inferiority, shiftlessness, and hopeless unfitness for full participation in the white man's civilization. Such expressions doubtless did much to add to the reconciliation of North and South, but they did so at the expense of the Negro. Just as the Negro gained his emancipation and new rights through a falling out between white men, he now stood to lose his rights through the reconciliation of white men.

The cumulative weakening of resistance to racism was expressed also in a succession of decisions by the United States Supreme Court between 1873 and 1898. . . . In the *Slaughter House Cases* of 1873 and in *United States* v. *Reese* and *United States* v. *Cruikshank* in 1876, the court drastically curtailed the privileges and immunities recognized as being under federal protection. It continued the trend in its decision on the *Civil Rights Cases* of 1883 by virtually nullifying the restrictive parts of the Civil Rights Act. By a species of what Justice Harlan in his dissent described as "subtle and ingenious verbal criticism," the court held that the Fourteenth Amendment gave Congress power to restrain states but not individuals from acts of racial discrimination and segregation. The court, like the liberals, was engaged in a bit of reconciliation—reconciliation between federal and state jurisdiction, as well as between North and South, reconciliation also achieved at the Negro's expense. Having ruled in a previous case (*Hall* v. *de Cuir*, 1877) that a state could not *prohibit* segregation on a common carrier, the Court in 1890 (*Louisville, New Orleans, and Texas Railroad* v. *Mississippi*) ruled that a state could constitutionally *require* segregation on carriers. In *Plessy* v. *Ferguson*, decided in 1896, the Court subscribed to the doctrine that "legislation is powerless to eradicate racial instincts" and laid down the "separate but equal" rule for the justification of segregation. Two years later, in 1898, in *Williams* v. *Mississippi* the Court completed the opening of the legal road to proscription, segregation, and disfranchisement by approving the Mississippi plan for depriving Negroes of the franchise. . . .

Then, in the year 1898, the United States plunged into imperialistic adventures overseas under the leadership of the Republican party. These adventures in the Pacific and the Caribbean suddenly brought under the jurisdiction of the United States some eight million people of the colored races, "a varied assortment of inferior races," as the *Nation* described them, "which, of course, could not be allowed to vote." As America shouldered the White Man's Burden, she took up at the same time many Southern attitudes on the subject of race. "If the stronger and cleverer race," said the editor of the *Atlantic Monthly*, "is free to impose its will upon 'new-caught, sullen peoples' on the other side of the globe, why not in South Carolina and Mississippi?" The doctrines of Anglo-Saxon superiority by which Professor John W. Burgess of Columbia University, Captain Alfred T. Mahan of the United States Navy, and Senator Albert Beveridge of Indiana justified and rationalized American imperialism in the Philippines, Hawaii, and Cuba differed in no essentials from the race theories by which Senator Benjamin R. Tillman of South Carolina and Senator James K. Vardaman of Mississippi justified white supremacy in the South. The Boston Evening *Transcript* of 14 January 1899, admitted that Southern race policy was "now the policy of the Administration of the very party which carried the country into and through a civil war to free the slave." And *The New York Times* of 10 May 1900 reported editorially that "Northern men . . . no longer denounce the suppression of the Negro vote [in the South] as it used to be denounced in the reconstruction days. The necessity of it under the supreme law of self-preservation is candidly recognized."

In the South leaders of the white-supremacy movement thoroughly grasped and expounded the implication of the new imperialism for their domestic policies. "No Republican leader," declared Senator Tillman, "not even Governor Roosevelt, will now dare to wave the bloody shirt and preach a crusade against the South's treatment of the negro. The North has a bloody shirt of its own. Many thousands of them have been made into shrouds for murdered Filipinos, done to death because they were fighting for liberty." And the junior Senator from South Carolina, John J. McLaurin, thanked Senator George F. Hoar of Massachusetts "for his complete announcement of the divine right of the Caucasian to govern the inferior races," a position which "most amply vindicated the South." Hilary A. Herbert, an advocate of complete disfranchisement of the Negro in Alabama, rejoiced in May 1900 that "we have now the sympathy of thoughtful men in the North to an extent that never before existed."

At the very time that imperialism was sweeping the country, the doctrine of racism reached a crest of acceptability and popularity among respectable scholarly and intellectual circles. At home and abroad biologists, sociologists, anthropologists, and historians, as well as journalists and novelists, gave support to the doctrine that races were discrete entities and that the "Anglo-Saxon" or "Caucasian" was the superior of them all. It was not that Southern politicians needed any support from learned circles to sustain their own doctrines, but they found that such intellectual endorsement of their racist theories facilitated acceptance of their views and policies.

At the dawn of the new century the wave of Southern racism came in as a swell upon a mounting tide of national sentiment and was very much a part of that sentiment. Had the tide been running the other way, the Southern wave would have broken feebly instead of becoming a wave of the future.

. . . If the psychologists are correct in their hypothesis that aggression is always the result of frustration, then the South toward the end of the 'nineties was the perfect cultural seedbed for aggression against the minority race. Economic, political, and social frustrations had pyramided to a climax of social tensions. No real relief was in sight from the long cyclical depression of the 'nineties, an acute period of suffering that had only intensified the distress of the much longer agricultural depression. Hopes for reform and the political means employed in defiance of tradition and at great cost to emotional attachments to effect reform had likewise met with cruel disappointments and frustration. There had to be a scapegoat. And all along the line signals were going up to indicate that the Negro was an approved object of aggression. These "permissions-to-hate" came from sources that had formerly denied such permission. They came from the federal courts in numerous opinions, from Northern liberals eager to conciliate the South, from Southern conservatives who had abandoned their race policy of moderation in their struggle against the Populists, from the Populists in their mood of disillusionment with their former Negro allies, and from a national temper suddenly expressed by imperialistic adventures and aggressions against colored peoples in distant lands.

The resistance of the Negro himself had long ceased to be an important deterrent to white aggression. But a new and popular spokesman of the race, its acknowledged leader by the late 'nineties, came forward with a submissive philosophy for the Negro that to some whites must have appeared an invitation to further aggression. It is quite certain that Booker T. Washington did not intend his so-called "Atlanta Compromise" address of 1895 to constitute such an invitation. But in proposing the virtual retirement of the mass of Negroes from the political life of the South and in stressing the humble and menial role that the race was to play, he would seem unwittingly to have smoothed the path to proscription.

Having served as the national scapegoat in the reconciliation and reunion of North and South, the Negro was now pressed into service as a sectional scapegoat in the reconciliation of estranged white classes and the reunion of the Solid South. The bitter violence and bloodletting recrimination of the campaigns between white conservatives and white radicals in the 'nineties had opened wounds that could not be healed by ordinary political nostrums and free-silver slogans. The only formula powerful enough to accomplish that was the magical formula of white supremacy, applied without stint and without any of the old conservative reservations of paternalism, without deference to any lingering resistance of Northern liberalism, or any fear of further check from a defunct Southern Populism.

The first step in applying the formula was the total disfranchisement of the Negro. In part this was presented as a guarantee that in the future neither of the white factions would violate the white man's peace by rallying the Negro's support against the other. In part disfranchisement was also presented as a progressive reform, the sure means of purging Southern elections of the corruption that disgraced them. The disgrace and public shame of this corruption were more widely and keenly appreciated than the circuitous and paradoxical nature of the proposed reform. To one Virginian, however, it did seem that disfranchising the Negroes "to prevent the Democratic election officials from stealing their votes" would be "to punish the man who has been injured"—a topsy-turvy justice at best. In no mood for paradoxes, Southerners generally accepted Negro disfranchisement as a reform, without taking second thought.

The standard devices for accomplishing disfranchisement on a racial basis and evading the restrictions· of the Constitution were invented by Mississippi, a pioneer of the movement and the only state that resorted to it before the Populist revolt took the form of political rebellion. Other states elaborated the original scheme and added devices of their own contriving, though there was a great deal of borrowing and interchange of ideas throughout the South. First of all, the plan set up certain barriers such as property or literacy qualifications for voting, and then cut certain loopholes in the barrier through which only white men could squeeze. The loopholes to appease (though not invariably accommodate) the underprivileged whites were the "understanding clause," the "grandfather clause," or the "good character clause." Some variation of the scheme was incorporated into the constitutions of South Carolina in 1895, Louisiana in 1898, North Carolina in 1900, Alabama in 1901, Virginia in 1902, Georgia in 1908, and Oklahoma in 1910. The restrictions imposed by these devices were enormously effective in decimating the Negro vote, but in addition all these states as well as the remaining members of the old Confederacy—Florida, Tennessee, Arkansas, and Texas—adopted the poll tax. With its cumulative features and procedures artfully devised to discourage payment, the poll tax was esteemed at first by some of its proponents as the most reliable means of curtailing the franchise—not only among the Negroes but among objectionable whites as well.

But if the Negroes did learn to read, or acquire sufficient property, and remember to pay the poll tax and to keep the receipt on file, they could even then be tripped by the final hurdle devised for them —the white primary. Another of the fateful paradoxes that seemed to dog the history of the progressive movement in the South, the primary system was undoubtedly an improvement over the old convention system and did much to democratize nominations and party control. But along with the progressively inspired primary system were adopted the oppositely inspired party rules, local regulations, and in some cases state laws excluding the minority race from participation and converting the primary into a white man's club. This perverse "reform" usually followed hard upon, though sometimes preceded, the disfranchisement "reform." The state-wide Democratic primary was adopted in South Carolina in 1896, Arkansas in 1897, Georgia in 1898, Florida and Tennessee in 1901, Alabama and Mississippi in 1902, Kentucky and Texas in 1903, Louisiana in 1906, Oklahoma in 1907, Virginia in 1913, and North Carolina in 1915.

The effectiveness of disfranchisement is suggested by a comparison of the number of registered Negro voters in Louisiana in 1896, when there were 130,334 and in 1904, when there were 1,342. Between the two dates the literacy, property, and poll-tax qualifications were adopted. In 1896 Negro registrants were in a majority in twenty-six parishes—by 1900 in none.

In spite of the ultimate success of disfranchisement, the movement met with stout resistance and succeeded in some states by narrow margins or the use of fraud. In order to overcome the opposition and divert the suspicions of the poor and illiterate whites that they as well as the Negro were in danger of losing the franchise—a suspicion that often proved justified—the leaders of the movement restored to an intensive propaganda of white supremacy, Negrophobia, and race chauvinism. Such a campaign preceded and accompanied disfranchisement in each state. In some of them it had been thirty years or more since the reign of the carpetbagger, but the legend of Reconstruction was revived, refurbished, and relived by the propagandists as if it were an immediate background of the current crisis. A new generation of Southerners was as forcibly impressed with the sectional trauma as if they had lived through it themselves. Symbols and paraphernalia of the Redemption drama were patched up and donned by twentieth-century wearers. Boys who had been born since General U. S. Grant was laid in his tomb paraded in the red shirts of their fathers, and popular Southern novelists glamorized the history of the Ku Klux Klan, the Knights of the White Camelia, and the heroes of the struggle for Home Rule.

In Georgia and elsewhere the propaganda was furthered by a sensational press that played up and headlined current stories of Negro crime, charges of rape and attempted rape, and alleged instances of arrogance, and impertinence, surly manners, or lack of prompt and proper servility in conduct. Already cowed and intimidated, the race was falsely pictured as stirred up to a mutinous and insurrectionary pitch. The Atlanta *Journal*, edited by Hoke Smith while he was a candidate for governor on a disfranchisement platform, was one of the worst offenders in this regard. Throughout his campaign Smith's paper kept up a daily barrage of Negro atrocity stories.

It was inevitable that race relations should deteriorate rapidly under such pressure. The immediate consequences in two states were bloody mob wars upon the Negro. Shortly after the red-shirt, white-supremacy election of 1898 in North Carolina a mob of four hundred white men led by a former congressman invaded the colored district of Wilmington, set fire to buildings, killed and wounded many Negroes, and chased hundreds out of town. The sequel to Hoke Smith's white-supremacy victory in Georgia in 1906 was a four-day rule of anarchy in Atlanta, during which mobs roved the city freely looting, murdering, and lynching.

This ugly temper did not pass with the white-supremacy campaigns. Indeed the more defenseless, disfranchised, and intimidated the Negro became the more prone he was to the ruthless aggression of mobs. Three years after Tillman had completed his work of crushing Negro rights in South Carolina, colored people were victims of atrocities. While the state had accustomed itself peacefully to dozens of Negro postmasters before, the appointment of one in 1898 at Lake City touched off a mob that burned the postmaster up in his own house and shot down his family as they escaped. The same year mobs of "white cap" riders ranged over the countryside of Greenwood County shooting and hanging an undetermined number of Negroes. Two years after the white-supremacy campaign had disfranchised the race in Louisiana, uncontrolled mobs took over the city of New Orleans and robbed and assaulted Negroes for three days. The number of lynchings per year was fortunately on the decline during the first decade of the century in the country as a whole and in the South. But the proportion of lynchings committed in the South was at the same time increasing, and so was the proportion of Negro victims of the lynchings committed.

A few of the old conservatives still spoke out against the savage turn that events had taken in race relations. Wade Hampton announced during the disfranchisement campaign in South Carolina that he had "no fear of Negro domination," that the Negroes had "acted of late with rare moderation," and that race prejudice was being exploited for the purposes of demagogues. But Hampton's influence had waned and he could do nothing to stop the Tillmanites. Ex-Governor Oates of Alabama, known as "a conservative among conservatives" and once the nemesis of Populism in his state, declared that he was shocked at "the change in public opinion in regard to the status of the Negro" that had occurred by 1901. "Why, sir," he declared to the disfranchising constitutional convention of Alabama, "the sentiment is altogether different now, when the Negro is doing no harm, why the people want to kill him and wipe him from the face of the earth." But it was Governor Oates who had admitted to the same body that in the heat of the Populist revolt he had said, "Go to it, boys. Count them out." The admission weakened his moral position, as the conservative tactic generally had undermined the authority of conservative influence on race relations.

Other representatives of the old conservative school, such as Senator John T. Morgan of Alabama, gave aid and comfort to the racists; or like Hoke Smith went over to them lock, stock, and barrel, and became one of their leaders. Younger men whose background, associations, and ideas would have normally drawn them to the conservative Hamptonian position on race in earlier days—men such as John Sharp Williams of Mississippi, or Furnifold M. Simmons of North Carolina, or later James F. Byrnes of South Carolina—were swept up in the tide of racist sentiment and gave voice to it.

White-supremacy leaders, however, measured their success not by the number of conservative converts to their cause, but by the response of the old Populists. For if the racist strategy for the reconciliation of alienated white men and the restoration of the Solid South were to work, it would have to win the insurgents. Populists were shrewdly watched for their reaction. In 1898, while the Populists were still in control of the North Carolina government, Josephus Daniels reported with elation seeing "quite a number of white Populists and white Republicans" taking part in a red-shirt parade for white supremacy. The following year when several Populist members of the Legislature cast their votes for the disfranchisement amendment, "the applause was long and deafening, shouts and yells being added to the hand clapping." The reported yells were probably of the well-known "rebel" variety, for they hailed a closing of the white man's ranks—white solidarity again.

Tom Watson, Populist candidate for President in 1904, was slower than some of his party to close ranks on the race issue and capitulate to the extremists. He had indignantly denounced the South Carolina disfranchisement campaign in 1895 with the statement that "All this reactionary legislation is wrong" and that "Old fashioned democracy taught that a man who fought the battles of his country, and paid the taxes of his government, should have a vote." Bruised and embittered by another decade of futile battles, he still believed that "the bugaboo of negro domination" was "the most hypocritical that unscrupulous leadership could invent." But by 1906 he had persuaded himself that only after the Negro was eliminated from politics could Populist principles gain a hearing. In other words, the white men would have to unite before they could divide. Watson optimistically believed that disfranchisement was the way to break up, rather than to unite, the Solid South. With that in mind he offered to swing the Populist vote to any progressive Democratic candidate for governor who would run pledged to a platform of Populist reforms and Negro disfranchisement. Hoke Smith, a recent convert to progressivism from conservative ranks, took up the challenge and Watson delivered the Populist vote, with the results we have already viewed. The picture of the Georgia Populist and the reformed Georgia conservative united on a platform of Negrophobia and progressivism was strikingly symbolical of the new era in the South. The campaign made Watson the boss of Georgia politics, but it wrote off Populism as a noble experiment, and launched its leader as one of the outstanding exploiters of endemic Negrophobia. . . .

Partisan politics was not the only index of the new trend in Southern race policy. A look at the contrast between Southern letters in the 1880's and in the 1900's also reveals something of the same development. The literary treatment that the Negro received in the fiction of Joel Chandler Harris and George Washington Cable was no doubt often patronizing, sentimentalized, and paternalistic, but there was never anything venomous or bitter about the Negro in their pages.* Rather the total picture that emerges is one that inspires a kind of respect, certainly sympathy, and more often an indulgent tenderness and affection. A stock figure to draw Southern tears was Uncle Remus with the little white boy in his lap, or the faithful black retainer of Marse Chan. It is instructive to compare the picture of the Negro painted by these authors who lived through Reconstruction themselves with the picture of the Negro during Reconstruction that emerges in the pages of Thomas Dixon, who was born the last year of the Civil War. Dixon was not of the same caliber as the earlier writers, but he accurately reflects the changed temper of the twen-

* This claim cannot be advanced with the same assurance if extended to Harris's editorial writings, unsigned for the most part, in the Atlanta *Constitution*.

tieth-century South. His trilogy: *The Leopard's Spots: A Romance of the White Man's Burden—1865–1900*: (1902); *The Clansman: An Historical Romance of the Ku Klux Klan* (1905); and *The Traitor: A Story of the Fall of the Invisible Empire* (1907) was the perfect literary accompaniment of the white-supremacy and disfranchisement campaign, at the height of which they were published.

Scholarship of the period, particularly its sociology, anthropology, and history, likewise reflected the current deterioration in race relations and the new Southern attitudes. Charles Carroll, *"The Negro a Beast"*; or, *"In the Image of God"* (1900); William P. Calhoun, *The Caucasian and the Negro in the United States* (1902); William B. Smith, *The Color Line: A Brief in Behalf of the Unborn* (1905); and Robert W. Shufeldt, *The Negro, A Menace to American Civilization* (1907) were a part of the then current national racist literature of the "Yellow Peril" school and the flourishing cult of Nordicism. Southern historians during the first decade and a half of the century completed the rewriting of Reconstruction history. Their work did not yield completely to the contemporary atmosphere of the white-supremacy movement, but some of it did not entirely escape that influence.

Public-spirited professional people of a humanitarian bent who gathered at periodic conferences to discuss the race problem took a deeply pessimistic or despairing view of the Negro. They laid great stress on the alarming increase in Negro crime as the race flocked to the cities and packed into crowded, filthy slums. They were convinced that the race was rapidly deteriorating in morals and manners, in health and efficiency, and losing out in the struggle for survival. They resolved that the Negro was incapable of self-government, unworthy of the franchise, and impossible to educate beyond the rudiments. They devoted much time and effort to the promotion of Negro education, but the limitations of their aims are indicated by Booker T. Washington when he said in welcoming a conference of white Southern University presidents to Tuskegee in 1912: "We are trying to instil into the Negro mind that if education does not make the Negro humble, simple, and of service to the community, then it will not be encouraged." . . .

Within this context of growing pessimism, mounting tension, and unleashed phobias the structure of segregation and discrimination was extended by the adoption of a great number of the Jim Crow type of laws. Up to 1900 the only law of this type adopted by the majority of Southern states was that applying to passengers aboard trains. And South Carolina did not adopt this until 1898,* North Carolina in 1899, and Virginia, the last, in 1900. Only three states had required or authorized the Jim Crow waiting room in railway stations before 1899, but in the next decade nearly all of the other Southern states fell in line. The adoption of laws applying to new subjects tended to take place in waves of popularity. Street cars had been common in Southern cities since the 'eighties, but only Georgia had a segregation law applying to them before the end of the century. Then in quick succession North Carolina and Virginia adopted such a law in 1901, Louisiana in 1902, Arkansas, South Carolina, and Tennessee in 1903, Mississippi and Maryland in 1904, Florida in 1905, and Oklahoma in 1907. These laws referred to separation within cars, but a Montgomery city ordinance of 1906 was the first to require a completely separate Jim Crow street car. During these years the older seaboard states of the South also extended the segregation laws to steamboats.

The mushroom growth of discriminatory and segregation laws during the first two decades of this century piled up a huge bulk of legislation. Much of the code was contributed by city ordinances or by local regulations and rules enforced without the formality of laws. Only a sampling is possible here. For up and down the avenues and byways of Southern life appeared with increasing profusion the little signs: "Whites Only" or "Colored." Sometimes the law prescribed their dimensions in inches, and in one case the kind and color of paint. Many appeared without requirement by law—over entrances and exits, at theaters and boarding houses, toilets and water fountains, waiting rooms and ticket windows. . . .

Much ingenuity and effort went into the separation of the races in their amusements, diversions, recreations, and sports. The Separate Park Law of Georgia, adopted in 1905, appears to have been the first venture of a state legislature into this field, though city ordinances and local custom were quite active in pushing the Negro out of the public parks. Circuses and tent shows, including side shows, fell under a law adopted by Louisiana in 1914, which required separate entrances, exits, ticket windows, and ticket sellers that would be kept at least twenty-five feet apart. The city of Birmingham applied the principle to "any room, hall, theatre, picture house, auditorium,

* For first-class coaches only, and not until 1900 was the law amended to apply to second class as well.

yard, court, ball park, or other indoor or outdoor place" and specified
that the races be "distinctly separated . . . by well defined physical
barriers." North Carolina and Virginia interdicted all fraternal orders
or societies that permitted members of both races to address each
other as brother.

Residential segregation in cities, still rare in the older seaboard
towns, developed along five different patterns in the second decade of
the century. The type originating in Baltimore in 1910 designated
all-white and all-Negro blocks in areas occupied by both races. This
experiment was imitated in Atlanta and Greenville. Virginia sought
to legalize segregation by a state law that authorized city councils to
divide territories into segregated districts and to prohibit either race
from living in the other's district, a method adopted by Roanoke
and Portsmouth, Virginia. The third method, invented by Richmond, designated blocks throughout the city black and white according to the majority of the residents and forbade any person to live in
any block "where the majority of residents on such streets are occupied by those with whom said person is forbidden to intermarry."
This one was later copied by Ashland, Virginia, and Winston-Salem,
North Carolina. A still more complicated law originated in Norfolk,
which applied to both mixed and unmixed blocks and fixed the color
status by ownership as well as occupancy. And finally New Orleans
developed a law requiring a person of either race to secure consent
of the majority of persons living in an area before establishing a residence therein. After these devices were frustrated by a Supreme Court
decision in 1917, attempts continued to be made to circumvent the
decision. Probably the most effective of these was the restrictive covenant, a private contract limiting the sale of property in an area to
purchasers of the favored race.

The most prevalent and widespread segregation of living areas was
accomplished without need for legal sanction. The black ghettos of
the "Darktown" slums in every Southern city were the consequence
mainly of the Negro's economic status, his relegation to the lowest
rung of the ladder. Smaller towns sometimes excluded Negro residents completely simply by letting it be known in forceful ways that
their presence would not be tolerated. In 1914 there were six such
towns in Texas, five in Oklahoma, and two in Alabama. On the other
hand there were by that time some thirty towns in the South, besides
a number of unincorporated settlements, inhabited exclusively by
Negroes. In August 1913, Clarence Poe, editor of the *Progressive
Farmer,* secured the unanimous endorsement of a convention of

the North Carolina Farmer's Union for a movement to segregate the races in rural districts.

The extremes to which caste panalties and separation were carried in parts of the South could hardly find a counterpart short of the latitudes of India and South Africa. In 1909 Mobile passed a curfew law applying exclusively to Negroes and requiring them to be off the streets by 10 p.m. The Oklahoma legislature in 1915 authorized its Corporation Commission to require telephone companies "to maintain separate booths for white and colored patrons." North Carolina and Florida required that textbooks used by the public-school children of one race be kept separate from those used by the other, and the Florida law specified separation even while the books were in storage. South Carolina for a time segregated a third caste by establishing separate schools for mulatto as well as for white and Negro children. A New Orleans ordinance segregated white and Negro prostitutes in separate districts. Ray Stannard Baker found Jim Crow Bibles for Negro witnesses in Atlanta courts and Jim Crow elevators for Negro passengers in Atlanta buildings.

A search of the statute books fails to disclose any state law or city ordinance specifying separate Bibles and separate elevators. Right here it is well to admit, and even to emphasize, that *laws are not an adequate index of the extent and prevalence of segregation and discriminatory practices in the South.* The practices often anticipated and sometimes exceeded the laws. It may be confidently assumed— and it could be verified by present observation—that there is more Jim Crowism practiced in the South than there are Jim Crow laws on the books.

To say that, however, is not to concede the position so often taken by Southern as well as Northern writers that the laws were of little consequence anyway. This view consciously or unconsciously voices a laissez-faire bias and often leans for support upon the authority of William Graham Sumner. It was the contention of Sumner's classic *Folkways*, published in 1907, that "legislation cannot make mores" and that "stateways cannot change folkways." Sumner described these "folkways" as "uniform, universal in the group, imperative, and invariable." Perhaps it was not his intention, but Sumner's teachings lent credence to the existence of a primeval rock of human nature upon which the waves of legislation beat in vain. This concept as it was applied to Southern race practices and caste penalties was further buttressed by an American apostle of Herbert Spencer, the sociologist

Franklin Henry Giddings. His emphasis upon "consciousness of kind" in works appearing in 1896 and the decade following gave aid and comfort to the followers of Summer. So did the racist interpretations of the psychologist William McDougall, whose *Introduction to Social Psychology* appeared in 1908.

Since the works mentioned represented the dominant American social theory of the early twentieth century, and since they appeared in the years when the wave of Southern and American racism was reaching its crest, it was natural that they should have influenced thinking upon the South's major social preoccupation. Their influence was to encourage the notion that there was something inevitable and rigidly inflexible about the existing patterns of segregation and race relations in the South; that these patterns had not been and could not be altered by conscious effort; and that it was, indeed, folly to attempt to meddle with them by means of legislation. These early twentieth-century theories have been characterized by a present-day psychologist, Kenneth B. Clark, as "the modern attempt at acceptable restatement of the medieval doctrine of *innate ideas*." Conceived of as biological or social imperatives, these modern "innate ideas" were presented as "folkways" or "mores" which explained and, by inference, justified the existing structure of society, the privileges and policies of the dominant race, and the subordination of the minority race. . . .

At any rate, the findings of the present investigation tend to bear out the testimony of Negroes from various parts of the South, as reported by the Swedish writer Gunnar Myrdal, to the effect that "the Jim Crow statutes were effective means of tightening and freezing—in many cases instigating—segregation and discrimination." The evidence has indicated that under conditions prevailing in the earlier part of the period reviewed the Negro could and did do many things in the South that in the latter part of the period, under different conditions, he was prevented from doing.

. . . In the 'seventies, 'eighties, and 'nineties the Negroes voted in large numbers. White leaders of opposing parties encouraged them to vote and earnestly solicited their votes. Qualified and acknowledged leaders of Southern white opinion were on record as saying that it was proper, inevitable, and desirable that they should vote. Yet after the defranchisement measures were passed around 1900 the Negroes ceased to vote. And at that time qualified and acknowledged leaders of white opinion said that it was unthinkable that they should ever be permitted to vote. In the earlier decades Negroes still took an active, if modest, part in public life. They held offices, served on the jury, sat on the bench, and were represented in local councils, state legislatures, and the national Congress. Later on these things were simply not so, and the last of the Negroes disappeared from these forums.

It has also been seen that their presence on trains upon equal terms with white men was once regarded in some states as normal, acceptable, and unobjectionable. Whether railways qualify as folkways or stateways, black man and white man once rode them together and without a partition between them. Later on the stateways apparently changed the folkways—or at any rate the railways—for the partitions and Jim Crow cars became universal. And the new seating arrangement came to seem as normal, unchangeable, and inevitable as the old ways. And so it was with the soda fountains, bars, waiting rooms, street cars, and circuses. And so it probably was with the parks in Atlanta, and with cemeteries in Mississippi. There must even have been a time in Oklahoma when a colored man could walk into any old telephone booth he took a notion to and pick up the receiver.

What was once said in extenuation of the harshness of the black codes of slavery times—that they were more honored in the breach than in the observance—cannot be said of the Jim Crow codes. Any Southerner of middle age, of course, could think of expectations: the old "auntie" who came to talk with one's grandmother on Saturday afternoons when the weather was nice; the privileged "uncle" who preferred and was permitted to attend the white church; the defiant "mammy" on the white day coach; and the old retainer who lorded it over the family larder and put the grocer's white delivery boy in his place. But we recognize them all as belated survivors of the old times—relics now gone with the second wind of history.

Barring those disappearing exceptions, the Jim Crow laws applied to *all* Negroes—not merely to the rowdy, or drunken, or surly, or ignorant ones. The new laws did not countenance the old conservative tendency to distinguish between classes of the race, to encourage the "better" element, and to draw it into a white alliance. Those laws backed up the Alabamian who told the disfranchising convention of his state that no Negro in the world was the equal of "the least, poorest, lowest-down white man I ever knew"; but not ex-Governor Oates, who replied: "I would not trust him as quickly as I would a negro of intelligence and good character." The Jim Crow laws put the authority of the state or city in the voice of the street-car conductor, the railway brakeman, the bus driver, the theater usher, and also into the voice of the hoodlum of the public parks and playgrounds. They gave free rein and the majesty of the law to mass aggressions that might otherwise have been curved, blunted, or deflected.

The Jim Crow laws, unlike feudal laws, did not assign the subordinate group a fixed status in society. They were constantly pushing the Negro farther down. In seeking to distinguish between the Southern white attitudes toward the Negro during Reconstruction and the era following and the attitudes later developed, Edgar Gardner Murphy in 1911 called the one "defensive" and "conservative" and the other "increasingly aggressive" and "destructive." "The new mood," he wrote, "makes few professions of conservatism. It does not claim to be necessary to the state's existence. . . . These new antipathies are not defensive, but assertive and combative . . . frankly and ruthlessly destructive." The movement had proceeded in mounting stages of aggression. "Its spirit is that of an all-absorbing autocracy of race, an animus of agrandizement which makes, in the imagination of the white man, an absolute identification of the stronger race with the very being of the state."

We have come a long way since that time and since that mood prevailed in the South. But most of the distance we have traveled has been covered in very recent years. The most common observation upon recent developments in race relations by intelligent white people of the South is almost invariably prefaced by the phrase: "Ten (or twenty) years ago I would never have believed that. . . ." And, indeed, there was then little reason to believe, or to expect, that things would change in the South at any more than a glacial pace. For as recently as that the doctrine according to Sumner prevailed almost unchallenged in the mind of the laity—as well as in the minds of a good part of the "experts" on social problems. And that doctrine had it that however crying the need for change, those immovable "folkways" and irresistible "mores" made the whole idea impracticable, or slowed down change to the pace of evolution.

When a scientific theory ceases to account for the observed facts of common experience, however, it would seem to be time to discard the theory. In lieu of another to offer in its place, we can at least try to understand what has happened.

IV: THE PROGRESSIVE FAILURE,

1900–1919

The Paradox of W. E. B. Du ·Bois

• The last quarter of the nineteenth century has aptly been termed "The Nadir" of Afro-American history by Rayford W. Logan. When the twentieth century began there was just cause for despair among the small black bourgeoisie as well as among the debt-ridden black peasantry. Nevertheless Negro spokesmen sought some formula of accommodation that would deflect impact of white racism and offer some real hope for the future. Booker T. Washington offered the dominant formula, an overwhelmingly accommodationist one which seemed eminently practical to most whites: acquiescence in segregation and political disbarment, coupled with a slow rise in Negro economic status through vocational education. Washington obtained substantial support from white char-ities and became a favorite of paternalistic politicians like Theodore Roosevelt. But Washington's program did not produce startling economic improvements in the lives of the Negro masses, nor was it intended to. Other black leaders grew impatient with "Tuskeegeeism." The most brilliant and effective dissenter during the early twentieth century was W. E. B. Du Bois. August Meier's perceptive essay examines the changing nature of Du Bois's thought, his initial agree-ment with most of Washington's views and his subsequent rejection of the Tuskeegee philosophy's major thrust. With an incisiveness and brilliance that provides models for today's black intellectual vanguard, Du Bois developed many themes of Negro protest thought that are still relevant today. How-ever, Meier also points up the counter-stream of accommoda-tionist content and potential that existed in Du Bois's ideas.

If, of the great trio of Negro leaders, Frederick Douglass best ex-pressed the aspirations toward full citizenship and assimilation, and

From August Meier, *Negro Thought in America, 1880–1915* (Ann Arbor: University of Michigan Press, 1963), pp. 190–206 (footnotes omitted). Copy-right © 1963 by The University of Michigan Press. Reprinted by permission.

Booker T. Washington the interest in economic advancement, it was Du Bois who most explicitly revealed the impact of oppression and of the American creed in creating ambivalent loyalties toward race and nation in the minds of American Negroes. As Du Bois said in 1897:

> One feels his two-ness—an American, a Negro, two souls, two thoughts, two unreconciled strivings, two warring ideals in one dark body. . . .
> The history of the American Negro is the history of this strife,—this longing to attain self-conscious manhood, to merge his double self into a better and truer self. . . . He would not Africanize America for America has too much to teach the world and Africa. He would not bleach the Negro soul in a flood of white Americanism, for he knows that Negro blood has a message for the world. He simply wishes to make it possible for a man to be both a Negro and an American, without being cursed and spit upon. . . .

More than any other figure Du Bois made explicit this ambivalence—an ambivalence that is perhaps the central motif in his ideological biography. Even Du Bois has described himself as integrally a part of European civilization, and "yet, more significant, one of its rejected parts; one who expressed in life and action and made vocal to many, a single whirlpool of social entanglement and inner psychological paradox."

A proud and sensitive youth reared in a western Massachusetts town, Du Bois had occasion to know the sting of prejudice and early realized that "I was different from others; or like, mayhap in heart and life and longing, but shut out from their world by a vast veil." Subsequently he therefore found the segregated community of Fisk University, which he attended from 1885 to 1888, an enriching experience. Though he yearned for the full recognition of his American citizenship, he was also, he later recollected, "thrilled and moved to tears," and recognized "something inherently and deeply my own" as a result of his association there with a "closed racial group with rites and loyalties, with a history and a corporate future, with an art and a philosophy." By the time he received his A.B. from Fisk and entered Harvard as a Junior in 1888, "the theory of race separation was quite in my blood," and the lack of social acceptance he experienced at Harvard, he recalled later, did not disturb him. Yet it certainly was his sensitivity to discrimination that led him at this time to view Negroes as a "nation"—Americans, but rejected in the land of their birth.

Meanwhile, Du Bois had been expressing himself on other subjects. As a correspondent for Fortune's New York *Globe* during the early 1880's and as editor of the Fisk *Herald*, he displayed an interest in industriousness and ambition. Furthermore, as a student at Fisk and at Harvard—where he received his Ph.D. in 1895—and as a professor at Wilberforce University (1894–96), Du Bois proved more than willing to meet Southern whites half way. He told both Fisk students and his white associates in the Tennessee prohibitionist movement that the interests of the two races were essentially the same. To his Fisk audience he proposed the admittedly unorthodox idea that Negroes should divide their vote in order not to exacerbate race relations. He assured Southern whites that they could depend on the friendship of Negroes if only the whites would grant them citizenship rights and adequate educational facilities. Since the Negro's condition was such as to encourage prejudice, for their part Negroes must stress duties as well as rights, and work for their own advancement. At both Harvard and Wilberforce he could, in a single speech, lash out at America's immoral and un-American treatment of Negroes (and at Harvard suggest that Negroes would revolt if other means failed) and at the same time adopt a conciliatory position. Since Negroes had not yet achieved what it took the Anglo-Saxons a millennium to do, they were not yet equipped to vote. What he objected to was not the disfranchisement of the Negro masses, but of intelligent, law-abiding Negroes; and what he advocated was a franchise limitation fairly applied to both races along with adequate educational opportunities for all. In 1891 it was even reported in the *Age* that Du Bois had asserted that the whole idea underlying the Lodge Elections Bill was wrong, for it was proposed on the assumption that

> law can accomplish anything. . . . We must ever keep before us the fact that the South has some excuse for its present attitude. We must remember that a good many of our people . . . are not fit for the responsibility of republican government. When you have the right sort of black voters you will need no election laws. The battle of my people must be a moral one, not a legal or physical one.

It was no wonder then that after Washington's address Du Bois wrote the *Age* suggesting "that there might be the basis of a real settlement between whites and blacks."

Meanwhile, Du Bois was formulating his notion of leadership by a college-educated elite, which he regarded as necessary for the advancement of any group. In 1891 he deplored the South's effort to make common and industrial schools rather than colleges the basis of its educational system. For only a liberally educated white leadership could perceive that, despite the justification for overthrowing the Reconstruction governments, to permanently disfranchise the working class of a society in the process of rapid industrialization would, as socialists from Lassalle to Hindman had said, result in economic ruin. And only a liberal higher education could create an intelligent Negro leadership. Thus, while still a student at Harvard, Du Bois had suggested his theory of the talented tenth, foreshadowed his later concern with the working class, and adumbrated the thesis he later stressed so much—that without political rights Negroes, primarily a working group, could not secure economic opportunity. Furthermore, it should be noted that his educational views were not unrelated to his ethnocentric feelings. As he said at Wilberforce, the educated elite had a glorious opportunity to guide the race by reshaping its own ideals in order to provide the masses with appropriate goals and lift them to civilization.

After two years at Wilberforce, Du Bois accepted a one-year research appointment at the University of Pennsylvania. Then in 1897 he became professor of sociology at Atlanta University, where he remained until 1910, teaching and editing the annual Atlanta University Studies on the American Negro.

At no time in his life did Du Bois place greater and more consistent stress upon self-help and racial solidarity than during the last four years of the century. Like many of his contemporaries he fused this emphasis with one on economic advancement; and like a few of them he synthesized it with his educational program for the talented tenth. To Du Bois in fact, the race prejudice which isolated the Negro group and threw upon it "the responsibility of evolving its own methods and organs of civilization" made the stimulation of group co-operation "the central serious problem."

It was his appointment to the University of Pennsylvania that provided Du Bois with his first opportunity to begin a scientific study of the race problem. He had long awaited such an opportunity because he believed that presentation of the facts derived from scientific investigation would go a long way toward solving the race problem. The resulting monograph, *The Philadelphia Negro*, leaned toward the blame-the-Negro, self-help point of view. Yet Du Bois did describe what it meant to be snubbed in employment and in social intercourse, and he judged that the Negro's participation in politics had been, in net effect, beneficial to the city and to the Negro himself. Above all, he felt that Negroes must uplift themselves, and by racial co-operation open enterprises that would provide employment and training in trades and commerce. Whites had their duty to help but society had too many problems "for it lightly to shoulder all the burdens of a less advanced people." Negroes ought to constantly register strong protests against prejudice and injustice, but they should do so because these things hindered them in their own attempt to elevate the race. And this attempt, Du Bois held, must be marked by vigorous and persistent efforts directed toward lessening crime and toward inculcating self-respect, the dignity of labor, and the virtues of truth, honesty, and charity.

Like Washington, then, Du Bois combined an enthusiasm for racial solidarity with one for economic development and the middle-class virtues. In fact, he regarded a college education as "one of the best preparations for a broad business life" and for the making of "captains of industry." Likening Negroes to other nationalities, he chided them for being ashamed of themselves, and held that such success as had been achieved by other nations no larger in population than the American Negroes could be accomplished only through a badly needed co-operation and unity. In view of the poverty of the Negro and the economic spirit of the age, it was most important to achieve success in business. Because of race prejudice the major opportunity for such achievement lay in commercial activity based on Negroes pooling their earnings and pushing forward as a group. Though their collective capital be small, thrift and industry could succeed even under the handicaps of prejudice. Under the circumstances a penny savings bank would be more helpful than the vote. Negroes should patronize and invest their money in Negro-owned enterprises, even at a personal sacrifice. For "we must cooperate or we are lost. Ten million people who join in intelligent self-help can never be long ignored or mistreated."

It should be noted, of course, that Du Bois did not, during the *fin de siècle* years, give up all interest in political rights, though like the majority of articulate Southern Negroes of the day he was willing to compromise on the matter. He was among those who in 1899 petitioned the Georgia legislature not to pass the Hardwick disfranchisement bill, though like Booker T. Washington he was willing to accept an educational and/or property qualification as long as free school facilities were open to all.

During this period Du Bois was more emphatic than at any other time about the value of racial integrity. Speaking on "The Conservative of Races" in 1897 he asserted that there existed subtle psychic differences, which had definitely divided men into races. Like his racist contemporaries, he was certain of the universality of "the race spirit," which he regarded as "the greatest invention for human progress." Each race had a special ideal—the English individualism, the German philosophy and science, and so forth. Therefore, "only Negroes bound and welded together, Negroes inspired by one vast ideal, can work out in its fullness the great message we have for humanity." To those who argued that their only hope lay in amalgamating with the rest of the American population, he admitted that Negroes faced a "puzzling dilemma." Every thoughtful Negro had at some time asked himself whether he was an American, or a Negro, or if he could be both; whether by striving as a Negro he was not perpetuating the very gulf that divided the two races, or whether Negroes "have in America a distinct mission as a race." Du Bois' answer was what is now called cultural pluralism. Negroes were American by birth, in language, in political ideas, and in religion. But any further than this, their Americanism did not go. Since they had given America its only native music and folk stories, "its only touch of pathos and humor amid its mad money-getting plutocracy," it was the Negroes' duty to maintain "our physical power, our intellectual endowment, our spiritual ideas; as a race, we must strive by race organizations, by race solidarity, by race unity to the realization of the broader humanity which freely recognizes differences in men, but sternly deprecates inequalities in their opportunity of development." To this end, separate racial educational, business, and cultural institutions were necessary. Despised and oppressed, the Negroes' only means of advancement was a belief in their own great destiny. No people that wished to be something other than itself "ever wrote its name in history; it must be inspired with the Divine faith of our black mothers, that out of the blood and dust of battles will march a victorious host, a mighty nation, a peculiar people, to speak to the nations of the earth a Divine truth that should make them free." Washington, it should be pointed out, while advocating race pride and race integrity, did not glory so much in the idea of a distinctive Negro culture (though he was always proud of the spirituals or "plantation melodies"). Nor did he exhibit Du Bois' sense of identification with Africans, evident in Du Bois' advocacy of "pan-Negroism" in this same address.

During the last years of the century Du Bois developed his educational theories at considerable length, attempting to construct "A Rational System of Negro Education" by reconciling the two widely diverging tendencies of the day—training for making a living and training for living a broad life. All agreed, he said, on the necessity of universal common school training, and on the contribution Hampton, Tuskegee, and the Slater Fund had made in stressing the building of an economic foundation, the freedmen's primary concern. But unfortunately only three or four schools made broad culture their chief aim. Du Bois criticized the talk of rosewood pianos in dingy cabins, of ignorant farmers, of college graduates without employment, though he agreed that more stress had been placed on college training than the economic condition of the race warranted. But the vogue for industrial education had become so great that the colleges were hard-pressed for funds. This was particularly deplorable because the isolation of the Negro community demanded the creation of an indigenous leadership of college-trained captains of industry and scholars, who would advance the masses economically and culturally, and who could view the race problem from a broad perspective.

There were remarkable similarities between Du Bois and Washington during the late 1890's—a period when more Negro leaders than at any other time adopted a conciliatory tactic. Both tended to blame Negroes largely for their condition, and both placed more emphasis on self-help and duties than on rights. Both placed economic advancement before universal manhood suffrage, and both were willing to accept franchise restrictions based not on race but on education and/or property qualifications equitably applied. Both stressed racial solidarity and economic co-operation. Du Bois was, however, more outspoken about injustices, and he differed sharply with Washington in his espousal of the cause of higher education.

The years from 1901 to 1903 were years of transition in Du Bois' philosophy, years in which he grew more critical of industrial education and more alarmed over disfranchisement. Writing in 1901 he engaged in sharp protest against the Southern race system, even while recognizing that Negroes must adjust to it. He denied that the "many delicate differences in race psychology" excused oppression. He complained of the economic discrimination that retarded the development of a substantial landowning and artisan class. He bemoaned the lack of contact between the races that increased prejudice by preventing the best classes of both races from knowing each other. Yet he felt that, since Negroes must accept segregation, the road to uplift and economic improvement lay in the development of college-educated leaders: "Black captains of industry and missionaries of culture" who with their knowledge of modern civilization could uplift Negro communities "by forms of precept and example, deep sympathy and the inspiration of common kindred and ideals." But while Negroes would have to temporarily acquiesce in segregation, they could not acquiesce in disfranchisement. Du Bois did not object to "legitimate efforts to purge the ballot of ignorance, pauperism and crime," and he conceded that it was "sometimes best that a partially developed people should be ruled by the best of their stronger and better neighbors for their own good," until they were ready to stand on their own feet. But since the dominant opinion of the South openly asserted that the purpose of the disfranchisement laws was the complete exclusion of Negroes from politics, the ballot was absolutely necessary for the Negro's safety and welfare. Moreover, as European experience had demonstrated, workers under modern industrial conditions needed the vote in order to protect themselves; Negroes, laboring under racial discrimination, needed it even more.

Du Bois developed further his educational views and the theme of the talented tenth. He agreed that it was most important to train Negroes to work, and he conceded that industrial schools would play an important role in achieving this end. He also approved of the compromise function of industrial education, which had brought together races and sections; and although industrial education would not solve the problem he asserted that "it does mean that its settlement can be auspiciously begun." Yet he had come to criticize the overinsistence of industrial schools upon the practical, the unfortunate opposition of their advocates toward colleges, the fact that industrial schools were preparing their students in obsolete crafts, and the fact that they produced few actual artisans. Du Bois defended Negro colleges from charges that they had erred in training school teachers and professional men before turning to industrial training. He pointed out that historically the European university had preceded the common school, and that out of the liberal arts institutions came the backbone of the teaching force of the Negro common schools and of industrial schools like Tuskegee, where almost half of the executive council and a majority of the heads of departments were college graduates. All races, he held, had been civilized by their exceptional men; "the problem of education, then, among Negroes, must first of all deal with the Talented Tenth."

It is evident that Washington and Du Bois had come to disagree not only in their educational philosophy, but also on the fundamental question of the immediate importance of the ballot. By 1903 Du Bois was not only pleading for higher education, but had begun to criticize the work of the industrial schools. Both men spoke of captains of industry, but where the Tuskegeean emphasized economic skills, th[e] Atlanta educator stressed a high grade of culture. And unlike W[ash]ington, Du Bois had come to believe that educational and qualifications for voting would not be equitably applied Bois never gave up his belief that, in the face of white p discrimination, group solidarity was necessary, especially in econom[ic] matters. But all that really remained to make the two men irreconcilable ideological opponents was for Du Bois to advocate the importance of protest rather than accommodation. This he did in his opening attack on Washington in 1903.

During the 1890's Washington and Du Bois had been cordial in their relationships. Upon returning to the United States from Germany in 1894 Du Bois accepted a position at Wilberforce, having had to turn down a somewhat later offer from Tuskegee. Again in 1896, 1899, and as late as 1902 Du Bois seriously considered invitations to Tuskegee. In his correspondence with Washington, through his articles and speeches, and by attending the Hampton and Tuskegee Conferences he exhibited his sympathetic interest in Washington's work. He had, it is true, mildly criticized the Tuskegeean in an article in 1901. In it he said that some of the most prominent men of the race regarded the Hampton-Tuskegee approach as only a partial approach to the race problem, in that they stressed the highest aspirations of the race, advocated college education, and believed that Negroes should enjoy suffrage equally with whites. But as late as July 1902 the *Guardian* denounced Du Bois for siding with Washington at the St. Paul meeting of the Afro-American Council. "Like all the others who are trying to get into the bandwagon of the Tuskegeean, he is no longer to be relied upon," declared the editor, Monroe Trotter.

Kelly Miller has asserted that Trotter wove a "subtle net" around Du Bois and captured him for the radical cause. It would be difficult to test the truth of this statement. Certain it is, however, that by January 1903 Trotter was praising Du Bois as a brilliant leader who, despite temptations, "has never in public utterance or in written article, betrayed his race in its contest for equal opportunity and equal rights." Du Bois himself has recalled that he was gradually growing more disturbed after 1900—less by the ideological difference between him and Washington (which he remembered as mainly one of emphasis) than by the immense power over political appointments, over philanthropic largess, and over the press wielded by what Du Bois has labeled the "Tuskegee Machine." Du Bois found Washington's influence over the press especially deplorable, in view of the Tuskegeean's soft-pedaling of agitation on segregation and disfranchisement. Yet whatever his actual motivation for criticizing Washington, his first public statement on the matter was confined to ideological issues.

This statement was Du Bois' famous essay, "Of Booker T. Washington and Others," in *Souls of Black Folk*, published in the spring of 1903. "Easily the most striking thing," began Du Bois, "in the history of the American Negro since 1876 is the ascendancy of Mr. Booker T. Washington." Others had failed in establishing a compromise between the North, the South, and the Negroes. But Washington, coming with a simple though not entirely original program of industrial education, conciliation of the South, and acceptance of disfranchisement and segregation, had succeeded. For with "singular insight" he had grasped the spirit of the age—"the spirit and thought of triumphant commercialism."

Du Bois went on to criticize the Tuskegeean because his policy "practically accepted the alleged inferiority of the Negro," allowed economic concerns to dominate over the higher aims of life, and preached a "submission to prejudice." Although Washington had made some statements about lynching and the franchise, generally his speeches purveyed the "dangerous half-truths" that the Negro's lowly condition justified the South's attitude and that the Negro's elevation must depend chiefly on his own efforts. Du Bois perceived paradoxes in Washington's attempt to make Negro workers businessmen and property owners when it was impossible for workers to defend themselves without the ballot; in his preaching self-respect while counseling accommodation to discrimination and in his advocacy of industrial and common schools while depreciating the colleges that supplied their teachers. Furthermore, Washington's propaganda had undoubtedly hastened the disfranchisement, the increased segregation, and the decreased philanthropic concern for higher education that accompanied his ascendancy.

Washington's popularity with whites, Du Bois held, had led Negroes to accept his leadership, and criticism of the Tuskegeean had disappeared. The time was ripe therefore for thinking Negroes to undertake their responsibility to the masses by speaking out. In addition to the few who dared to openly oppose Washington, Du Bois thought that men like Archibald and Francis J. Grimké, Kelly Miller, and J.W.E. Bowen could not remain silent much longer. Such men honored Washington for his conciliatory attitude, and they realized that the condition of the masses of the race was responsible for much of the discrimination against it. But they also knew that prejudice was more often a cause than a result of the Negro's degradation; that Negroes could not gain their rights by voluntarily throwing them away, or obtain respect by constantly belittling themselves; and that, on the contrary, Negroes must speak out constantly against oppression and discrimination.

Du Bois had indeed moved away from his conciliatory ideology of the 1890's. Yet attempts at co-operation between him and Washington were not quite at an end. In the summer of 1903 Du Bois spoke at Tuskegee. The two men also continued their collaboration—begun in 1902—in an effort to prevent the exclusion of Negroes from Pullman cars. Nevertheless, after the "Boston Riot" Du Bois was—with reservations—lining up with Trotter. He did not, he said, agree with Trotter's intemperate tactics, but he admired his integrity and purpose, which were especially needed in view of Washington's backward steps. The Carnegie Hall Meeting of January 1904 and Du Bois' appointment to the Committee of Twelve temporarily restored an uneasy working relationship between him and Washington, but he soon resigned from the Committee and in 1905 was chiefly responsible for inaugurating the Niagara Movement. Meanwhile, he has recollected, he found it increasingly difficult to obtain funds for his work at Atlanta, experienced criticism in the Negro press, and in other ways "felt the implacability of the Tuskegee Machine." He was one of the most active members of the Conference on the Negro in 1909, and when the N.A.A.C.P. was organized in 1910 he became director of publicity and research and editor of the *Crisis*.

Thus by 1905 Du Bois had definitely come to the parting of the ways with Washington. And it is in the Niagara Movement manifestoes and in the pages of the *Horizon* and *Crisis* that one can best observe Du Bois as the consistent agitator, the ardent and brilliant fighter for integration and citizenship rights. For example, he insisted that disfranchisement retarded the economic development of the Negro because the voteless could not protect their property rights. He cited cases of persecution of prosperous Negroes as evidence that Washington's program would not obtain the respect of the white man and the rights of citizenship. In a typical editorial he pointed out that in spite of Washington's conciliatory policy conditions had grown worse. True, as Washington said, Negroes had continued to accumulate property and education, but how Washington could assert that discrimination and prejudice were decreasing was incomprehensible to Du Bois. Horrible as race prejudice was, it could be fought if faced frankly. But "if we continually dodge and cloud the issue, and say the half truth because the whole stings and shames . . . we invite catastrophe." Elsewhere he insisted that opportunism was a dangerous policy that gave moral support to the race's enemies, and he denounced the stress on sycophancy, selfishness, mediocrity, and servility at the expense of the best education, the highest ideals, and self-respect. Naturally he criticized industrial schools. On one occasion he attacked Hampton for its opposition to the work of the Negro colleges, and described it as "a center of that underground and silent intrigue which is determined to perpetuate the American Negro as a docile peasant," lacking political rights and social status. Du Bois was unequivocal in his stand on segregation. He scathingly denounced the separate-but-equal doctrine: "Separate schools for Whites and Blacks, and separate cars for Whites and Blacks are not equal, can not be made equal, and . . . are not intended to be equal." He charged that what the South wanted was not mere separation but subordination, and insisted that no "square deal" was possible as long as segregation existed. And unlike Washington he opposed a colored Episcopal bishop to work only among Negroes, even though this would have elevated a Negro to a high church office.

It is evident from a reading of Du Bois' less publicized scholarly and nonpolemical statements that throughout these years he still maintained his interest in racial solidarity and self-help, in the group economy, and in the American Negro's ties to Africa. On occasion he was most explicit about his concept of economic nationalism. Just as a country can by tariffs build up its separate economy to the point where it can compete in international trade, so the Negro should create a group economy that would "so break the force of race prejudice that his right and ability to enter the national economy are assured." His enthusiasm for the group economy was indeed at times interpreted as implying a favorable attitude toward segregation, and in an exchange of letters on the subject with the editor of the Boston *Transcript*, Du Bois was finally prompted to declare that while opposed to physical separation he was prepared to accept for some time to come a "spiritual" separation in economic life that would involve Negroes trading only among themselves. True, he shifted his support from the creation of captains of industry who would exploit the Negro proletariat to the building up of a consumers' and producers' co-operative movement among Negroes. But inevitably he had to reconcile his espousal of a group economy with his demands for full integration. In 1913, replying to a communication which claimed it was hard to meet the argument that segregation forced Negroes to develop themselves, Du Bois agreed that undoubtedly thousands of Negro businesses, including the *Crisis*, had developed because of discrimination, capitalizing, in a sense, on race prejudice. But this did not make discrimination a "veiled blessing." While Negro enterprises had done creditable work under the circumstances, and although Negroes must make the best of segregation, turning even its disadvantages to their advantage, they "must never forget that none of its possible advantages can offset its miserable evils, or replace the opportunity . . . of free men in a free world."

A similar paradox was involved in Du Bois' stand on intermarriage. Writing in the *Independent* in 1910 he held that a person had the right to choose his spouse, that the prohibition of intermarriage was not justified when it arbitrarily limited friendships, and that where satisfactory conditions prevailed, race mixture had often produced gifted and desirable stocks and individuals, such as the Egyptians, and Hamilton, Pushkin, Douglass, and Dumas. He believed, however, that for the present widespread intermarriage would be "a social calamity by reason of the wide cultural, ethical and traditional differences" between the races, and predicted that if Negroes were accorded their rights and thus encouraged to build up their racial self-respect, the two races would continue to exist as distinct entities, perhaps forever, and this not "at the behest of any one race which recently arrogantly assumed the heritage of the earth, but for the highest upbuilding of all peoples in their great ideal of human brotherhood."

Nor was Du Bois consistent in his views on race differences. Earlier, while never accepting any idea of Negro inferiority, he had referred to Negroes as a backward, childlike, underdeveloped race, and he had accepted the idea of inherent racial differences. But in March 1908 he attacked the "glib" Darwinist interpretations about undeveloped races and the survival of the fittest. After the Universal Races Congress in London in 1911 Du Bois enthusiastically reported its conclusion that there was no proven connection between race and mental or cultural characteristics. Yet in 1913 he harked back to the idea of inherent racial differences and described the Negro as primarily an artist, possessing a "sensuous nature . . . the only race which has held at bay the life destroying forces of the tropics," gaining thereby an unusual aesthetic sensitivity. This quality explained the artistic achievements of the Egyptians and the Ommiads, the literature of Pushkin, the bronze work of Benin, and the "only real American music."

As a matter of fact Du Bois maintained his strong feeling of identification with other colored peoples, especially Africans. At one time he was secretary of a company which aimed to participate in the economic advancement of East Africa. Years before Melville J. Herskovits cited anthropological evidence for African origins of the culture of American Negroes, Du Bois held that their religious life and institutions, family life, burial and beneficial societies, the roots of economic co-operation, and the skill of Negro artisans all had their origins in Africa. Finally, *The Negro*, published in 1915, dealt with Negro history from ancient Egypt to the United States and was especially notable for its discussion of the history and culture of West Africa. In it he also adopted the Italian anthropologist Giuseppe Sergi's thesis that an ancient rather dark-skinned race spawned all of the ancient Mediterranean civilizations. Moreover, he predicted the emergence of a pan-African movement, uniting Negroes everywhere, and a growing unity of the darker races against the intolerable treatment accorded them by the white man. Since the colored races were in a majority, the future world would probably be what colored men make it, and "in the character of the Negro race is the best and greatest hope. For in its normal condition it is at once the strongest and gentlest of the races of men."

A new theme in the pages of the *Horizon* and *Crisis* was Du Bois' interest in the labor movement and in socialism. At one time he had viewed the white working class as the Negro's "bitterest opponent." By 1904 he had come to believe that economic discrimination was in large part the cause of the race problem, and to feel sympathetic toward the socialist movement. Three years later, he was writing favorably of the socialists in the *Horizon*. Elsewhere he advised the socialists that their movement could not succeed unless it included the Negro workers, and wrote that it was simply a matter of time before white and black workers would see their common economic cause against the exploiting capitalists. Though in 1908 Du Bois did not vote for the socialists because they had no chance of winning, in 1911 he joined the party. In a Marxist exegesis in the concluding pages of *The Negro*, Du Bois viewed both American Negroes and Africans, both the white workers and the colored races, as exploited by white capital which employed the notion of race differences as a rationalization of exploitation, segregation, and subordination. And he predicted that the exploited of all races would unite and overthrow white capital, their common oppressor.

Du Bois' espousal of the cause of labor was so deep-seated that he had the *Crisis* printed by members of a union that did not admit Negroes, and in its pages he welcomed the rare signs that white and Negro workers might be getting together. In this regard he was certainly ahead of his time, and even he finally expressed discouragement after the 1917 East St. Louis riot in which white unionists played such a striking role. Thus Du Bois' attempts to woo union labor had succeeded no better than his related attempt to woo the Democratic party. . . . But Du Bois never gave up his vision of a union of white and black workers creating a society of economic and racial justice. He had in fact shifted from pinning his faith on the intellectuals or talented tenth of professional and business men to pinning in on the actions of the black working classes, though quite likely they were to be led, as has been suggested, by a talented-tenth intelligentsia.

In W.E.B. Du Bois then, the most distinguished Negro intellectual in the age of Booker T. Washington, we find explicitly stated most of the threads of Negro thought at that time. On the one hand he had a mystic sense of race and of the mission of the Negro, which made him sympathetic toward ideas of racial pride and solidarity as sentiments useful for racial uplift. On the other hand he held explicitly and constantly, especially after 1901, to the ideal of waging a struggle for full acceptance in American society. While at times he seemed to view segregated institutions as good in themselves, actually he regarded them as second-best instruments in the struggle for advancement and citizenship rights. He envisaged not amalgamation but cultural pluralism as the goal. He was inconsistent on the question of innate race differences, but he never admitted that Negroes were inferior. Above all he insisted that Negroes wanted to be both Negroes and Americans, maintaining their racial integrity while associating on the freest terms with all American citizens, participating in American culture in its broadest sense, and contributing to it in fullest freedom.

It is notable that though Du Bois expressed the views held by most of the articulate Negroes of the age of Booker T. Washington, both in his stress on racial solidarity and economic co-operation and in his demand for full citizenship rights, nevertheless he frequently found himself in the minority. Few articulate Negroes exhibited the same extent of political independence; not many Northern Negroes agreed

with his accommodating tactic of the late ninetheenth century; relatively few championed the cause of liberal education as enthusiastically as he did; few either dared or cared to follow him in the extent
to which he championed the protest movement during the first years
of the twentieth century; and few embraced socialism or the cause
of the black workers and interracial working-class solidarity. It is important to note, however, that many times people, who at heart agreed
with his point of view, were not courageous enough to flout the power
structure both within and outside of the Negro community as he did.

Of the great trio of Negro leaders, Douglass was the orator, Du Bois
the polished writer, and Washington the practical man of affairs. Like
Douglass, Du Bois has been known primarily as a protest leader,
though he was not as consistent in this role as Douglass. Like Douglass, too, he exhibited a marked oscillation in his ideologies—in fact
his was more marked than that of Douglass. Like Douglass he clearly
stated the ultimate goals which Washington obscured. Yet Du Bois
displayed more of a sense of racial solidarity than Douglass usually
did. Nor did he envisage the degree of amalgamation and the loss of
racial consciousness that Douglass regarded as the *summum bonum*.
On the contrary he, like Washington, emphasized race pride and solidarity and economic chauvinism, though after 1905 he no longer
championed support of the individualist entrepreneur but favored instead a co-operative economy. Where Washington wanted to make
Negroes entrepreneurs and captains of industry in accordance with
the American economic dream (a dream shared with less emphasis
by Douglass), Du Bois stressed the role of the college-educated elite
and later developed a vision of a world largely dominated by the colored
races which would combine with the white workers in overthrowing
the domination of white capital and thus secure social justice under
socialism. All three emphasized the moral values in American culture
and the necessity of justice for the Negro if the promise of American
life were to be fulfilled. But of the three men it was Douglass who was
pre-eminently the moralist, while Washington and Du Bois expressed
sharply divergent economic interpretations. Where Douglass and
Washington were primarily petit-bourgeois in their outlook, Du Bois
played the role of the Marxist intelligentsia. Where the interest of
Douglass and Washington in Africa was largely prefunctory, Du Bois
exhibited a deep sense of racial identity with Africans. Above all,
though only Douglass favored amalgamation, all three had as their goal
the integration of Negroes into American society.

Scholar and prophet; mystic and materialist; ardent agitator for political rights and propagandist for economic co-operation; one who espoused an economic interpretation of politics and yet emphasized the necessity of political rights for economic advancement; one who denounced segregation and called for integration into American society in accordance with the principles of human brotherhood and the ideals of democracy, and at the same time one who favored the maintenance of racial solidarity and integrity and a feeling of identity with Negroes elsewhere in the world; an equalitarian who apparently believed in innate racial differences; a Marxist who was fundamentally a middle-class intellectual, Du Bois becomes the epitome of the paradoxes in American Negro thought. In fact, despite his early tendencies toward an accommodating viewpoint, and despite his strong sense of race solidarity and integrity, Du Bois expressed more effectively than any of his contemporaries the protest tendency in Negro thought, and the desire for citizenship rights and integration into American society.

Support Your Local Mob

• A racist community and a peaceful community are incompatible. America learned that fact again, only to neglect it, during the Progressive Era, just as similar recognition had been forgotten in previous periods of great social unrest. The number of lynchings decreased in the twentieth century, as C. Vann Woodward noted in a previous selection, and they became primarily if not exclusively a southern phenomenon, inflicted overwhelmingly upon black victims. Early in this century, however, racial tensions mounted dangerously in all sections of the country, as midwestern and eastern communities where many Negroes began to migrate joined the accustomed Deep South place names as the sites of lynchings and violence stemming from race hatred. The following selection by Charles Crowe describes one such slaughter in Atlanta.

A great many Americans on all educational levels assume that serious and sustained urban racial violence began in this country about 1964 or 1965. Yet the only truly novel features in this long established form of social conflict spring from the fact that the initiative of violence has passed from the whites to the blacks in new ghetto rebellions which involve both the revolution of rising black expectations and spontaneous explosions of anger and despair. In the decades since the beginning of the Civil War few years passed without at least one race riot, but Americans have always insisted on regarding this kind of violence as extraordinary. During 1906, for example, commentators across the country followed the national custom by discussing the Atlanta riot as a singular episode without general implications. Nevertheless, many hundreds of riots have taken place, nearly all of them share at least some common characteristics and all fit into a few basic patterns. First of all, prior to 1964, white assaults on isolated

From Charles Crowe, "Racial Massacre in Atlanta, September 22, 1906," *Journal of Negro History*, LIV (April 1969), 150–68 (footnotes omitted). Reprinted by permission of Associated Publishers, Washington, D. C.

blacks or white invasions of black neighborhoods generally began the conflicts.

Northern riots between 1862 and 1865 in New York, Cincinnati, and other cities were largely massacres of blacks as were the political riots in the South during Reconstruction, but in a significant number of Reconstruction disorders black men made extensive efforts for self-defence and retaliation. During the retreat from Reconstruction that reached a nadir in the Progressive era, black self-defence and retaliation declined sharply. While whites continued to be the aggressors in most disturbances of the First and Second World Wars, blacks mounted even stronger defensive and retaliatory actions than they had in Reconstruction.

In the First and Second World Wars, riots sprang from white opposition to a major redistribution of population in which blacks moved toward "better" cities, jobs, homes and schools. Earlier conflicts did not involve any major population shifts. Racial disturbances during Reconstruction originated in the efforts of Southern white supremacists to deny blacks freedom and power, and the riots of the Progressive era were rooted in the common white desire to arrest Negro progress and to drive blacks into greater docility and subjugation. Although the Progressive period marked the political nadir for American Negroes, the continuing black educational and economic gains coupled with the rising tide of white demands for racial repression and the perfection of the color caste system made a large number of riots inevitable. The characteristics which distinguish Progressive riots from disorders in other historical periods are real enough, but it is easy to overstress them. "Political" riots, for example, certainly did not end in 1877. Conservative Democrats in Danville, Virginia instigated a race riot during 1883 to insure the triumph of a white supremacy regime. Democrats of Wilmington, North Carolina in 1898 used a race riot as a smokescreen for the revolutionary seizure of the city from Fusionist Republicans and Populists, and the Atlanta riot of 1906 had clear political overtones. As late as 1921 whites in Ocoee, Florida started a riot when a small group of Negroes tried to vote. Moreover, Northern responses to the great migrations of the two world wars were foreshadowed in disorders such as the Springfield, Illinois riot of 1908.

In the final analysis, however, it is possible to find patterns into which the riots of the four different periods fit. During the age of reform, blacks had virtually no political power, but they continued to seek educational and economic gains in the face of mounting white opposition. The Atlanta riot of 1906 was a representative riot of the Progressive era, and Southern riots differed from Northern disorders only in two respects: both barbarous atrocities on the one hand and the paternalistic rescue of some servants on the other hand were far more likely in the South.

Like other cities, Atlanta in 1906 had been hearing increasingly insistent trumpet calls of repression. When the riot burst into reality with the full impact of a long expected nightmare on "bloody Saturday" September 22, white Atlanta seemed to be surrendering to its own sense of inevitability. Two days earlier the sense of impending violence led a lawyer to inform *Harper's Weekly* that racial conflict might shatter an uneasy peace and engulf the city at any moment. Even more pessimistic Negro leaders tried vainly with accommodating words and deeds to stem the tide of white aggressiveness produced by Hoke Smith's vituperative Negro baiting campaign for the governorship which lasted eighteen months and left in its wake inflamed emotions and unsatiated desires for more repression. Throughout the summer civic leaders and evangelists made the situation worse by clamoring for new restrictive measures against Negroes, and the press contributed to tensions by giving much lurid coverage to racial conflict.

On July 30, when an Atlanta mob lynched an innocent Negro for "rape," the city press took a sympathetic stance toward the mob and editor Charles Daniels of the *Evening News* formally congratulated the killers for having given the community "general satisfaction." For months lynchings in Georgia and adjacent states dominated public discussion, particularly after a Chattanooga mob murdered a "sexual assailant" under the protection of a U.S. Supreme Court order signed by Justice Oliver Wendell Holmes. The lynchers and their conspiratorial allies in public office gained public approval from many white Georgians.

Despite mounting tensions in Atlanta, publicists used "the Chattanooga lesson" to "show" Georgia Negroes the drastic measures white men would commonly take "to protect our women." In this climate of opinion even the most trivial encounters between black men and white women inspired hostile and lurid discussion about the "sexual animality" of the black man, and the idea of a "rape menace" became an obsession strong enough to compel economy minded officials to double the number of local police. While civic leaders continued to demand new anti-Negro measures, their more impetuous fellow citizens roamed the streets at night in armed Klan-like bands. Fear gripped the Negro community as an angry belligerence increasingly characterized the behavior of many white people in a city destined for mass violence.

Between Monday September 17 and Thursday September 19, scattered and largely inconsequential incidents between Negro men and white women were transformed by press and public discussion into "an intolerable epidemic of rape" which had to be ended "immediately." On Friday evening, September 20, a white man whose daughter had been "assaulted" tried to organize a lynch mob inside the city criminal court, and during the same evening police narrowly averted a lynching outside the station house. As a general sexual hysteria took possession of white Atlanta, violent and well armed men began to gather at the center of the city during the afternoon of September twenty-second. A final burst of police and press activity on Saturday against Negro "vagrancy" and "dives" as "the sources" of "sexual crime" added the final ingredient to the development of an emotionally explosive situation.

Saturday's anger crystallized around "Decatur Street dives," the "breeding ground of Negro lust and crime." Only two blocks from busy Peachtree Street, the central traffic artery and the pride of the city, solid Decatur Street stone and brick gave way to decaying structures and poorly built wooden buildings which sheltered ordinary boarding houses, restaurants and clubs as well as "dime bed dives," pawnshops, gambling dens, and houses of prostitution. To the area came drifters, "criminals," and, for the main part, ordinary black people seeking entertainment. White people came also, for in Atlanta as in other American cities vice was integrated and largely confined to the central Negro section.

The police, who ruled the Decatur Street area with methods reminiscent of both political terrorists and barbarian overlords, operated from a centrally located station which bore a formidable resemblance to a robber baron's castle. Extortion and bribery had become well used customs, but "protection" went largely to the Greek, East European Jewish, and Negro proprietors of integrated saloons and seldom to the Negro customers. Carelessly repaired windows in some saloons and clubs revealed traces of terrified Negro flight before the onslaught of police raids. Actual arrest, which depended on the whim of the police, led almost invariably to conviction and usually to the city stockade, the dreaded Georgia chain gang, or the even more oppressive convict lease camp. During "a routine investigation" several weeks before the Atlanta riot two fear ridden men had leaped from a third floor saloon to avoid detention. This dread of arrest sprang partly from convict death rates of nearly ten percent a year which made a ten year term equivalent to a death sentence. The guards at the Atlanta stockade, accustomed to dealing brutally with black prisoners, sometimes extended the same treatment to white men. The *Atlanta Georgian* on December 4, 1906 reported the circumstances of three white prisoners convicted on the minor charge of drunkenness: the first spent five months on the critical list in a hospital recovering from a week's sentence; the second had to do the most back breaking prison labor while gravely ill; and the third after narrowly escaping death left the stockade ill, emaciated, with a badly cut left hand and a right hand swollen to twice its normal size. Under these conditions the doom of many black men was sealed.

To most white Atlantans the stockade existed for righteous reasons and the Decatur Street dive lacked reason for existing at all. If the dives in "normal" times represented social evil and a standing insult to the color caste system, they seemed on September 22 to be an intolerable offense which merited destruction. At approximately six o'clock in the evening bands of white men began to collect around Peachtree and Decatur Streets on the fringe of the central Negro district to discuss angrily the black "sexual assaults" reported in the inflammatory newspaper extras which appeared on the streets between five and nine o'clock. The alarmists, following the long established custom, earnestly reported news of plans for a great "Negro uprising." In the same general vicinity small groups of Negroes gathered to deny crime and conspiracy and to denounce the sensational headlines.

At first the more aggressive white men satisfied themselves by sporadically jeering and shoving passing messengers and delivery men. Rumors of black and white encounters rapidly circulated through the crowds—a Negro man had forced a white woman from the sidewalk or stolen her purse, or insulted her. Although these stereotyped reports on the origins of race conflict invariably circulated in times of tension, credulous reporters traced the riot to several of these tales. Stories that a white man "insulted" by a Negro woman "punished" her "impudence" violently and that a scuffle between two men ended with the black man stabbing his white adversary seem more authentic but only the existence of scattered incidents between 8:30 and 9:00 p.m. can be asserted with certainty.

About 8:30 p.m. near Decatur and Marietta Streets in the midst of much angry shouting about "vengeance" on "the rapists," a self-appointed leader mounted a dry goods box brandishing a newspaper extra which read in bold headlines "THIRD ASSAULT."

"Are WHITE men going to stand for THIS?" The speaker asked rhetorically until the mob began to respond with "No! Save our Women!" and "Kill the niggers!" As the rhetoric continued the outer fringe of the crowd began to experiment with more vicious Negro baiting. In several instances a dozen white men encircled a Negro tormenting him alternately by kicks and blows with a barrel stave until loss of self-control led the man to fight back, thus "provoking" the mob to surge forward beating and kicking their victim into unconsciousness.

Shortly after 9:00 p.m., Mayor James Woodward, who had been on the scene for hours, reported "a demonstration of citizens" and asked for police and fire units. The mayor did not command a great deal of public respect, and at one city council session, so rowdy as to require police intervention, Woodward was described as a "flunky" of the saloons and the Atlantic Traction Company and "a dirty vulgar liar . . . reeking with slime." Thus when the mayor standing on a box before several thousand violent men, "implored" them—perhaps ironically—to "consider the honor of the city," "the citizens" paid little attention to his token protests and responded jeeringly, "Oh, go home yourself Jim. We're after niggers." A few minutes later James W. English, head of the police commission, made another futile attempt to calm the crowd in front of the Piedmont Hotel but was quickly shouted down as a "nigger lover."

Even as the mayor and the commissioner spoke, at least 5,000 persons had gathered in the streets and the riot was underway. One mob ruthlessly assaulted a messenger and left him for dead; several gangs beat and chased Negroes from key intersections, and at least one band of lynchers organized "to clean up Decatur Street dives." At this point Fire Chief and Mayor-elect Joyner came riding dramatically into Decatur Street with all the city's hose carts trailing him. The mob allowed the firemen to pass but ran hooting after them. When the chief had six jets turned on the largest mob, many men indignantly shouted their regrets for having voted in his favor. The chief did not repeat the attack and the mob dispersed only to come together again at a safe distance. Then the hose company advanced down Decatur Street forcing several hundred Negroes, who had fearfully and defensively grouped together, to retreat into an open plaza where a wild gathering of some two thousand white men waited for them. For a few minutes the two groups fought with clubs and fists before the outnumbered Negro line broke and gave way to a frantic scramble for refuge.

Meanwhile a large force of police perfunctorily "held" a second mob until the sight of a substantial number of Negroes coming around a corner "maddened" mob leaders enough to brush aside police lines and rush forward in a jagged, uneven line. A second skirmish developed but the numerical odds were even more disproportionate and the Negroes soon fell back before a wave of clubs, iron pipes, and brickbats. One group of black people by retreating toward the central train station temporarily drew the mob away from lower Decatur Street where many hundreds of Negroes waited and a major confrontation might have taken place. Later, when another mob entered lower Decatur, most of the Negroes had fled to safety outside the city.

Between nine-thirty and eleven o'clock thousands of white men bought arms. A single hardware store sold sixteen thousand dollars worth of weapons, and the ten o'clock closing of saloons, clubs and theaters sent more mob recruits in search of weapons. Although the Sheriff of Fulton County called for an end to gun sales, he personally signed hundreds of permits for "respectable citizens." (Later the sheriff "handled" two hundred aggressive white men by deputizing them!) City police, executing quite a different policy on the other side of the color line, took weapons from legally armed Negroes and later in the evening brutally disarmed five men at a time when nearby white mobs were trying to kill black people. Thus by 10:30 more than 10,000 rioters, many of whom had rifles and pistols, hunted unarmed Negroes. Unsympathetic police, professing a general "helplessness," refused to use guns, nightsticks or fists to stop assault and murder. Some policemen rescued individual Negroes when the task was easy; and a few made heroic efforts to save lives but others joined the rioters in clubbing, robbing, and, in several instances, killing. The most popular stance, however, seemed to be one of non-involvement. The general quality of the force can be judged by the fact that nearly a quarter of it was dismissed between October 1 and December 31 for drunkenness on the beat, neglect of duty, robbery and other charges. Indeed, as the southern writer and *Atlantic Monthly* editor Walter Hines Page observed, the city government itself was "a standing invitation to crime."

After making one of the few arrests of the evening, five policemen fled with their prisoner from a mob which gave pursuit shouting "Let him go! He's a white man!" The police did not often repeat this experiment but on the contrary failed to take advantage of superior numbers in a great many instances. It is difficult to say why the police arrested some violent men and left a vastly larger number ·

alone, unless they acted on caprice or against rioters who annoyed them. Had it not been for the Orwellian doublethink implicit in white supremacy, the failure of the police to arrest more "criminals" might have been embarrassing to the post-riot consensus of white Atlanta which held that the violence had been done only by "lawless elements and excitable boys." In fact the police failed to detain even one well known person; but disinterested action was hardly to be expected from so corrupt and inefficient a force. Policemen did arrest a prosperous Mississippian in transit as well as Atlantans with some fairly high status occupations. While the mob was typically youthful, it contained many adults of all ages and social types including professional people, storeowners, business school students, and skilled workers. A leading officer of the Southern railroad insisted that "members of the best families" joined the fray, a visiting actor described the expensive dress worn by many in the mob, and Dr. R. R. Kline urged the Atlanta Sociological Society "to be honest" by admitting that "respectable saloons" as well as dives provided rioters. Post-mortems, of the riot commonly had more to do with social role playing than with current events, and the tale of "the aristocracy" rallying as a group to protect Negroes from "the rabble" sprang from a tradition in which higher status whites demonstrated the existence of "quality" by "patriarchal" descriptions of "race relations" or the allegedly genteel pronunciation of the word "Negro." The actual treatment received by the Negro before, during and after the riot often bore no more than a modest resemblance to the rhetoric of the upper status white people.

When the rioters—gentleman, rabble and others—gained control of the street from the "helpless" police about 10:30, they added to assault and murder the systematic destruction of restaurants, clubs, saloons and pool rooms frequented by Negroes. Several gangs invaded Auburn Avenue (then in the process of becoming the economic Mecca for ambitious Negroes of the Southeast) but found the street nearly deserted. The rioters did pursue and mistreat a Greek merchant despite his loud protestations about white identity, and they drove a terrified Negro tailor through the glass door of his shop before beating him with iron bars. Soon, however, the frustrated gangs drifted back to Decatur Street. One Decatur gang leader, George W. Blackstock, arriving from suburban Oakland "to hunt niggers," spoke obsessively to one and all of his passion to take part in the killing. Blackstock, who had been heard exclaiming rapturously over the "beauty" of a mutilated Negro corpse, spent most of the evening leading raids on black establishments. The first to suffer was a restaurant keeper with twenty years at the same location who saw Blackstock's gang coming and barred the door. Mattie Adams and her daughter stood inside petrified with fear as Blackstock exhorted his group to "kill every damned nigger in sight" and led the charge against the door with a battering ram. After smashing in the door, the mob beat Mrs. Adams and her daughter repeatedly with wagon wheel spokes, used a small grandson for target practice with revolvers, and broke dishes, glasses, furniture and everything in sight which could be destroyed. Blackstock attacked other Negro establishments and his gang represented only one of many groups engaged in assault and destruction. Mobs, selecting certain kinds of establishments as favorite targets, invaded every Negro owned barber shop as well as most "dives" and pool rooms with a black clientele. Although rioters destroyed some white property, damaged a train, smashed a dozen trolley cars, and raided two hardware stores for guns, they visited most of the destruction on places owned or used by Negroes.

Between nine and eleven o'clock a general exodus of Negroes took place, and cab drivers, bell boys, maids, delivery men, barbers, Decatur Street residents and visitors fled "as only those can who know that a second's delay may mean death." A suburban Negro picking up his mother at work on Peachtree Street got a bullet wound for his efforts to protect her from physical attack. Dozens of large and small mobs roaming the inner city greeted every Negro on sight with "Nigger! Kill the black devil!" One mob pursued a Negro from the North Side of the Forsyth Street Bridge with guns until a gang on the South side yelled their determination to stop the man. The victim collapsed from a club blow on the head so heavy that it could be heard across the bridge. At the main entrance to the Piedmont hotel in the presence of hundreds of witnesses a roving gang stabbed two Negroes and a few minutes later two large mobs trapped a victim whom they tortured to death. Several men concentrated on breaking heavy bottles over the man's head while others sliced the torso with knives. The tormenting continued for fifteen minutes until impatient men in the rear of the crowd began to yell "Burn him! Kill the nigger!" and those closest to the scene rushed in for the kill with knives and hatchets. After the murder had been completed one of the killers triumphantly held over the corpse the newspaper extra that read "Third Assault." Then in a frantic scramble souvenir hunters ripped the dead man's clothing to shreds and cut off his fingers and toes. In two minutes' time the mob had moved on to search for more black people leaving a bloody pavement littered with small pieces of cloth, tattered fragments of felt hats, and scraps of shoe leather.

As the black population thinned out the mobs became even more blood-thirsty and relentless in the pursuit of victims. Mob members who failed to secure shotguns, rifles or revolvers armed themselves with canes, iron bars, heavy umbrellas, and rocks. From the peak of violence and destruction on Decatur Street we have the account of the Negro journalist, Max Barber. who described vividly the sinister play of rapidly moving shadows around the electric lights in an atmosphere ridden with swirling dust and powdersmoke. For a long time Barber would recall the glitter of blue steel, the roar of guns, the crack of shattering glass, the trails of blood along the sidewalks, and the limp bodies of the wounded, the dying and the dead scattered at the intersection.

In the quest for victims, rioters entered a barbershop then open and filled with white customers. The barbers, too frozen with fear to utter a sound, tried to continue cutting hair until the mob began to beat them. When another mob crashed through the plate glass window of a fashionable Peachtree Street barber shop, the barber closest to the door held up his hands until a mob leader threw a brick in his face. In this fray, dozens of rioters beat a barber and a boot-black to death with heavy weapons, slashed the faces and bodies, and carved initials on the back of one corpse. The mob then carried the bodies to the Henry Grady monument with the idea that this constituted a proper tribute to "the statesman of the New South," who had lectured so often on the need to keep the Negro in his place. White leaders then discovered, crouching fearfully behind the monument, a Negro man who had taken refuge there. A short burst of gunfire rang out until a leader shouted "Don't shoot—you'll kill good white men!" and the crowd obeyed the imperative cry by beating the man to death. The frenzied clubbing continued until the exhausted killers allowed a party of men to carry the corpse to the front of the monument and dump it with the other two bodies. During the night souvenir hunters mauled and mutilated the dead men, but they lay in the same locations the next morning.

On Peachtree just a few hundred yards from the Grady monument the violent hours were given over to macabre mixture of carnage and carnival. The shocked but fascinated Arthur Hofman of Field's Minstrel Show watched throngs of well dressed men, women and children on the sidewalks cheer and applaud mob activists beating Negroes in the streets. Frequently men left the sidewalks to join the rioters or returned from mob action to become spectators. To amuse the sidewalk galleries rioters would give a captured Negro a five yard start and then take up an armed chase with clubs and knives as the only policeman in sight energetically joined the assaults. In the excitement the actor Hofman began shouting until "the best people," among whom he had chosen to stand, noticed the Northern accent and demanded his assent to the "agreeable" nature of the evening's "diversion." "It didn't seem so bad at the time . . ." said Hofman, "and besides the crowd might have killed me. . . . What was I to do?"

The mobs, after driving all Negroes from Peachtree, began to gather at the streetcar stops to catch uninformed and unsuspecting black people as they rode into the maelstrom of conflict. Although the police at first "interfered" by occupying some boarding platforms and rescuing a few Negro passengers, they tended increasingly to ignore Negroes until after they had been assaulted. In the first attack a large mob on Peachtree spotted two Negroes seated on a car behind two white women and ignoring the women's screams clubbed the men to the floor before dragging them out for a more savage assault. A few minutes later at a nearby stop the same mob halted a car half filled with Negroes. By cutting the trolley ropes the rioters plunged passengers into darkness and abruptly forced the front end of the car high into the air. With the black and white occupants reduced to hysterical fright the invaders frantically spilled into the car stabbing and clubbing, and striking women as well as men. Two Negro men fought back so effectively that four or five whites fell but sheer numbers brought them down with a special ferocity as payment for their resistance. Although the majority escaped with bloody heads and cut arms, two dead men lay on the floor and three more were unconscious from critical wounds when the mob finally allowed the car to proceed. In a third car a Negro man fired two shots into the riotous crowd before making a successful escape. The mob that rushed car 207 on Peachtree encountered a Negro woman who "fought like a wildcat" striking men right and left with an umbrella before going down. With this woman vanquished the invaders beat a man until his death seemed a certainty before they allowed themselves to be "persuaded" to leave the car. As the car began to move off one white man yelled "He ain't dead! Beat him again!" and two men cut the power off by yanking the trolley rope down. Not until the rope had been removed and replaced several times did the car go off at full speed with dozens of rioters "clambering on the sides like rats." After two hours of violence the traction company finally stopped all cars before they entered the riot zone, but by that time twelve cars had been attacked, three men were dead, six lay critically wounded and more than thirty men and women had been injured.

After the violence ended on Peachtree, wagon drivers carted away the wounded to Grady Hospital until that overcrowded institution had to send new patients to the police. Before the night ended the packed police station used all the available space and the injured had no public place to go. The station house became not only an auxiliary hospital but a general gathering place for thousands of white Atlantans who drifted from Peachtree or Decatur Streets. Nearly all night the crowd on the street watched police units come and go, commented on the wounded as they arrived, and listened for word of the newest scene of racial conflict. Inside the station house the idle and the curious wandered freely and reporters answered calls from half-hysterical suburban white women who demanded "protection" because of the absence of husbands and fathers.

If chaos prevailed at the station house and policemen frequently failed to do their duty in the streets, police units did in two rare instances act forcefully and effectively. In the first case a police company deflected a Decatur Street mob from their march on a skating rink where five hundred Negroes had taken refuge. Badly frightened women and children huddled in the center of the rink but a substantial number of men along with some women guarded the entrances until news arrived that the mob had gone in another direction and people could slip away from the center of town through the back streets. In the second instance a white mob of four hundred stormed a hardware store and seized hundreds of weapons as preparation for marching on the central train station to attack the porters on the eleven thirty train. The coaches held not only porters but also black refugees from the streets and jammed waiting rooms contained many white women and children stranded because of the flight of Negro cab drivers. The charge on the station grounds evoked terrified screams from the waiting rooms but the mob passed on swiftly toward the eleven thirty train. A single Negro-occupied coach provided the major target for the howling onslaught of attackers who hurled bricks and fired revolvers as they smashed into the car windows with gun butts. Although six people fell into the hands of the mob at once, the majority fled trying to dodge bullets and the deluge of clubs and other objects thrown at them. The station grounds now resembled embattled Decatur Street and the damage would have been even greater had not fifteen mounted policemen arrived to disperse the mob with one aggressive charge. After the disorderly flight of the rioters the police recovered nearly a hundred stolen weapons.

From the train station most members of the broken mob drifted back to Decatur Street where just before midnight frenzied street orators organized a mob to assault Peters Street establishments. With a burst of enthusiasm and loud, sustained rebel yells, the crowd surged in the direction of their targets, seizing lumber, rocks and clubs as they went. "Moving like a river," the mob turned into Peters Street smashing windows and hammering doors with lumber beams. When a female storekeeper peered out to investigate the roar in the street and then fearfully began to bar the door, her actions caught the attention of riot leaders who proceeded to lead a charge with axes and timber beams. Bursting through the flimsy barrier the rioters attacked the woman and her helpers and made a shambles of the interior before rushing out to find new opportunities for assault and destruction. A few minutes later a segment of the mob encountered a Negro man with a pistol, knocked him down before he could use it, and quickly killed him. When a second black man fired from a high window and wounded a white man on the street, many of the marauders moved off toward the nearest store to get more bullets and guns. Hundreds of men looted a hardware store of weapons and other items. Just as the raiders returned to Peters Street a hapless coal company employee turned into the street, and men closest to the scene began to beat him with clubs until gunfire forced them to step back and allow the victim to be nearly torn apart by the barrage.

For every actual casualty of the raids many Negroes narrowly escaped death and sometimes white men gave vital assistance. The owner of the largest downtown stable averted the probable murder of two Negro helpers by using a shotgun and great presence of mind to turn away an armed gang of several hundred men. In a second instance a Bijou Theater employee, named J. D. Belsa, reached his baggage men almost simultaneously with a murderous mob and daringly rushed them to safety behind locked doors. When the rioters tried to storm the theater doors, Belsa, armed with a shotgun, forced them to retreat and stood guard the rest of the night. About the time of the theater incident, an undertaker's barouche crossed nearby Marietta Street at a furious pace with three Negro men in the back and a white driver who alternately lashed the horses and made powerful swoops with a whip at the pursuing rioters. This rescue and others like it rested on a foundation of the sense of partial ownership ("*my* Negroes") and of the general unwillingness of the mob to kill or injure white people. The second factor proved to be strong enough to enable a very frail white woman to save a black man from a hundred assailants merely by standing before her door and "refusing" to allow anyone to cross her threshold until the police arrived. In one curious incident a Negro hack driver saved a crippled white passenger by racing bravely through two mobs in scrapes so narrow that both men arrived at the police station still trembling with fear. Ironically, the driver's efforts led to a short jail term because the police failed to make distinctions in all cases between Negroes charged with crimes and those who had sought sanctuary from attack.

The white household was a far safer place than the police station for Negroes trapped in the central city and fortunate enough to have a well disposed white employer. In truth, several hundred white families did keep Negroes in their houses. However, the fact that the dominant caste had the prerogative of giving or refusing shelter had nothing to do with mitigating the factors that caused and sustained the riot. If human compassion inspired a few to befriend the black stranger, most men who gave refuge were moved by the quasi-feudal motives which led even violent Negrophobes to "do favors" for the "deserving" Negro dependant.

The feudal protection extended to several hundred Negroes did not affect the fate of several thousands frightened, injured or driven from the city by the murderous white mobs. Undoubtedly many black people regarded the riot as a war of white against black which justified both defensive and retaliatory action, but violence came like a sudden and destructive storm which allowed no time for organized efforts. Moreover, the scattered and isolated instances of resistance which did take place only seemed to make death or grave injury more certain. At no time did confrontations take place on numerically equal terms, and in two conflicts involving a substantial group of Negroes the preponderance of white power made the battles brief. In a significant number of incidents, women urged retaliation, "fought like Amazons," and even led small bands of men and women into combat. One young woman, described by reporters as "a firebrand" "parading" on Cain Street, denounced white oppression and called on black men to rise up and take a life for a life. A second young woman later served a jail sentence for helping a male friend in efforts to organize an offensive band. (She insisted that she "would fight until the last pea is out of the dish.") A few men formed and led resistance groups or seized houses to barricade as stations for snipers. In one instance nine Negro men on the edge of the inner city occupied a building which commanded a major car line and stopped all traffic with rifle fire for nearly an hour before escaping. Near the downtown area a group of armed and aggressive Negroes attacked the Inman Park car before a much larger police force overwhelmed them, and an hour later a second band of twenty-five men with weapons organized to rescue Negroes was surrounded and taken into custody. Although Negroes inflicted injuries on about a dozen white men in conflicts during the night, no white fatalities were reported.

As news of the riot spread through Negro neighborhoods and rumors circulated about mass killing on the street cars, some young people turned out with guns to fire at the passing cars. By 1:00 A.M. half a dozen cars with white drivers had ridden through a "hail of fire" and motormen refused to go out any more. In Negro districts all over the city bands of black men attacked street lights with rocks and revolvers, both to express general anger and to make white invasion more difficult. Informal assemblies here and there considered means of coping with the menace and in some gatherings militants threatened leaders who counseled "moderation." For ill or for good the various Negro colleges and seminaries of Atlanta had not begun the fall term and many professors such as W.E.B. Du Bois were out of town. President J.W.E. Bowen of Gammon Theological Seminary and his colleagues at Clark University opened college buildings as places of refuge and stayed with the frightened women and children who came to take shelter. J. L. Price, storekeeper and postmaster who served the college community, sold or lent his entire stock of guns. Indeed every Atlanta Negro who could buy, borrow or steal a weapon did so in fear of his life.

A thousand Negroes fled the city and many thousands more spent the night armed and tensely waiting for the mobs. The future NAACP leader Walter White, then a boy of eleven, remembered all of his life that evening of "terror and bitterness" in which "I learned who I was." Walter's father, after sending wife and daughter to the rear of the house, waited with his son at the windows of the darkened front room with a generous supply of guns and ammunition at hand. A great number of families vainly waited in a similar fashion for the mob. In the three days of sporadic racial violence yet to come, some families had tragic encounters with white gangs, and blacks fought a bloody clash with whites near Clark University; but on the evening of September 22 only a few white gangs ventured cautiously beyond the central city.

If rumors about the massacre of Negroes by the hundreds swept the city, some stories of large white casualty lists could also be heard during and after the riot. A few Negro weeklies published reports of numerous white deaths, and a Negro minister from Atlanta told a Northern audience that both white and black people had secretly buried some of their dead. When Monroe Trotter, the militant editor of the *Boston Guardian*, first got word of the conflict it was his understanding that Federal troops from Ft. McPherson had been used to salughter a large number of Negroes. Most of these rumors and reports had little foundation in reality, but Trotter's news did not depart from the truth so wildly as many supposed. The commanding officer at Ft. McPherson did offer troops and if Negroes had counter-attacked or sponsored much retaliatory violence the offer would undoubtedly have been accepted. In the Atlanta riot as before and after, state troops stood behind the police and behind them were U.S. soldiers—a situation which hardly encouraged retaliation or rebellion. Nor could anything be expected of President Roosevelt personally since he had on several occasions followed the precedent of McKinley by failing to intervene when mobs attacked black soldiers and Federal officials. Roosevelt would not even publically condemn the riot.

With no hope for effective help from city or nation peace-makers could seek relief only from the state, but so little was expected of the governor that no one thought to awaken him until eleven o'clock. Then he refused to declare martial law and delayed a few precious minutes before reluctantly calling out the militia. While a few soldiers reported as early as midnight, two o'clock arrived before several companies had been deployed and at five in the morning only five companies patroled the streets. The troops won the highest praise from civic leaders and did indeed represent an improvement over the police but they gave the Negro populace few reasons for gratitude. Aside from the fact that a few joined the clubbing and plundering, many refused to interfere seriously with the violence and the troops as a whole played no significant part in ending the riot during the first evening. As the *New York Times* reporter properly described the situation, Southern mobs paid little attention to soldiers because they felt strong bonds of common emotion and sympathy with the troops and did not expect forceful military action. Although the troops failed to cope with the riot, the ranks of the rioters were thinned after one o'clock by physical exhaustion, the lack of victims in the central city, and a partial satiation of the lust for blood. The first and bloodiest night of rioting was brought to an end when the rain began to fall mercifully at three o'clock clearing the streets of the last violent men and leaving the riot area deserted except for scattered bands of soldiers.

On Sunday September 23 white mobs killed two more black men and on Monday evening county employees and other armed civilians invaded the Negro colleges in the "Brownsville" area of South Atlanta. Nearly all the professors and students were on vacation but a clash between the resentful residents and the white invasion party quickly developed into a gun battle in which at least half a dozen blacks and whites fell to the street from gunshot wounds. The embattled whites fell back only to return a few hours later with hundreds of troops and police, and before the night ended at least four more black men had been added to the casualty lists. With characteristic partisanship the troops ignored the white aggressors and arrested nearly every young black man in Brownsville. On Tuesday and Wednesday sporadic fistfights and gunfire shattered the uneasy calm and on Thursday, September 27, a sullen peace returned to the city. As a result of the riot, one white person died and several dozen were hurt. Twenty-five black men perished, about one hundred and fifty suffered serious wounds, hundreds had less critical injuries, and more than a thousand black men, women and children fled the city. For several months to come white leaders busied themselves with public apologetics as black people concentrated on the restoration of "normal" patterns of work and life. The Atlanta race riot was not soon forgotten by black people who remembered with particular vividness the evening of September 22 as the terror-ridden night of the white assassins.

The Negro and the New Freedom

• *The recodification of racism in the Progressive Era South,
which came at height of scholarly and popular belief in the
myth of Anglo-Saxon superiority, inevitably influenced the
actions of the federal government. Since Negroes voted Republican, GOP's national ascendancy during the Gilded Age
preserved a few scattered pockets of political influence and
patronage for blacks. Then, in 1912, a southern-born Democrat, Woodrow Wilson, won the Presidency on a progressive
platform. Initially, Negroes thought that progressivism of
Wilson's New Freedom might have a place for them. The
new administration soon scotched that hope. For reasons
both of partisanship and Wilson's own racism, the few remaining black officeholders faced removal, and the Wilson-
ians appointed very few blacks in their place. In addition,
segregation in the civil service and in public buildings became
official government policy. Nancy Weiss describes the fruit-
less attempts of blacks and the interracial NAACP to reserve
this trend. With the pronounced southern presence in the
higher echelons of Wilson's administration and of Congress,
the course of events should have surprised no one. After four
decades of averting its eyes from the problems of black
America, the federal government turned its back completely
on the Negro.*

If broadened opportunities, political democracy, and social justice
describe Wilsonian Progressivism, the man on the furthest fringe of
that movement was surely the American Negro. Woodrow Wilson's
first administration inaugurated officially-sanctioned segregation in the
federal departments and witnessed ill-concealed moves to cut into already meager Negro patronage.

From Nancy J. Weiss, "The Negro and the New Freedom: Fighting Wilsonian Segregation," *Political Science Quarterly*, LXXXIV (March 1968), 61–79
(footnotes omitted). Reprinted by permission.

White liberals and Negroes alike worried over the same question: how could Progressivism find room for race discrimination? Or, how could one explain the introduction of official shackles on the black man at a time when America was legislating the liberation and protection of the individual? The President, liberal publicist Oswald Garrison Villard declared, "fails utterly to see that to discriminate in his democracy against anyone, is to bring his whole carefully reared edifice crashing to the ground."

Yet, federal segregation was less a new departure than the logical culmination of a decisive Southern—and national—trend. Moreover, despite the anomaly of a New Freedom bringing a new bondage, Progressivism and racism were in many respects interdependent. The early years of the Progressive era coincided with widespread Negro disfranchisement and the birth of full-scale, state-level Jim Crow legislative discrimination. Accustomed by imperial design and judicial decision to thoughts of racial superiority, white America linked Progressive democracy and equality to greater separation from Negroes.

By the election of 1912 most Southern states had succeeded in purging their political systems of Negro voters and office-holders. Those Negroes retaining the franchise generally aligned themselves as a bloc with the party of emancipation. But 1912 marked a turning point in national Negro political participation. Angry at Theodore Roosevelt's "lily white" Progressivism and alienated by incumbent William Howard Taft's concessions to racism, Negroes were fair game for Democratic efforts to split the solidarity of the bloc vote.

Democratic candidate Woodrow Wilson was a Southerner who concurrrd in this wife's outspoken belief in social separation of the races, a college president who barred Negroes from Princeton (and who later told darky stories in Cabinet meetings). Prominent Negroes faced the issue squarely: "We do not believe that Woodrow Wilson admires Negroes," W.E.B. Du Bois wrote with considerable understatement. And yet, he told readers of the NAACP's magazine *Crisis*, Negroes might well expect such a "cultivated scholar" to treat them with "farsighted fairness." Leaders of the race secured a much-publicized campaign pledge "to see justice done them in every matter, and not mere grudging justice, but justice executed with liberality and cordial good feeling." "Should I become President of the United States," Wilson promised in 1912, "[Negroes] may count upon me for absolute fair dealing and for everything by which I could assist

in advancing the interests of their race in the United States." Even
Villard proclaimed himself "quite delighted" with the candidate's
position.

Thus, the election of 1912 saw the curious spectacle of the champions of the Negro lining up, albeit hesitantly, behind a symbol of
Southern Democracy. "We sincerely believe," the *Crisis* intoned,

> that even in the face of promises disconcertingly vague, and in the
> face of the solid caste-ridden South, it is better to elect Woodrow
> Wilson President of the United States and prove once and for
> all if the Democratic party dares to be Democratic when it comes
> to black men.

Although there is no way of measuring the Negro vote, observers
speculated that roughly half a million black men would exercise
the franchise in 1912. Du Bois has written that Wilson won the votes
of nearly 100,000 Negroes in the North alone. While many Negroes
voted for Roosevelt, Professor Arthur Link states that Wilson got
"more [Negro votes], probably, than any other Democratic presidential candidate had ever received." In any event, it appears that influential Negro leaders and a significant part of the rank and file did
break away from their traditional Republican affiliations.

After Wilson took office Negroes quickly discovered that their support packed little bargaining power. By the summer of 1913 segregated toilets, lunchroom facilities, and working areas had been ordered
in the Departments of the Treasury and the Post Office, among
others. Job segregation was especially evident in cases where Negro
men had previously supervised white women. Some construed the
new policies as a backhanded way of phasing out all Negro civil service
employes, and pointed to cases where Negroes were shifted into
separate departmental divisions later slated for dissolution. For the
first time photographs were required on all civil service applications.
The impact was so great that Booker T. Washington could write
of an August visit to the nation's capital: "I have never seen the
colored people so discouraged and bitter as they are at the present
time."

Secretary of the Navy Josephus Daniels relates that the question of
federal segregation was first introduced in high administration circles at a Cabinet meeting in April 1913, when Postmaster General
A. G. Burleson brought up complaints over integration in the railway
mail service. Burleson, a Southerner like Daniels, "was anxious to
segregate white and negro employees in all Departments of the Gov-

ernment. . . . he believed segregation was best for the negro and best for the Service." Secretary of the Treasury William Gibbs Mc-Adoo (another Southerner) especially seemed to agree with him. Then, Daniels recalls, the Cabinet discussed the general question of Negro appointments. "The President said he made no promises in particular to Negroes, except to do them justice, and he did not wish to see them have less positions than they now have; but he wished the matter adjusted in a way to make the least friction." Although no action was taken, the Cabinet certainly made no effort to halt the beginnings of deliberate segregation.

Departmental segregation was a conspicuous reversal of a fifty year tradition of integrated civil service. With racism having infiltrated state and local systems, easily-delineated pressures pushed the Wilson administration toward federal discrimination. The administration, itself obviously Southern, paid considerable attention to senatorial influence from the James K. Vardamans, Benjamin R. Tillmans and Hoke Smiths. Moreover, organizations like the National Democratic Fair Play Association worked as powerful lobbies for a racist outlook on the civil service. And the capital itself, as the New York *Evening Post's* Washington correspondent wrote, was "essentially a Southern city," where "the great majority of the white people . . . hold the Southern view of the negro. . . ." "The white men and women in the Government service," he continued, "have resented being compelled to associate with the negroes. *Never before has there been an Administration that dared to cater to this feeling, except in surreptitious ways. . . .* There has always been . . . a *wish* to do it, but not the *courage.*" Forces defending racial equality finally gave way to long-latent desires for discrimination.

While segregation orders were conceived and issued by subordinates, it is clear that Wilson made little or no effort to stop them. He summed up his own attitude in a letter to the editor of the *Congregationalist.*

> . . . I would say that I do approve of the segregation that is being attempted in several of the departments. . . . I certainly would not . . . have . . . if I had not thought it to their [Negroes'] advantage and likely to remove many of the difficulties which have surrounded the appointment and advancement of colored men and women.

Federal appointment policy, on the other hand, initiated directly from the White House. Certain federal positions—like Register of the

Treasury, Recorder of Deeds and Customs Collector for the District of Columbia, and Auditor of the Navy Department—as well as diplomatic assignments to black nations, were traditionally held by Negroes. Given their support for the Democrats in 1912, Negro leaders expected increased patronage. When Wilson took office the *Negro Year Book* reported that Negroes held thirteen significant federal offices and filled eleven posts in the diplomatic and consular service. By the end of 1915 nine of the former (plus four officials not listed in the original account) and three of the latter had "retired from office and white men . . . [had] been appointed to fill their places." Three years later just six diplomatic representatives and one judge were left. Wilson made only two key Negro appointments: Minister to Liberia and Municipal Court Judge of the District of Columbia. Negroes were especially incensed when the black Register of the Treasury was replaced by an Indian. Wilson lamely noted the difficulty of pushing Negro nominations past a Vardaman-Tillman-Smith Senate, but failed to explain his predecessors' perseverance in pursuing the same end. Negro leaders underlined the irony of an administration preaching social separation of the races, but sending a white envoy to a black nation.

Executive discrimination found considerable sympathy on Capitol Hill. During the first Wilson administration nearly two dozen anti-Negro measures were introduced in the House and Senate, "the greatest flood of bills proposing discriminatory legislation against Negroes" ever to come before the Congress. They ran the gamut from Jim Crow transportation regulations and armed forces enlistment to prohibition of miscegenation, civil service segregation, and repeal of the Fifteenth Amendment. Their sponsors were Southerners, and they made little or no progress, with only the miscegenation bill being reported by a committee.

Incorporating a remarkable ethnic, social, and occupational diversity, the youthful National Association for the Advancement of Colored People seemed the logical forum for liberals of every cast who challenged the thinking of those supporting segregation. As chairman of its executive committee, Oswald Garrison Villard, grandson of famed Abolitionist William Lloyd Garrison, led off with a steady letter-writing campaign designed to clarify the administration's stand on the race issue. He urged the President to repudiate a disastrous policy, due, he hoped, "to the individual initiative of department heads without your knowledge and consent." But Wilson insisted that departmental segregation was "in the interest of the negroes. . . . " "My own feeling," he wrote, "is, by putting certain bureaus and sections of the service in the charge of negroes we are rendering them more safe in their possession of office and less likely to be discriminated against." This gave spokesmen for the Negro grounds for open attack. On August 15, 1913, the NAACP filed an official protest at the White House against the "drawing of caste lines." Negroes "desire a 'New Freedom,' too, Mr. President," they asserted. The organization called for public response to their appeal for social justice.

Villard mobilized his liberal *Nation* and New York *Evening Post;* Boston *Guardian* editor William Monroe Trotter led off the Negro press reaction; and the NAACP's branches organized nationwide protest meetings. The press, both Northern and Southern, white and Negro, answered the call. Responding to suggestions for a letter-writing marathon, countless citizens flooded the White House mail-bags. Hundreds of letters bore the signatures of Negroes of every station. More notably, however, the NAACP's appeal brought forth vocal support from white clergymen, professors, social workers, philanthropists, Progressive politicians, and leaders of other minority groups like Jews and women. The "harsh and humiliating discrimination," they wrote, was "an insult and an outrage upon American citizenship," "violating the spirit of the Constitution and opposed to the teachings of Jesus Christ." From all corners there arose cries of dismay over the "unjust and disheartening" measures instituted "in plain derogation of the policy favored by our fundamental law."

Beyond letters and editorials, white liberals exerted little, if any, more active pressure. Some appealed to their spokesmen in Congress to influence the President, and touched off critical communications from Capitol Hill to the White House. Congressman John J. Rogers of Massachusetts introduced resolutions urging investigation of treatment of Negro employes in the Treasury and Post Office Departments, but both measures died on committee calendars without gaining so much as a hearing. Some whites debated arranging a peaceful protest at the White House by representatives of the segregated employes, but nothing ever materialized. In short, white liberals spoke up vociferously for the Negro cause, but the issue never packed enough political leverage to evoke more effective tactics.

Negroes appealed to Wilson not only on grounds of humanitarianism, campaign pledges, constitutionalism, and plain American decency, but also on the basis of political expediency. The precarious

Democratic strength established among members of their race in 1912 crumbled rapidly in the face of the President's policies, so that Negro Democratic politicians found themselves "in a political wilderness of dispair [sic]." The men who decried segregation were fighting for their very political lives. "We are constantly being called traiters [sic] and being threatened with bodily harm," the secretary of the National Colored Democratic League wrote to presidential secretary Joseph P. Tumulty. "We are publically [sic] and frequently charged with having sold the Race into slavery. . . ."

But these men were talking about more than their own careers. What they saw was a fast-disappearing opportunity to capitalize on Negro disaffection from the Republican fold. They continually emphasized that Wilsonian discrimination would mean political suicide for any vestiges of Negro Democracy in 1916. And Wilson countered just as consistently by insisting that segregation was not a matter of politics, but of humanitarianism. Certainly the size of the Negro vote, and the political leverage it wielded, were small, so that the immediate political benefits of courting Negroes were limited. But the chances for constructive reconciliation and for a useful precedent were not insignificant.

The future, and not only the political future, was very much on the minds of those who cried for a change in policy. What were the implications of the new caste system for future generations? There was no telling, protesters noted, what measures others might justify on the basis of the Wilsonian precedent. "Should the National Government adopt this seemingly simple provision," a prominent Negro professor wrote, "it would thereby sanction all of the discriminatory legislation on the statute books of the several states and would suggest and justify all such enactment in the future." Hand in hand with this caution went a curiously ambivalent attitude toward the President himself. Carefully noting Wilson's sincerity and highmindedness, many tried to rationalize his program as the work of underlings unbeknownst to him. What they feared more than anything, however, was the future election of a less scrupulous, less principled chief executive who would tailor Wilsonian segregation policies to more disastrous, far-reaching ends, affecting not only Negroes but possibly other minority groups like Jews.

With the public "campaign of making the White House just as uncomfortable as possible" gaining in momentum, Villard continued his own efforts at private persuasion. Finding Tumulty sympathetic to his arguments, he nevertheless had great difficulty in establishing any

real understanding with the President on the race issue. While justifying departmental segregation, Wilson admitted that "in several instances the thing has been managed in a way which was not sufficiently
thoughtful of their feelings . . . ," which provoked Villard to retort:
"Believe me, it is not a question of handling segregation awkwardly or
tactfully, or otherwise, it is a question of right and wrong." The interchange ended temporarily with the President pleading for time and
tolerance:

> I hope . . . that by the slow pressure of argument and persuasion
> the situation may be changed and a great many things done
> eventually which now seem impossible. . . . I appeal to you
> most earnestly to aid at holding things at a just and cool equi-
> pose until I can discover whether it is possible to work out any-
> thing or not.

Shifting focus from the White House to the departments proved no
more rewarding. Villard informed Treasury Secretary McAdoo of a
speech he intended to give concerning segregation instituted under
McAdoo's jurisdiction. The ambivalence of the Secretary's reply
summed up the sheer frustration encountered by those who tried to
reverse the discriminatory policies. "There is no 'segregation issue' in
the Treasury Department," McAdoo insisted. "It has always been a
mischievous exaggeration." And yet, in the same letter he confessed,

> . . . I shall not be a party to the enforced and unwelcome juxta-
> position of white and negro employees when it is unnecessary
> and avoidable without injustice to anybody, and when such en-
> forcement would serve only to engender race animosities detri-
> mental to the welfare of both races and injurious to the public
> service.

From the Negro's point of view, departmental segregation was anything but a "mischievous exaggeration." In November 1913 a group
of prominent Negroes representing the National Independent Political
League and sponsored by Massachusetts congressmen went to the
White House to deliver a petition of protest against discrimination in
the government service. Wilson seemed impressed by the protest and
surprised at the conditions they mentioned. He assured the delegation
that "segregation had not been decided upon as an administration
policy," and promised further investigation. The protests reputedly
made some impact, so that in December the New York *Evening Post*
could write, "it seems plain that the word has gone forth that the

segregationists must take the back track. . . . it appears that a return to former conditions is underway all along the line."

Despite token efforts, like removal of some signs on toilets, there seems to have been little concrete evidence of actual reversal of policies. In November 1914 the delegation of Negro leaders called again at the White House to discuss the situation. Headed by Boston *Guardian* editor Trotter, the group detailed instances of continued segregation, charged certain officials with race prejudice, asked for investigation and redress by executive order, and predicted Negro opposition to the Democrats in 1916. Wilson, dismissing any political considerations, "said that the policy of segregation had been enforced for the comfort and best interests of both races in order to overcome friction." The President ended the interview abruptly, announcing that he was insulted by Trotter's approach, and warning that any future meetings would have to be conducted by another Negro spokesman. The so-called Trotter incident provoked a new flurry of editorials and correspondence; even those who found Trotter's conduct objectionable agreed on the positive results of reintroducing the segregation issue into public discussion. Whether Trotter actually did anything out of order is open to doubt; Tumulty told Villard that the Negro's speech was "one of the most eloquent he had ever heard," and the President later admitted privately to Tumulty that "he was very sorry he had lost his temper as he had made a great mistake."

As the controversy over the Trotter interview died down another issue arose to take its place on Negro and white liberal editorial pages. President Wilson and his Cabinet had attended a private White House showing of "The Birth of a Nation," the controversial D. W. Griffith film based on Thomas Dixon's *The Clansman*. Featuring vicious distortions of Negro activities during the Reconstruction era, the movie was a potent weapon for inflaming white hatred of blacks. Indignant at this so-called "work of art," Negroes organized nationwide protests calling either for censorship of particularly offensive scenes or for total banning of the film. In only a smattering of communities were they at all successful. The movie's producers delighted in justifying its value by noting that it had been screened without objection before the President and his Cabinet. Wilson, driven into a corner by persistent inquiries, lamely directed Tumulty to explain that "the President was entirely unaware of the character of the play before it was presented, and has at no time expressed his approbation of it. Its exhibition at the White House was a courtesy extended to an old acquaintance."

While "The Birth of a Nation" and federal segregation bred loud public protest, a private effort in behalf of the Negro was also taking shape. Largely unsuccessful at curbing Wilson's negative policies, white liberals and Negro leaders put forth a constructive suggestion of their own to grapple with the Negro's place in an expanding American democracy. The idea of a National Race Commission was first developed by R. H. Leavell, professor of economics at Texas A & M, and later taken up by Villard and the NAACP. The plan called for a presidentially-appointed, privately financed, biracial, multi-sectional commission to investigate every phase of Negro life in the country, "with particular reference to his economic situation." Hopefully, the inquiry might ease racial tensions and provoke legislative recommendations from the White House. Moreover, the investigation would be in the best tradition of Progressive concern for social justice; it "would be of great service to the white South as well as to Negroes," for "a situation in which millions of people were living on the border line of destitution in the slums . . . ought to be intolerable in civilized communities. . . ."

The Race Commission plan spoke the purest language of Progressivism. Its primary objective—"to promote realization of democracy in America"—could be attained "by providing adequate opportunity for self-realization by all individuals of all classes or all races in ways beneficial both to the individual and to society." Those who drafted the proposal fully understood the American reform tradition of widening avenues of opportunity for the disadvantaged.

Villard took the plan to the White House in May 1913. He left the interview enthusiastic over Wilson's reaction; the President, he wrote to Professor Leavell, was "wholly sympathetic," promising to consider the proposal in the light of "his relations with the Senate and Congress, and what it will mean to him to antagonize the reactionary Southern politicians. As to the necessity of some such inquiry he was quite clear. . . ." Wilson postponed subsequent interviews throughout the summer, insisting that the Mexican crisis kept him too preoccupied for other considerations. Villard repeatedly sought authorization to proceed with the fund-raising; "I am particularly urging this upon you now," he wrote in August, "because of the intense dissatisfaction of the colored people at the treatment by your Administration thus far."

A few days later Wilson rejected the suggestion. With the balance of his legislative program still awaiting congressional action, he shrank from alienating powerful Southern congressional leaders. An investigation, he maintained, inevitably implied an indictment. Recalling his earlier receptivity, he admitted, "I never realized before the complexity and difficulty of this matter in respect of every step taken here."

Strikingly, the President's stand on the Race Commission sparked absolutely no public protest. Villard had purposely avoided any publicity of the negotiations, fearing that outside pressure might force Wilson's hand. At the same time, departmental segregation and appointments more than occupied the efforts of those championing the Negro cause. Indeed, the Race Commission "lobby" consisted of only one man—Villard himself. Various professionals and NAACP leaders made comments on the original draft, but the organization itself remained officially silent. The only recriminations after Wilson's refusal came in bitter letters from Villard. "Frankly, I feel very sorry that you find yourself 'absolutely blocked by the sentiment of senators,'" he wrote. "I believe that like your most immediate predecessors, the time will come when you will find it necessary to go ahead and do what is right without considering their feelings. . . ." But "[bowing] down to the god Expediency," Villard warned, ought not to demand continued segregation and non-appointment of Negroes. Unless Wilson faced squarely the place of the Negro in his New Freedom, the liberal editor predicted, "the feeling of bitterness among the colored people towards your Administration and the Democratic party shall steadily increase."

Villard was right. The election of 1916 justified warnings that segregation policies spelled the end of an unusual opportunity to convert Negroes to the Democratic party. Unfortunately, there are no satisfactory statistics to indicate just how many Negroes broke away to vote for Wilson in 1912, or how many deserted the Democrats in 1916. Beyond just holding their own, the Democrats seemed unable to absorb any significant portion of the Negro voters who had defected from Republicanism to support the Progressive ticket in 1912. General contemporary comment indicates that Negroes "returned en masse to the party of liberation." In Negro Harlem, for instance, the Democratic vote slipped from 23.29 to 20.23 per cent, while the Republican share jumped from 17.67 to 77.99 per cent, undoubtedly including the 56.63 per cent who had voted for Roosevelt in 1912. More important than the overall tallies, leaders of the race who stumped for the Democrats in 1912 faced the 1916 election with nothing but distaste for Wilson. Their continued allegiance, promising future Democratic dividends of large-scale Negro support, would have been especially valuable.

Surely, Negroes in general found in their press little reason to stick with the Democrats. The New York *Age*, expressing the philosophy of Booker T. Washington and a supporter of Taft in 1912, declared for Charles Evans Hughes, as did the Washington *Bee*. The NAACP solicited explicit statements on the race question from both candidates. Tumulty responded for Wilson with a noncommittal "he stands by his original assurances. He can say with a clear conscience that he has tried to live up to them, though in some cases his endeavors have been defeated." Hughes never answered the NAACP's letter, and left himself to be judged on the basis of a Nashville campaign pledge of "equal and exact justice to all. I stand for the maintenance of the rights of all American citizens, regardless of race or color." At first Association leaders reluctantly found Hughes "practically the only candidate for whom Negroes can vote." The *Crisis* eventually urged Negroes to disown both major party candidates, suggesting formation of an all-Negro party and ultimately advising abstention or a vote for the Socialist candidate.

In sum, in 1916 Negro leaders found their race courted by neither party. Despite years of agonizing controversy over their place in Progressivism, the political establishment was again trying its best to ignore the Negro question. Looking back on the election the *Crisis* summed up best of all the frustrating lack of progress toward enlisting those in power in the cause of a democracy not limited by the color line. By the peak of the Progressive era the President had proven "satisfactory as a reducer of the tariff, a promoter of currency reform, and as a man of Peace." "But," the editors wrote, "he was still the representative of the southern Negro-hating oligarchy, and acknowledged its leadership." By the same token, "Mr. Hughes was the author of several of the best decisions in favor of the Negro that the reluctant Supreme Court has ever handed down. At the same time, on specific Negro problems he was curiously dumb."

Why were Negroes and white liberals unsuccessful in extending the boundaries of a Progressivism limited "to whites only"? Wilson argued that his sentiments were on the side of the protesters, but that courting Southern senatorial support for his Progressive legislative package made it impossible for him to act in their behalf. Yet he straightforwardly advocated "separate but equal" as mutually beneficial to both races.

It is too easy, however, to attribute the stalemate to executive inhibitions alone. The key still seems to lie in the nature of the protest. Negro groups lacked a cohesive, tightly organized program. Gaining the right to vote, and fighting lynching, preoccupied much of their effort. This was the decade of landmark Supreme Court decisions striking down the Grandfather Clauses in state voting requirements and levelling an initial blow at residential segregation. For many, these struggles were much more important than gaining political positions. But Negroes disagreed over more than just priorities affecting their race alone. Looking at the national scene, many played down their grievances; "we believe," a North Carolina cleric told Wilson after Trotter's White House demands, "that he should not have approached you with a minor domestic protest when you are filled with graver responsibilities. . . ."

These disavowals were well calculated to cripple the effectiveness of any organized protest. The Negroes who wrote to the President claiming that "Mr. Trotter does not represent the Negroes of the United States," or that "the more thoughtful" members of the race "don't approve of Mr. Trotter's insult to you," may honestly have been ashamed of his reported disrespect. But they also testified to the exceptional fragmentation of Negro leadership. Theirs was largely the fading gasp of a Washingtonian theory of Negro conduct, reflecting the growing split in Negro philosophies of self-advancement.

In previous Republican administrations Booker T. Washington had been recognized as "the office broker for the race," or chief consultant on Negro patronage and policies. Publicly conciliatory toward the white South, the Tuskegee educator subordinated eventual attainment of political and civil rights to the more immediate goals of moral and economic progress through self-help and vocational training. The Wilson administration found Washington newly out of favor not only in official circles, but also among the ranks of leading Negroes. New expectations and new spokesmen came to prominence with the Democrats. Seriously challenging the old, more accommodating outlook, fathers of the Niagara Movement, like Du Bois and Trotter, stressed immediate equality—social, economic, *and* political—and urged agitation to reach these goals. The inability of these men to agree among themselves contributed to a proliferation of loose factions and formal groups all in the same fight without meaningful coordination of efforts.

The protest movements petered out, too, because they eventually lost even their divided leadership. Villard, certainly their most influential white spokesman, became preoccupied with keeping the United States out of World War I. Washington died early in 1915, and Bishop Alexander Walters ("the new political leader of his race for the incoming Democratic administration at Washington") was dead before Wilson's second inaugural. Discredited (however unfairly) among Negroes and whites alike after the White House incident, Trotter quickly began to "slip . . . out of the main current of the protest movement." A foe of accommodation, he nonetheless divorced himself from the activist Du Boisian camp, and never took full advantage of cooperation with white liberals. Du Bois, too, had already generated considerable friction with white NAACP leaders. In 1916 he decisively curbed his effectiveness when he told Negroes, in effect, to throw away their votes and abandon the regular political process, surely their best hope for any kind of influence on the status of the race in Wilsonian Progressivism.

Even if we accept this analysis of deficiencies in the protest movement, it is still important to ask whether we may not be overstating the case. In short, could Negroes have been expected to make much of a dent in Wilsonian segregation policies? The national apotheosis of Jim Crow militated strongly against any possible hope of success for the champions of the Negro cause. But the generation of the current Negro revolution may still wonder over the striking lack of militancy in the protests of the Progressive era. The afflicted exercised unusual restraint and self-discipline, engaging in thoroughly polite, deferential opposition. In the second decade of this century, hardly more than a generation removed from the demise of Reconstruction, Negroes were in considerable part an ex-slave population. Their educational level and political consciousness were still barely above a minimum. It is a commonly accepted principle of social science that a submerged group must reach a certain plateau before it can even begin to rebel, and most Negroes of the Wilson era were still struggling toward that level. The birth of the NAACP, fusing white liberal strength into the Niagara Movement, was barely three years past when Wilson took office. The transition in Negro thinking from a Washingtonian to a Du Boisian approach was an important one, and one whose earliest stages coincided with the birth of the New Freedom. Negro protest, symbolized and centralized chiefly in the NAACP, was a very new, highly improvised instrument in the Wilson era—an instrument which took nearly forty years to impress upon the nation the gravity and sincerity of its purpose.

V: THE NEED FOR IDENTITY,

1919–1929

Marcus Garvey: Black Is Beautiful

• Repeated disappointments suffered by American blacks during the first two decades of this century inevitably provoked strong protest. On the one hand the Negro's increasing urbanization, with the accelerated movement from southern countryside to northern ghetto, produced black urban leaders attuned to the powerful but latent collective consciousness of the growing black communities. On the other, the basic irrelevance of white Progressivism to the Negro created an opportunity for the rise of militant separatist spokesmen. During the 1920's the man who capitalized most effectively on Negro frustrations, stepping into a vacuum left by the failure of traditional Negro leadership to reach the black masses, was Marcus Garvey. This flambouyant Jamaican created a black organization, the Universal Negro Improvement Association, which served a vital function in fusing the themes of racial pride and social protest for the average Negro of his era. His skillful use of press-agentry and passionate oratory made Garvey a leader among those blacks (including the father of Malcolm X.)who remained unmoved by the more restrained and legalistic appeals of groups like the NAACP. If Garvey's economic enterprises, particularly the ill-starred Black Star Steamship Line, fell far short of their original goals, he nevertheless preached a notable doctrine of racial pride—not racial hate—at a time when such sermonizing was in short supply among beleaguered American blacks. Considering the indifference to Negro ambitions during the early decades of this century, the emergence of Garveyism as a desperate secular faith for millions of blacks was both plausible and useful. But Garvey's effective career ended suddenly. He served two years in federal prison for mail fraud and was then deported in 1927. His final years in London could not recapture the spirit or support of his Harlem days.

Abridged from E. David Cronon, *Black Moses: The Story of Marcus Garvey* (Madison: The University of Wisconsin Press, 1955), pp. 39–72 (footnotes omitted). © 1955 by the Regents of the University of Wisconsin. Reprinted by permission.

Harlem in 1916 was the logical place to begin any organization of American Negroes. Within the crowded confines of the Negro section of New York City a would-be leader could find support for almost any type of movement. A compact black ghetto, Harlem boasted more publications than any other Negro community and could rightfully claim to be the seat of Negro urban society. Here were to be found representatives of all elements in the colored world, a sable mélange of sensitive artists, successful businessmen, self-anointed preachers, poorly paid day laborers, and ignorant sidewalk loafers. Although its teeming tenements were already jammed to groaning capacity, the next few years would see the arrival of many thousands more immigrants from the West Indies and the American South as northern industry expanded to meet the demands of World War I. These new arrivals would be for the most part poorly educated agricultural workers, Negro peasants who would find urban life new and strange and who could therefore be reached by an emotional appeal that might be ignored by more sophisticated Harlemites. A movement that offered gaudy uniforms, colorful parades, high-sounding titles, and grandiose dreams would make a strong appeal to this lower strata of Harlem society.

At first skeptical Harlemites paid but scant attention to the stocky black Jamaican whose big ideas on race redemption had sounded so impressive in Kingston. The sidewalk crowds loitering on Lenox Avenue ignored his harangues and dismissed him as just another West Indian carpetbagger. Even the brief but favorable notice of Garvey's visit printed in the *Crisis* failed to arouse more than a casual interest in the Jamaican stranger. Not daunted by this seeming indifference on the part of his future legions, Garvey made a tour of the country, visiting some thirty-eight states in order to study Negro conditions in America. He went to see some of what he scornfully termed the "so-called Negro leaders" and was shocked to discover "that they had no program, but were mere opportunists who were living off their so-called leadership while the poor people were groping in the dark." The fact that some of these leaders were light-skinned mulattoes may well have been one of the reasons for Garvey's distrust. Another reason was the reliance of many Negro leaders upon the support of white philanthropists. Garvey feared such dependence upon white charity and contemptuously termed this type of Negro leader "the most dangerous member of our society" because of his willingness "to turn back the clock of progress when his benefactors ask him to do so.". . .

In Harlem Garvey found not only a mass of Negroes overshadowed by the larger white world but also a large number of West Indians isolated from the native American Negro population. As a West Indian himself, Garvey quite naturally turned to this group as a focal point for the establishment of his organization. Garvey had been brought up in the Roman Catholic faith and carried letters of introduction from officials of the Jamaican church. Seeking support in this direction, he arranged to hold his first American meeting in the annex of St. Mark's Roman Catholic Church in Harlem. Apparently the gathering was rather poorly attended. . . .

Garvey made a new start and in two months claimed to have built up a new organization of about 1,500 members. Once again the politicians attempted to acquire control of the association and managed to split the group into two factions. At this juncture, thirteen of the loyal members, most of them Jamaicans, came to Garvey with the request that he take over the active leadership of the Harlem organization until it could be consolidated. . . .

During 1919 and 1920 the Universal Negro Improvement Association enjoyed a remarkable growth. Garvey traveled extensively throughout the United States and established branches of the association in most urban centers of Negro population. The spread of the movement was not confined to the United States, moreover, as Garvey made every effort to interest Negroes in the West Indies and Central America in his ideas. He now dropped the fiction that the headquarters of the U.N.I.A. was in Jamaica and it was obvious that the headquarters of the movement was wherever its founder happened to be, that in fact Marcus Garvey was the U.N.I.A. By the middle of 1919, Garvey was making the dubious claim of more than two million members and thirty branches. . . .

The movement received unexpected publicity when in October, 1919, Garvey was attacked by an insane former employee. . . . Two of his shots found their mark, one grazing Garvey's forehead and narrowly missing his right eye, and the other imbedding itself in Garvey's right leg. . . . Garvey's attractive secretary and future wife, Amy Ashwood, had wrestled with the intruder and had courageously placed herself between her employer and the gunman. Garvey himself had rushed after the assassin with blood streaming down his face. The assault assumed heroic proportions in the Negro press and Garvey became overnight a persecuted martyr working for the salvation of his people. Harlem began to take a deeper interest in Marcus Garvey and his newly reorganized branch of the Universal Negro Improvement Association.

One of the important reasons for Garvey's amazing success in the rapid organization of the Negro masses was his establishment in January, 1918, of the *Negro World*, the U.N.I.A.'s New York newspaper. This was one of the most remarkable journalistic ventures ever attempted by a Negro in the United States, and it drew from Claude McKay, a sometime Garvey critic, the grudging praise of being "the best edited colored weekly in New York." . . .

The character of this newspaper merits some consideration. Separating the two words *Negro* and *World* was a sphinxlike seal bearing the motto of the organization, "One Aim, One God, One Destiny." Under this was the phrase, "A Newspaper Devoted Solely to the Interests of the Negro Race." The paper was priced within the low-income range of Garvey's followers and generally sold for five cents in New York, seven cents elsewhere in the United States, and ten cents in foreign countries. Certain sections of the *Negro World* were printed in French and Spanish for the benefit of those West Indian and Central American Negroes who could not read English. The front page of the paper always carried a lengthy editorial proudly addressed to the "Fellowmen of the Negro Race" and signed, "Your obedient servant, Marcus Garvey, President General." These editorials covered a wide variety of subjects, ranging from grand visions of the past glories of Negro history to undisguised promotional appeals on behalf of the association. "Africa must be redeemed," Garvey asserted in an early editorial, "and all of us pledge our manhood, our wealth and our blood to this sacred cause. Yes, the Negroes of the world have found a George Washington, yea more; they have found a Toussant L'Overture [*sic*], and he will be announced to the world when the time comes." . . .

. . . The paper made a great effort to remind its readers of their glorious history, with particular emphasis on the regal splendors of ancient Africa. Garvey proudly recalled for his followers, though not always with complete accuracy, the stirring heroism of such leaders of American slave rebellions as Denmark Vesey, Gabriel Prosser, and Nat Turner. The struggles of Zulu and Hottentot warriors against European rule, the histories of Moorish and Ethiopian empires, and the intrepid exploits of Toussaint L'Ouverture against the French in Haiti were not neglected in the effort to make Negroes conscious and proud of their racial heritage. Garvey delighted in references to the greatness of colored civilizations at a time when white men were only barbarians and savages. This emphasis on racism was one of the reasons that the *Negro World* was cited by the Department of Justice and the Lusk Committee of New York in two separate reports on Negro radicalism in 1919 and 1920.

The newspaper also carried news of the activities of the various divisions and branches of the Universal Negro Improvement Association, and the *Negro World's* wide circulation helped to direct and unify the efforts of the component parts of the organization. Readers were urged to write and speak on behalf of race equality and unity. . . .

The *Negro World* prided itself on its refusal to accept advertising for such race-degrading items as skin-whitening and hair-straightening compounds, lucrative sources of advertising revenue for most Negro papers. These chemical beauty aids had long provided a sizable share of the advertising income of the Negro press. As far back as 1885 the *Nation* had jocularly noted this "solution" of the race problem, as advertised in a New York Negro newspaper. While Garvey refused to accept any advertisements that tended to degrade the Negro race, the *Negro World* did occasionally carry commercial plugs for hair-growing compounds similar to products that claimed ability to straighten hair. The emphasis was, however, always on growing "a wonderful head of hair." The policy probably tended to relax as the need for money, from any source, became ever more pressing. Scoffers referred to the *Negro World* as the "bulletin of the Imperial Blizzard" or "the *weakly* organ of Admiral Garvey's African Navy," but the paper was a potent force among Negroes in America and its influence extended far beyond American shores. . . .

In 1919 Garvey's organizational activities had progressed far enough for him to purchase a large auditorium located at 114 West 138 Street in Harlem. Originally the foundation of the uncompleted Metropolitan Baptist Church, the structure had been roofed over and enlarged to provide seating space for as many as 6,000 people. Rechristened Liberty Hall, this building became the American headquarters of the Universal Negro Improvement Association. At the dedication services on July 27, 1919, the U.N.I.A. membership was reminded that the name Liberty Hall was particularly appropriate, the more so in light of the recent bloody race riots in Washington, D.C. . . .

The work of the Universal Negro Improvement Association was more than speeches and meetings, however. Sometime early in 1919 Garvey projected the idea of an all-Negro steamship company that

would link the colored peoples of the world in commercial and industrial intercourse. The bold bid to enter the white-dominated maritime
industry quickly caught hold of the popular imagination and for several months money was collected at U.N.I.A. meetings to purchase
ships for this promised Black Star Line. News of this activity soon
reached the ears of Edwin P. Kilroe, assistant district attorney of New
York, and on June 16, 1919, he called Garvey in and warned him not
to attempt to sell stock unless the Black Star Line was organized as a
legitimate business enterprise. In compliance, ten days later Garvey
formally launched the Black Star Line by securing a broad charter of
incorporation from the State of Delaware, whose friendly laws had
long attracted businessmen and industrial entrepreneurs. Under its
charter the Black Star Line was explicitly authorized to own, charter,
operate, and navigate ships of various types in any part of the world
and to carry passengers, freight, and mails. . . . The B.S.L. was
capitalized at $500,000, composed of 100,000 shares of stock with a
par value of five dollars each. Garvey and four of his associates were
each listed as holding forty shares of capital stock, so that the company
commenced business with a stated capital of one thousand dollars. . . .

Sale of Black Star stock was limited to members of the Negro race,
and no individual could purchase more than two hundred shares.
Garvey's *Negro World* carried full-page advertisements exhorting its
readers to take a hand in guiding their destiny through "a direct line
of steamships, owned, controlled, and manned by Negroes to reach
the Negro peoples of the world." Ostensibly the Black Star Line was
established as a strictly commercial venture, and Garvey did not intend, as his critics sometimes claimed, that the line would merely be
the vehicle for the transportation of all Negroes back to their African
homeland. The publicity value of the venture, however, far exceeded
anything that it was likely to accomplish commercially; and Garvey,
always the master propagandist, skillfully exploited this aspect of the
undertaking to the fullest extent.

At first the scheme was laughed off by many Negroes as just another
attempt to extort money from the ignorant black masses. Garvey's vision of a fleet of ships manned by Negro crews and flying the Black
Star Line flag made little impression on Harlem business circles.
Skeptics pointed out the great difficulty of raising sufficient capital to
float one ship, let alone a whole fleet of merchant vessels plying the
African trade routes in competition with established white firms. Garvey was advised not to attempt the impossible. The critics were
struck into amazed silence, therefore, when in mid-September a B.S.L.

circular proudly announced that the first ship of the new line could be viewed at her berth at West 135 Street and the North River. "The Ship will fly the Black Star Line Flag," Garvey promised.

Two days after this announcement, Garvey was once again called to the office of Assistant District Attorney Kilroe, who had discovered that the Black Star Line was as yet only negotiating for the ship Garvey had indicated could be seen flying the company's flag. Kilroe warned Garvey that if any B.S.L. stock had been sold as a direct result of this misleading circular he and the corporation could be prosecuted for commercial fraud. As before, Kilroe's admonition brought swift results. The next day, on September 17, 1919, Garvey and the other directors of the Black Star Line closed the deal on the purchase of the company's first ship, a small freighter named the *S.S. Yarmouth*. The purchase price was a stiff $165,000, of which the company paid $16,500 down, with another $83,500 due when the B.S.L. took possession. The balance was to be spread over ten equal monthly installments of $6,500 each at 6 per cent interest.

The *Yarmouth* was a small ship of only 1,452 gross tons that had been built in 1887, the year of Garvey's birth. . . . During the war the *Yarmouth* had been used to transport cotton, but most recently it had carried a cargo of coal. The squat, grimy ship, its rakish funnel ridiculously tall, was scarcely the sort to inspire undue confidence in the future success of the Black Star Line or the business sagacity of its leaders. Garvey and the rest of his landlubber board of directors had accepted without question the word of his Negro maritime adviser, Captain Joshua Cockbourne, as to the suitability and seaworthiness of the vessel. Later it developed that adviser Cockbourne had been working both sides of the street and had received a commission of $1,600 from a ship brokerage firm for his help in arranging the sale. There is no doubt that the owner of the *Yarmouth*, a New York cotton broker named W. L. Harriss, was out to take the Black Star Line and its inexperienced officers for as large a sum as possible. . . .

The Black Star Line lacked the necessary funds, however, to carry out this first purchase agreement, and on October 31, 1919, Harriss obligingly agreed to a schedule of easier time payments for the *Yarmouth*, on condition that the total purchase price be jacked up to $168,500. . . . Garvey immediately appointed the double-handed Captain Cockbourne as master of the ship and scheduled an early sailing for the West Indies. The ship would, he announced, be renamed the *S.S. Frederick Douglass*, after the great nineteenth-century American Negro leader in the fight against slavery. . . .

Late in November, 1919, the *Yarmouth* was ready for its first voyage under the red, black, and green flag of the Black Star Line. To the line's 135th Street pier came fully five thousand Negroes to cheer this great moment in the race's commercial history. Hundreds paid a dollar to go aboard and watch the proud Negro crew make ready to cast off, while at pierside the smart U.N.I.A. band added to the holiday atmosphere with a gay martial serenade. Captain Cockbourne was about to give the order to sail when anxious Leo Healy, representing the interests of the *Yarmouth's* real owner, W. L. Harriss, arrived with an order forbidding the departure until the Black Star Line had furnished adequate insurance coverage. Rather than face the riot that might develop should it appear that a white man was trying to cheat the Negro crowd of its triumph, Healy reluctantly agreed to allow the *Yarmouth* to depart on schedule, provided that he and the white port captain of the North American Steamship Corporation went along as apprehensive chaperones. With its two uninvited and unwelcome passengers the *Yarmouth* finally got under way, but its first voyage was unexpectedly short. When the *Yarmouth* had arrived in the Hudson River opposite 23d Street, Healy halted the ship, and declaring it would go no further until properly insured, clambered into a boat and rowed grimly ashore. Several days later, after the Black Star Line had taken out insurance on the *Yarmouth*, the interrupted voyage was resumed.

Meantime Harlem knew nothing of these difficulties and the magic name Garvey was on everyone's lips. Faced with the actuality of a steamship managed by a Negro company and manned by a black crew, even onetime Garvey critics were forced grudgingly to admit that the little Jamaican had accomplished something unique in race history. During the winter of 1919/20 thousands of shares of Black Star Line stock were sold at five dollars a share to Negroes all over the country. . . .

In February, 1920, while the *Yarmouth* was on its second voyage to the West Indies, the Black Star Line was recapitalized at $10,000,000. Garvey announced to an admiring black world, "They told us when we incorporated this corporation that we could not make it, but we are now gone from a [$500,000] corporation to one of $10,000,000." As critics like W. E. B. Du Bois vainly tried to point out, this statement meant absolutely nothing, since under lax Delaware laws the larger capitalization merely involved the payment of an additional fee and had nothing to do with the actual solvency of the company. It did make excellent sales propaganda, however, and Garvey and the *Negro World* exploited it to the utmost. . . .

In line with the increased capitalization of the Black Star Line, in the spring of 1920 Garvey began looking around for additions to the B.S.L. merchant fleet. . . . The *Shadyside* was an old Hudson River excursion boat of 444 gross tons that had been built in 1873 and was therefore nearly a half century old. Nevertheless, a marine survey report of April 7, 1920, declared that the vessel had been thoroughly renovated, "her engines and boilers overhauled and put in good order, and passed by U.S. local inspectors," and was thus "a fair risk for annual hull insurance when confined to inland waters." Garvey agreed to pay $35,000 for the *Shadyside*, $10,000 down and the balance in monthly payments of $2,000. The small ferry boat was intended for use on summer excursions and for B.S.L. promotional purposes. . . .

In addition to the *Shadyside*, the persuasive Leon Swift also sold Garvey on the merits of another dubious vessel, the steam yacht *Kanawha*, formerly the expensive toy of Standard Oil magnate Henry H. Rogers, and most recently on government patrol duty during the war. . . . The *Kanawha*'s small size (length, 227 feet; beam, 25 feet; and depth, 15 feet) automatically precluded her successful operation as a cargo ship. Only a millionaire oil man or the United States Treasury could afford to run such a costly plaything. . . . The Black Star Line agreed to pay the asking price of $60,000 and to expend another $25,000 refitting the *Kanawha* for passenger and cargo service. Garvey informed the colored world that this ship would be rechristened the *S.S. Antonio Maceo*, after the Negro patriot of the Cuban struggle for independence from Spain, and as soon as refitting had been completed would depart on the first of a series of scheduled trips to the WestIndies. . . .

On July 20, 1920, Marcus Garvey presided over the first annual meeting of the stockholders of the Black Star Line in Liberty Hall, which was packed to capacity. "We entered as a people with but little experience in the running of steamships," Garvey declared, and for that reason, "we were satisfied to purchase small boats so as to show that we can run them. We have much to be thankful for, in that no unfortunate accident has befallen us." The Black Star Line might not be the biggest in the world, but the work of the past year had been of great benefit to the Negro people, "for it has brought recognition to us as a race—it has elevated our men." Loud cheers greeted Garvey's declaration that through skillful and determined management the

Black Star Line had closed its first year "as solvent and as intact as any corporation can be." . . . Nor did . . . B.S.L. officials raise the question of whether the corporation had chosen wisely in its ship acquisitions, whether in fact its invested assets were worth the large sums expended for them. Such questions were overlooked in the general rejoicing, however, and few Negroes had any doubt that Marcus Garvey was leading his people along the road to economic independence and social self-respect.

In addition to the Black Star Line, in 1919 Garvey also established another business enterprise, the Negro Factories Corporation, capitalized at $1,000,000 under a charter from the State of Delaware, the corporation offered "200,000 shares of common stock to the Negro race at par value of $5.00 per share." The purpose of the company, according to Garvey's *Negro World,* was to "build and operate factories in the big industrial centers of the United States, Central America, the West Indies, and Africa to manufacture every marketable commodity." . . .

Among the businesses developed by the corporation were a chain of co-operative grocery stores, a restaurant, a steam laundry, a tailor and dressmaking shop, a millinery store, and a publishing house. An effort was made to seek out good business opportunities and to interest Negroes in developing them. . . . Strong emphasis was placed on the need of greatly expanded Negro business activity. "No race in the world," Garvey warned, "is so just as to give others, for the asking, a square deal in things economic, political and social." . . .

The Universal Negro Improvement Association was itself organized on a business basis. Its membership was required to pay monthly dues of thirty-five cents, of which ten cents went to the parent organization headed by Garvey and twenty-five cents remained with the local division. In spite of a U.N.I.A. directive that prompt payment of dues was necessary for retention of membership in the organization, Garvey's constant appeals for the share belonging to the parent body indicated that collection of dues was never an easy task. The U.N.I.A. was modeled after other American fraternal orders in that its active membership was entitled to draw sickness and death benefits from the organization. Actually the association's central treasury rarely had enough money to meet current operating expenses, let alone any charges for benefits to ailing and deceased members. This fraternal aspect of the movement stemmed from Garvey's belief that the easiest and best approach to the black masses was through their universal search for security. . . .

From his headquarters in Harlem early in 1920 Garvey issued a call for a mammoth international convention of delegates representing the entire Negro race to be held in New York during the month of August, 1920. In banner headlines the *Negro World* proclaimed that the gathering would be the largest of its kind in the history of the race. . . . As August approached and word spread of the preparations being made for the convention in Harlem, the colored world was roused to a fever pitch of excitement. While whites had their attention fixed on Geneva, Switzerland, and the newly born League of Nations, the eyes of Negroes focused on Liberty Hall in New York City, where thousands of black delegates from each of the United States, the West Indies, Central and South America, and even Africa began to arrive for the meetings.

Judged by any standards, the 1920 convention of the Universal Negro Improvement Association was a magnificent affair. Even Harlem, long used to the spectacular, found it an extravaganza not soon to be forgotten, and for the first time white America began to take notice of Marcus Garvey. . . . The magic of Garvey's spell and the power of his organizational ability were never better demonstrated than at this first great international convention. Throughout the black world Negroes were stirred to a new sense of their power and destiny by the fierce nationalism that pervaded every activity of the gathering.

The convention opened on Sunday, August 1, with three religious services and a silent march of all members and delegates through the streets of Harlem. . . . The next afternoon business activity in Harlem came to a standstill as thousands of cheering onlookers lined the curbs of Lenox Avenue to view the massed units of the Universal Negro Improvement Association. All the splendor and pageantry of a medieval coronation were present at this greatest of Negro shows. In a parade that was the talk of Harlem for months to come, the component parts of the U.N.I.A. were for the first time revealed to an astonished black world. First came the African Legion, smartly dressed in dark blue uniforms with narrow red trouser stripes, its members proudly conscious of the effect of their colorful garb and marching precision on the enthusiastic sidewalk crowds. Although the African Legion was unarmed except for the dress swords of its officers, its existence hinted that the redemption of the Negro people might come through force. Another group, the Black Cross Nurses, two hundred strong and neatly attired in white, indicated the readiness of the U.N.I.A. to come to the aid of stricken peoples all over the world. . . .

On the night of August 2 the delegates gathered in Madison

Square Garden to hear Garvey address an estimated 25,000 Negroes, one of the largest gatherings in the history of the hall. Prominent among the delegates, and the objects of intense interest on the part of the assembled black host, were an African prince and several tribal chiefs and descendants of chiefs. Three massed bands accompanied the audience as it solemnly sang the new U.N.I.A. anthem, "Ethiopia, Thou Land of Our Fathers." . . . When Garvey finally stepped forward to speak, clad in a richly colored academic cap and gown of purple, green, and gold, he received a tumultuous ovation that lasted for fully five minutes. . . .

"We are the descendants of a suffering people," Garvey told his attentive listeners; "we are the descendants of a people determined to suffer no longer." Gazing out over the colorful sea of waving U.N.I.A. banners, the new Negro Moses promised, "We shall now organize the 400,000,000 Negroes of the world into a vast organization to plant the banner of freedom on the great continent of Africa."

> We do not desire what has belonged to others, though others have always sought to deprive us of that which belonged to us. . . . If Europe is for the Europeans, then Africa shall be for the black peoples of the world. We say it; we mean it. . . . The other races have countries of their own and it is time for the 400,000,000 Negroes to claim Africa for themselves.

This emphasis on African nationalism was to be repeated in every speech of this and future U.N.I.A. conventions. The gospel of Garveyism was now written for all to see and take warning. . . .

Later in the month in a speech delivered before the convention in Carnegie Hall Garvey spelled out his warning to the white man in more explicit terms:

> The Negroes of the world say, "We are striking homewards towards Africa to make her the big black republic." And in the making of Africa a big black republic, what is the barrier? The barrier is the white man; and we say to the white man who now dominates Africa that it is to his interest to clear out of Africa now, because we are coming not as in the time of Father Abraham, 200,000 strong, but we are coming 400,000,000 strong, and we mean to retake every square inch of the 12,000,000 square miles of African territory belonging to us by right Divine. . . . We are out to get what has belonged to us politically, socially, economically, and in every way. And what 15,000,000 of us cannot get we will call in 400,000,000 to help us get.

From now on, according to this belligerent Jamaican, the white man need expect no more Negro blood shed on his behalf. "The first dying that is to be done by the black man in the future," Garvey warned, "will be done to make himself free." And when this was accomplished, he continued, "if we have any charity to bestow, we may die for the white man." "But as for me," and the words had an ominous portent for every colonial government, "I think I have stopped dying for him." This speech was sufficiently frightening to white legislators in New York that it was cited in the Lusk report on radicalism and sedition in that State.

Getting seriously to work, the delegates next drafted the long-awaited "Declaration of the Rights of the Negro Peoples of the World," which was adopted by the convention on August 13, 1920. . . . The declaration went on to "demand and insist" upon certain basic rights "in order to encourage our race all over the world and to stimulate it to a higher and grander destiny." The enumerated Negro rights were embodied in a series of fifty-four articles covering such topics as political and judicial equality, complete racial self-determination, and a free Africa under a Negro government. Article 45 went so far as to declare the League of Nations "null and void as far as the Negro is concerned, in that it seeks to deprive Negroes of their liberty." This was a reference to the former German colonies in Africa that had been given to France and Great Britain under a mandate from the League. . . . Garvey, the driving force and inspiration for this Negro reformation, was designated by the convention Provisional President of the African Republic, a sort of government in exile. . . . The emphasis on African nationalism was further reflected in the official anthem of the movement, sung to the tune of a militant old Jamaican missionary hymn:

> Ethiopia, thou land of our fathers,
> Thou land where the gods loved to be,
> As storm cloud at night suddenly gathers
> Our armies come rushing to thee.
> We must in the fight be victorious
> When swords are thrust outward to gleam;
> For us will the vict'ry be glorious
> When led by the red, black, and green.
>
> Advance, advance to victory,
> Let Africa be free;
> Advance to meet the foe

With the might
Of the red, the black, and the green.

Stock of the various business enterprises of the U.N.I.A. was sold in large amounts during the convention. The *Negro World* stressed the importance of support for the Black Star Line and delegates were urged to patronize the shops of the Negro Factories Corporation. . . .

The convention also created a nobility and freely bestowed impressive titles upon the favored elite of the organization. Membership in such honorary orders as the Knights of the Nile or the Distinguished Service Order of Ethiopia was a reward for past services to the race and brought with it immeasurably enhanced prestige. Along with the prestige went added responsibility, and this nobility was generally a serious ruling caste with special duties to perform as district or sectional leaders of the U.N.I.A. Even the lowliest follower was not forgotten, moreover, and every black man could square his shoulders with pride when Garvey addressed him as a "Fellowman of the Negro Race." No ego need remain unbolstered in this crusade. . . .

Perhaps the most prominent American Negro to become interested in Garveyism was the registrar of Howard University, Dr. Emmett J. Scott. Scott had been Booker T. Washington's private secretary for many years and during the war had served as Secretary of War Newton D. Baker's special assistant in matters relating to Negro troops. His services to the Negro people were honored at a later convention when he was made a Knight Commander of the Sublime Order of the Nile. William Pickens, an educator active in the National Association for the Advancement of Colored People, for several years showed considerable interest in the Garvey movement. In 1922, however, Pickens repudiated the offer of a title similar to the one given Scott on the ground that "Americans would be foolish to give up their citizenship here for a one thousand year improbability in Africa or anywhere else."

. . . Cutting across national lines and banishing national allegiances, the racial doctrines of Marcus Garvey were infusing in Negroes everywhere a strong sense of pride in being black. . . . Garveyism had suddenly emerged as a movement of world significance, with a spiritual power that reached deep down into the colored peoples of the world and swept them along on the currents of a potent racism. "Up, you mighty race," Garvey thundered, "you can accomplish what you will," and the Negro people responded with an enthusiastic determination born of centuries of frustration and despair.

The striking triumph of the 1920 convention and the successful launching of the Black Star Line and the Negro Factories Corporation marked the peak of Marcus Garvey's influence and prestige in America. The initial successes of Garveyism might well be attributed to the daring magnitude of the plans and dreams of its founder. Even Negroes not active in the movement gloried vicariously in the achievements of the dedicated Garvey followers. To many the Universal Negro Improvement Association seemed the answer to the hopes and prayers of countless generations of oppressed and downtrodden blacks. Its inspiration was providing the basis for a regeneration of Negro life. Few could dispute Garvey's proud boast that "the nations of the world are aware that the Negro of yesterday has disappeared from the scene of human activities and his place taken by a new Negro who stands erect, conscious of his manhood rights and fully determined to preserve them at all costs." . . .

. . . Marcus Garvey's rapid rise to a position of great prominence as a world leader indicated, however, that his movement was built upon the unstable foundations of personal rather than organizational power. Consequently there was grave danger that the Universal Negro Improvement Association would collapse should its leadership ever falter. . . . Garvey's . . . dreams would need to be implemented by successful action if the initial impetus of his movement was to be maintained. Having launched a great program with bombast and grandiloquence, Garvey would have to continue to hold his followers with constantly expanding promises and ever more dazzling actions. And if his enterprises should fail or his leadership be discredited in any way, in all likelihood the daring dreams of 1920 would dissolve into a deep disillusionment that would mark the end of this promising chapter in the history of Negro aspirations.

The Quest for Community

• Residents of the expanding urban black ghettoes of the early twentieth century worked almost as hard to develop a sense of community as they did to provide themselves with food and shelter. The migration of 1910–20 created in the black ghettoes de facto communities, whose relation to the larger urban setting and whose place within the dominant white social structures remained uncertain. Although Garveyism helped unite many urban Negroes within a black-led racial movement, its contribution was more in the realm of psychological uplift than tangible economic gains. Garvey's own Harlem swelled to become the largest black ghetto during the 1920's, the unofficial capital of the American Negro nation, while Chicago and other cities in the East and Midwest attracted thousands of new black migrants. Allan Spear discusses below some aspects of the black quest for community in Chicago, then the nation's second largest city. Spear concentrates on the reactions of previously established black Chicagoans to their newer kinsmen, the assimilationist (though not always integrationist) agencies set up to aid and direct the migrants, and the changes wrought within the black religious community.

By 1915, most Negro leaders in Chicago were committed to the idea of a separate Negro community with civic institutions, businesses, and political organizations of its own. The debate between the militant integrationists and the advocates of self-help had begun to lose its edge. Some members of the old elite, who held strongly integrationist views, had actively participated in the establishment of a Negro YMCA, Negro social agencies, and cooperative business enterprises. On the other hand, some of the most vigorous exponents of separate development also advocated militant protest against racial discrimina-

From Allan H. Spear, *Black Chicago: The Making of a Negro Ghetto* (Chicago: University of Chicago Press, 1967), pp. 167–79 (footnotes omitted.) Copyright © 1967 by the University of Chicago Press. Reprinted by permission.

tion. They saw the need to modify the Tuskegee philosophy when it was transplanted to the North. Many accepted Booker T. Washington's ideas of racial solidarity and self-help but rejected his emphasis on accommodation with the white community. Robert Abbott, for instance, saw no contradiction in applauding Negro civic undertakings and business ventures while at the same time urging a direct attack on racial barriers. By the beginning of World War I, therefore, Chicago's Negro leaders were all Washingtonians and they were all Du Boisians.

Most of the leaders of black Chicago welcomed the migrants and urged the Negro community to aid them in adjusting to urban ways. "The new arrivals rapidly adjust themselves to their changed surroundings," said George Cleveland Hall, now perhaps the most universally esteemed leader on the South Side. But they must be "reached by the proper people and get the right tip." Robert Abbott, who had played a key role in stimulating the migration, described the movement as "merely one group of American citizens moving in their own home country to better their conditions."

As the migration progressed, Negro leaders became increasingly aware of the problems presented by the newcomers. The crude, rustic ways of many of the migrants, their inability to maintain accepted standards of cleanliness, and their traditionally sycophantic demeanor in the presence of whites antagonized the old settlers. Not only did the more established Negroes find the newcomers' habits personally offensive but they felt that they diminished the status of all Negroes in the eyes of the white community. The old settlers began to formulate a myth that became an article of faith in later years. Discrimination, they argued, was minimal before the migration and it was the behavior of the newcomers that induced it.

The *Defender*, the first champion of the migration, was also one of the first to criticize the migrants' behavior in Chicago. The paper declared:

> It is evident that some of the people coming to this city have seriously erred in their conduct in public places, much to the humiliation of all respectable classes of our citizens, and by so doing, on account of their ignorance of laws and customs necessary for the maintenance of health, sobriety and morality among the people in general, have given our enemies ground for complaint.

The *Defender* urged the newcomers "to strictly observe the laws, city ordinances and customs" and it submitted a list of twenty-six "don'ts" as a guide for public conduct. The rules ranged from general precepts, such as "don't use liberty as a license to do what you please" to specific admonitions as "don't appear on the street with old dust caps, dirty aprons and ragged clothes." On other occasions, the *Defender* printed blunt advice in bold type: "Keep your mouth shut, please! There is entirely too much loud talking on the street cars among our newcomers." "Go clean up north. . . . In the south a premium was put on filth and uncleanliness. In the north a badge of honor is put on the man or woman who is clean."

The task of helping the migrants adjust to urban life required not haphazard criticisms and admonitions, but concerted educational efforts by civic and welfare organizations. The *Defender* attacked "the glib assumption that matters will eventually adjust themselves"; the situation demanded "positive efforts of constructive social welfare work." At the very onset of the migration, some social workers and church leaders recognized that the migrants would place new demands upon the community. The Cook County Sunday School Association met early in 1917 to discuss "how to handle the . . . newcomers," and the Baptists set up a center for migrants at the Olivet Church. By far the most important organization to respond to the problems of the migration years was the Chicago Urban League. Not a social welfare organization itself, the League attempted to coordinate the efforts of existing agencies, help the newcomers find jobs, gather data on Negro living conditions, and represent Negro interests in the general community.

The Chicago Urban League was a branch of the National League on Urban Conditions among Negroes, which had been founded in New York in 1911. Like the NAACP, the League was an interracial group, reflecting the reform impulse of the progressive era. Unlike the NAACP, it envisaged itself not as a protest organization, but as an extension of the social work movement into the growing urban Negro enclaves. Before World War I, the League operated primarily in New York and in several southern and border cities, where the branches soon atrophied for lack of white cooperation. During World War I, however, the League came into its own by firmly establishing itself in the Northern industrial cities most affected by the migrants.

The president and associate director of the National League came to Chicago late in 1915 to interest local leaders in the establishment a Chicago Urban League. They called together three groups of people: (1) professional social workers, such as Sophonisba Breckinridge, Edith Abbott, and Celia Parker Woolley; (2) white progressives who had exhibited an interest in the Negro cause—Judge Edward O. Brown, president of the Chicago NAACP, Robert Park the eminent University of Chicago sociologist, and Horace Bridges of the Ethical Culture Society; and (3) Negro community leaders, such as George Cleveland Hall, Robert Abbott, A. L. Jackson, and several prominent Negro clubwomen. T. Arnold Hill, an organizer for the national body, agreed to serve as acting secretary of the new Chicago branch. He had originally planned to stay in Chicago for a month; he eventually stayed eight years and became a major figure in the Chicago Negro community.

Hill was primarily responsible for putting the League on an organizational basis. An able, articulate and tactful man, he won friends for the League in the Negro community and among white philanthropists, on whom the League depended for financial support. He made a strong impression on Julius Rosenwald, who described him as a "very conservative, vigorous, educated Negro"—all highly complimentary terms in the philanthropist's lexicon. Rosenwald agreed to underwrite one-third of the League's annual budget, and his secretary, William Graves, became a member of the executive board. Although 75 per cent of the League's membership was Negro, whites accounted for 90 per cent of the financial contributions. After a few months of operation in the YMCA building, the new organization moved to its own office on State Street, and shortly thereafter took over the building of the dying Frederick Douglass Center on Wabash Avenue.

The Chicago Urban League, according to its first president, Robert Park, was designed to do for Negroes what other social agencies were doing for immigrants, to help with "work and wages, health and housing, the difficulties of the adjustment of an essentially rural population to the conditions of a city environment, and to modern life." But Park also realized that racial prejudice made the Negro's problem distinct and engendered in Negroes a counter feeling of racial hostility. The Urban League, he hoped, would convert this racial feeling from "a liability into an asset" by directing "the energies aroused by racial antagonism into constructive channels." To achieve these aims, Park and Hill outlined a concrete program of coordination, investigation, education, and labor relations that the League attempted to follow throughout the migration period.

In trying to coordinate existing welfare programs, the League put its prime emphasis upon efficiency. Arnold Hill and many of the founders of the Urban League were products of the professional social work movement and frowned upon the haphazard manner in which the numerous church, settlement house, and private welfare programs were administered. Hill hoped to bring the various agencies together in order to avoid duplication, delineate areas of interest, and assist the weaker organizations in their work. Inevitably such a program aroused the antagonism of existing agencies that saw the new group as a threat to their own work. Nevertheless, the League achieved notable results. It took over the ailing Wendell Phillips Settlement, cooperated with the wartime agencies in operating a service men's club on the South Side, and acted as a Negro branch of general welfare agencies, such as the Social Service Department of the Cook County Hospital, the United Charities, and the Travelers Aid. According to William Graves, the League brought "cooperation from scores of Negro civic and philanthropic organizations which have been working at cross purposes with much jealousy." The League also operated several civic programs intended specifically for the migrants: Urban League representatives helped the newcomers find housing; League workers spoke at churches on such themes as thrift and hygiene; and a creed of cleanliness distributed by the League outlined simple rules of neatness and decorum. Utilizing Park's theory that racial feeling could be turned into constructive channels, the League organized block clubs and community improvement societies. Through these organizations, Negroes were encouraged to answer the white argument that Negroes depreciate property values by maintaining high standards in their homes and neighborhoods.

Another tenet of the progressive credo that motivated the Urban League was the belief that the compilation of factual data on social problems was the first step toward their solution. The League retained Charles S. Johnson, then a graduate student at the University of Chicago and later a prominent sociologist and educator, to direct its Bureau of Investigation and Records. Johnson investigated Negro migration for the Carnegie Foundation, conducted a study of juvenile delinquency among Negroes, and surveyed Negro housing conditions. He was called into the army in 1918 and his bureau then became moribund, but it was revived in the 1920's with the cooperation of the University of Chicago.

The most important phase of the Urban League's program was its work in the field of labor relations. In this area it received the widest acclaim and at the same time faced its most serious potential problem. The League's Industrial Department operated through the war period as an employment bureau. Migrants were encouraged to register with the Urban League for a job, and employers went to the League's office to obtain Negro labor. In addition to placing the newcomers in the plentiful unskilled jobs, the League also operated training courses for prospective workers and tried to find jobs for them in skilled and clerical work. In 1918, the Department of Labor assumed responsibility for the League's employment service, but it left the supervision of the bureau in the hands of the League staff. Federal assistance gave additional impetus to the program, and the League jealously guarded its prerogatives when the Labor Department's newly formed Bureau of Negro Economics threatened to set up a rival employment bureau.

The Urban League's labor program pleased its conservative white benefactors. William Graves told Julius Rosenwald that not only had the League "opened kinds of employment hitherto closed to Colored people," but it had also "been of assistance to many employers whose forces have been reduced by employees volunteering and being drafted for military service." The League identified itself, in most cases, with the interests of the large employers. During the war years, it could do this without contradiction. In labor disputes, the welfare of Negro workers was usually dependent upon the favor of management. When, however, the butchers' union made a real attempt to win Negro support, the League broke with its usual policy and encouraged the union's efforts. The end of the war ushered in a new set of conditions that severely tested the League's policy. Job scarcity and labor unrest made it more difficult to defend vigorously the interests of its Negro clients and at the same time satisfy its white supporters. The dilemma posed by an increasing need for militancy and continued dependence upon white contributions was to plague the Chicago Urban League throughout its history.

Despite this potential difficulty, the Urban League was a notable success in its early years. It brought to the field of community welfare a new kind of professionalism and competence and introduced to Chicago, in T. Arnold Hill, a new kind of Negro leader—the able, well-trained professional. In a period of increasing racial strife, it stressed interracial cooperation and yet recognized ethnocentric attitudes and tried to make constructive use of them. It provided a new focal point for Negro community life, replacing many of the struggling settlement houses, church social programs, and welfare agencies of the prewar years.

Not all of the older civic institutions disappeared. The Urban League absorbed the Frederick Douglass Center and took over the Wendell Phillips Settlement, but Provident Hospital and the Wabash Avenue YMCA—the most important of the prewar institutions

—broadened their programs as the migrants poured into Chicago. In 1916 and 1917, Provident conducted a $15,000 fund-raising drive for expansion to meet the new demands. Although it sought help from white benefactors, it solicited Negro support with a special appeal to race pride. Provident, said George Hall, "is the Colored people's hospital. It is an establishment in which, more and more each year, the Colored folks are taking personal pride." The money was raised by the end of 1918.

The YMCA tried to reach the newcomers by establishing industrial baseball teams, glee clubs, and social organizations in the factories, yards, and mills. Through these groups, the Association also conducted forums on thrift and vocational guidance. The directors of the YMCA, A. L. Jackson and George Arthur, were frequently characterized as tools of industrial management. They discouraged Negroes from joining unions, and Arthur admitted that "plant loyalty" was one aim of the Association's industrial program. The YMCA was supplemented by a YWCA, opened by a group of Negro clubwomen in 1915. Independent at first, the group subsequently affiliated with the Chicago YWCA. Its work paralleled that of the men's association. It operated vocational classes, a dormitory, employment bureau, summer camp, library, and recreational program.

Of all aspects of community life, religious activities were most profoundly changed by the migration. Before the war, the large, middle-class Baptist and Methodist churches had dominated Negro religious life in Chicago. Although they had not completely discarded the emotionalism of traditional Negro religion, these churches had moved toward a more decorous order of worship and a program of broad social concern. The migration, however, brought into the city thousands of Negroes accustomed to the informal, demonstrative, preacher-oriented churches of the rural South. Alienated by the formality of the middle-class churches, many of the newcomers organized small congregations that met in stores and houses and that maintained the old-time shouting religion. Often affiliated with the more exotic fringe sects, Holiness or Spiritualist, these storefront churches became a permanent force in the Chicago Negro community and secured a powerful hold on thousands of working-class Negroes.

The Holiness or Pentecostal churches were the most conspicuous of the new storefront congregations. Although a few churches of this type had existed before the war, they became numerous and prominent only with the migration. By 1920, there were twenty Holiness churches in Chicago, all meeting in storefronts or houses. Most were concentrated west of State Street, among the poorest of the recent migrants. All were small, usually with no more than fifty members, and their organization was highly personal. The preacher, or presiding elder, was commonly an uneducated migrant from the South, who had founded the church while working at another job. He held his congregation together through personal loyalty, and if he died or moved away, the church rarely survived. Doctrinally, the Holiness churches were fundamentalist. Their highly emotional services were marked by rolling, shouting, or "speaking in tongues." Often too the preachers claimed the power to heal. Members of these congregations spent most of their free time in religious activities: some churches held nightly services, and all of them, in addition to Sunday worship, conducted two or three mid-week prayer meetings and periodic revivals and healing campaigns.

Elder Lucy Smith was perhaps the most successful of the Holiness preachers; her All Nations Pentecostal Church became a landmark on the South Side in the 1930's. But despite her unusual success, she probably typified in background and motivation those who founded storefront churches during the migration years. A large, heavy-set woman with almost no formal education, Lucy Smith was born on a Georgia plantation in 1875, moved to Atlanta in 1909, and a year later migrated to Chicago. A Baptist by birth, she joined Olivet Church upon her arrival in Chicago. Soon dissatisfied with the formality of the large congregation, she began to attend the smaller Ebenezer Baptist Church, but here too she was unable to find the traditional kind of religion she sought. She then turned to the Stone Church, a predominantly white Pentecostal congregation. The Stone Church provided her with the inspiration she needed to begin her own religious career. "In 1914," she recalled, "I received my baptism and came into the works of the Lord. I continued going to the Stone Church until I received my calling, which is divine healing." Lucy Smith's calling coincided neatly with the arrival of the first wave of World War I migrants, who were receptive to her spiritual message. In 1916, she organized a one-room prayer meeting in her house; ten years later, after numerous moves and changes, she started to erect her own church building. Lucy Smith, according to one observer, was "a simple, ignorant, untrained woman with deep human sympathies, who believed absolutely in her own power to help and heal other people. Calm and serene in that faith, she has drawn together a following from the back streets of Chicago."

Not all of the little storefront churches that sprang up during the migration years were Pentecostal. Many called themselves Baptist, although they often closely resembled the Holiness churches in their uninhibited form of worship. Others were Spiritualist, a vague term used to identify those religious groups that believed in "communication of the spirit" and that attempted to relay messages to the spirits through mediums. Many Spiritualist churches were merely commercial enterprises that charged fees for readings and advice. But several true Spiritualist churches were organized between 1915 and 1920. These congregations combined the emotional worship service of the Pentecostal and Baptist storefronts with seances and spiritual readings.

A dearth of material makes it difficult to assess the social significance of storefront churches in Chicago. In all probability, they were primarily migrant churches; as the newcomers became acculturated to city ways, they moved to the more established churches, leaving the storefronts to the still more recent arrivals. One observer described the members of Lucy Smith's congregation, for instance, as "new arrivals from the South and those Negroes who have not [been] and probably never will be urbanized." In any case, the emergence of the storefronts was symptomatic of increasing differentiation within the Negro class structure. For the storefronts were decidedly lower-class churches. As some sophisticated upper-class Negroes had broken with the old-line churches to form Episcopalian and Presbyterian congregations, so now the southern-oriented lower class sought religious fulfillment in churches that more closely approximated their values and ideals. While the upper-class churches followed formal, decorous orders of worship and emphasized ethics and social concern, the storefronts allowed the widest range of personal expression and uninhibited emotionalism, and offered a salvation-centered religion that ignored and provided an escape from the problems of everyday life.

Despite the rise of the storefronts, the old-line Baptist and Methodist churches grew rapidly during the migration years. Olivet Baptist Church, for example, already the largest Negro church in the city, grew from an estimated membership of four thousand in 1915 to almost nine thousand in 1920. During this period it moved into a new and larger building and vastly expanded its already sizable social and recreational program. Lacey Kirk Williams, who became pastor of the church in 1915, tried to make Olivet a community center. By 1920, a full-time professional staff of sixteen operated a program that included a labor bureau, kindergarten, nursery, and welfare department, in addition to the usual club and athletic activities. For Olivet, as for many other northern churches that tried to provide facilities for the newcomers, this expansion resulted in heavy financial debt. The migrants were unable to contribute an amount commensurate with the new financial burdens they created. Quinn Chapel, the Methodist counterpart of Olivet, did not grow as rapidly. More sedate and formal than Olivet, Quinn Chapel soon gained a reputation as a "swank" church, not for the "common herd." The A.M.E. denomination in Chicago claimed a total membership increase of about five thousand during the migration years; this figure was matched by Olivet alone.

The Baptist churches, in general, outpaced the Methodist during this period and secured a preeminent position in Chicago, which they never lost. In 1916, Chicago had thirty-six Baptist churches and twenty-two Methodist. By 1920, the number of Methodist churches had increased to only thirty-four, while there were now eighty-six Baptist churches in the city. Many of the new Baptist congregations were ephemeral little storefronts, but others, although beginning in stores or private homes, grew into large and substantial congregations. Pilgrim, Progressive, Provident, Liberty, and Monumental Baptist Churches, all founded between 1916 and 1919, began as prayer meetings in the homes of migrants recently arrived from the South. Within a decade, all of these congregations had acquired their own buildings and boasted memberships of over five hundred. Primarily migrant churches, they provided a middle ground between the formal, old-line northern congregations and the emotional, uninhibited storefronts.

The churches affiliated with white denominations were least affected by the migration. Most of these were upper-class urbanized churches with little to offer the recent arrivals. But there was one exception. St. Monica's Roman Catholic Church had always drawn its membership chiefly from Negroes who had been Catholics in the South; the large migration from Louisiana swelled its ranks between 1915 and 1920. The growth in the Negro Catholic population in Chicago came at a time when anti-Negro sentiment among the white Catholic groups in the city was mounting rapidly. In deference to this feeling, Archbishop Mundelein formulated a policy that resulted in almost complete racial segregation within the Archdiocese of Chicago. In 1917, Mundelein announced that while "until now practically anyone who so desired could affiliate himself with St. Monica's," he now desired "St. Monica's to be reserved entirely for the colored Catholics of Chicago . . . ; all other Catholics of whatever race or color are to be requested not to intrude." The Archbishop said that he took this action so that his "colored children shall not feel uncomfortable in the

Catholic Church," and he quickly added that he had "no intention of excluding colored Catholics from any of the other churches in the district." In practice, however, the Archbishop's order provided white parishes with an excuse for excluding Negroes. Many white priests refused to marry or bury Negroes and, in some cases, would not even hear their confessions. Instead they ordered them to go to their own church, which the Archbishop had set aside for them.

The Negro Renaissance

• *The growth of new Negro ghetto communities soon stimulated the development of an autonomous yet viable black
urban culture. Earlier imitation of white cultural norms,
despite the Negro's recurrent exclusion from equal status
within white culture, made the rediscovery and celebration of
his own racial identity vital for black cultural survival in
white America. In this quest for black traditions, the new
Negro intelligentsia played a vital part. Robert A. Bone, in
a larger study of the Negro novel in America, describes the
background of the Negro Renaissance of the 1920's and the
peculiar conditions that guided its literary impulse and gave
it distinctive social meaning. Bone points out that just as
white American writers in the mid-nineteenth century discarded the shackles of commitment to European styles, Black
writers of the Renaissance began to draw inspiration from
the realities of Negro experience, rather than from the concerns and language of white America.*

Alain Locke has described the Negro Renaissance as "the mass movement of the urban immigration of Negroes, projected on the plane of
an increasingly articulate elite." The Great Migration to which Locke
refers was the most important event in the history of the American
Negro since his emancipation from slavery. In the course of this
migration, centuries of historical development were traversed in a few
decades. It was not merely a movement of the colored population from
South to North, or from country to city; it was the sudden transplant-
ing of a debased feudal folk from medieval to modern America.

From 1890 to 1920, while the business and professional class was
fighting for the right to rise, the base of the Negro social pyramid was
shifting from a peasantry to an urban proletariat. In these decades

From Robert A. Bone, *The Negro Novel in America*, revised edition (New
Haven: Yale University Press, 1965), pp. 53–67 (footnotes omitted). Copyright © 1958, 1965 by Yale University. Reprinted by permission.

more than 2,000,000 Negroes left the farm for the factory. As growing numbers of Negro sharecroppers were pushed off the land by erosion and drought, by an exhausted soil, and by the mechanical cotton-picker, they were drawn to the cities by the demands of American industry for cheap labor. Competition from the European immigrant was conveniently eliminated by World War I and by the immigration laws of 1924. At the same time, the war encouraged a vast expansion of American industry, creating a labor market for thousands of black workers. Under these circumstances, the urbanization of the American Negro took place at an unprecedented rate.

The Great Migration brought the Negro masses into contact with the quickened pulse of the modern city. There they were faced with a mass of strange experiences which forced them to revise their traditional ways of thinking. The crowded ghetto, unlike the isolated farm, provided a basis for a vigorous group life. A rising standard of living and better educational opportunities fostered new attitudes of self-respect and independence. In a word, the Negro's urban environment lifted him to a new plane of consciousness. Such a profound transformation could hardly occur among the masses without reverberations in the world of letters. The new group experience called for a new literary movement to interpret it.

It was a foregone conclusion that Harlem should become the center of the new movement. The largest Negro community in the world, Harlem was itself a product of the Great Migration. Doubling its population from 1900 to 1920, it was wrested from the whites by sheer weight of numbers. As it grew to metropolitan proportions, it gradually acquired the character of a race capital. Negroes from Africa and the West Indies, from North and South, and from all classes and backgrounds poured into the crucible of dark Manhattan. Harlem thus provided the Negro artist with an infinite variety of human subjects, as well as an opportunity to observe urban life at its maximum intensity.

Moreover, this black metropolis evolved within the womb of a city which was the literary, musical, and theatrical capital of America. Harlem meant proximity to Broadway, to the little magazines and the big publishing houses, to Greenwich Village and its white intellectuals, to avant-garde literary groups and successful, established writers. It offered a unique, cosmopolitan milieu, where artists and intellectuals of all kinds could find mutual stimulation. Under the circumstances, it is hardly surprising that Harlem became the cultural center of Negro America.

Before any group can prosper artistically, as Arthur Koestler notes, it must produce an intelligentsia. This social layer arises in bourgeois society, according to Koestler, when enough gifted individuals have broken with their middle-class background to form a community of emancipated intellectuals. Shortly after World War I just such an intellectual community began to form in Harlem. Young men and women of introspective leanings came to Harlem from every corner of the nation, drawn by the changing kaleidoscope of metropolitan life.

These young intellectuals were a different breed from the Negro writers of the prewar period. Like their contemporaries of the Lost Generation, they reached maturity in a world of crumbling values. "I had no reason to think," wrote Claude McKay, "that the world I lived in was permanent, solid, and unshakable." Lacking the comforting assurance of an integrated moral universe, they were forced to cope as best they could with what Henry Adams called 20th-century multiplicity. Unsure of their positive goals, they began by sweeping aside the moral debris of the previous era. At one stroke they cut through the taboos of the Victorian Age, demolished its shallow optimism, repudiated its value system, and entered the mainstream of contemporary intellectual life.

The significance of the Negro intelligentsia, which emerged for the first time in the 1920's, lay precisely in this realm of values. The middle-class writer, as Koestler suggests, is inclined not toward new hierarchies of values but toward climbing to the top of the existing hierarchy. The intelligentsia, more independent in outlook, debunks existing values and attempts to replace them with values of its own. Koestler's theoretical point may thus serve to sharpen the contrast between the early Negro novelist and his Renaissance successor. The early novelists were loyal members of the middle class who desired only equal rights within the status quo. The younger writers of the 1920's were the second generation of educated Negroes; they were the wayward sons of the rising middle class. In psychological terms, they were rebelling against their fathers and their fathers' way of life.

This pattern of rebellion appears in the lives of many Renaissance authors. Langston Hughes, for example, observes in his autobiography, "My father was what the Mexicans call *muy americano*, a typical American. . . . He was interested only in making money." Hughes' most vivid memory of his father was his constant injunction to hurry up. His father tried to hurry him through a course in bookkeeping and then through Columbia University, but Hughes left college to ship out, taking his Grand Tour on a tramp steamer. Claude McKay's rebellion carried him from Greenwich Village to the Left Bank, and from militant Negro nationalism to the early Communist party. Jean Toomer abandoned a law career for literature and the Gurdjieff Institute. Countee Cullen, whose father was a minister, has recorded his rebellion against religious formalism in his novel *One Way to Heaven*.

The rebellious mood of the emerging Negro intelligentsia is revealed by the little magazines they founded. *The Messenger*, for example, displayed as its credo:

> I am an Iconoclast
> I break the limbs of idols
> And smash the traditions of men.

Fire, according to one of its founders, was intended "to burn up a lot of the old, dead, conventional Negro ideas of the past." In their rebelliousness and defiance the Negro writers of the 1920's were no different from their white contemporaries, who were engaged in a similar labor of destruction in such little magazines as *Broom, Transition*, and *Secession*. The younger Negro intellectuals, whose consciousness was formed during the war years, were members of an uprooted generation. Critical, skeptical, iconoclastic, they raised the banner of the New Negro against the stubborn guardians of the Victorian tradition.

THE NEW NEGRO MOVEMENT

The term "New Negro" presents certain difficulties, for it has been used to describe both a racial attitude and a literary movement. The extension of the term from its original meaning was the work of Alain Locke, who in 1925 published an anthology of younger writers entitled *The New Negro*. The title struck a responsive chord, and it soon became the accepted designation of the new literary movement. From the standpoint of literary history this was unfortunate. "New Negro" is not a descriptive term in any literary sense; basically it indicates a rejection of racial conservatism on the part of those who employ it. It is nonetheless of considerable subject importance that Renaissance writers should think of themselves as "New Negroes." To establish the primary meaning of the term may therefore cast additional light on the period.

The New Negro, with his uncompromising demand for equal rights, was the end product of a long historical process which began when the Negro middle class emerged from slavery and entered upon a new kind of social relations. As the patriarchal relations of slavery were replaced by the contractual relations of bourgeois society, a corresponding psychological transformation took place. Feudal attitudes of servility and dependence were abandoned in favor of the sturdy bourgeois virtues of initiative and self-reliance. This psychological transformation crystallized politically when Du Bois challenged the "accommodating" leadership of Booker T. Washington in the name of universal manhood suffrage. Manhood suffrage, the basic aim of Du Bois' Niagara Movement, became a symbol of the new spirit which animated the Negro middle class. This sense of manhood, greatly enhanced by the Negro's participation in World War I, was passed on to the Renaissance generation as part of its spiritual heritage.

There is a direct line from the Niagara Movement of the early 1900's to the New Negro Movement of the 1920's. The descent may be traced through Negro defense organizations such as the NAACP and the National Urban League, and more precisely through their house organs, *Crisis* and *Opportunity*. These two periodicals and their editors, Jessie Fauset and Charles S. Johnson, did yeoman's work for the Negro Renaissance. They encouraged new talent, opened their pages to young writers, and offered cash prizes for outstanding literary achievement. In this manner, as well as through overt patronage, the Negro middle class made a substantial contribution to the birth of the New Negro Movement. Whether they were prepared to acknowledge the lusty and sometimes ungrateful infant which they sired is another matter.

As the Negro Renaissance gained momentum and its break with the tradition of Chesnutt and Dunbar became apparent, the term "New Negro" began to take on an additional connotation of modernism. As a result, it became intellectually fashionable to declare oneself a member of the New Negro coterie. Yet if the New Negro slogan created something of a vogue, it also provided the literary movement of the 1920's with a unifying idea. "New Negro" literary societies sprang up in several large cities; New Negro magazines were founded by avant-garde writers; and one novelist playfully christened his first-born "the New Negro"! This self-consciousness, this sense of belonging to a movement, made for a high group morale, and for an atmosphere which encouraged literary effort. Moreover, in its own way the New Negro Movement expressed that determination to ring out the old and ring in the new which was the central theme of the decade.

The years following World War I were marked by a sudden upsurge of interest in Negro life and culture among the white intelligentsia. Manifestations of this interest were numerous and varied. Throughout the 1920's books on the Negro by white authors appeared in ever-increasing numbers. *Survey Graphic* came out with an issue devoted entirely to Harlem, while Albert and Charles·Boni offered a prize of $1,000 for the best novel written by an American Negro. Musical reviews which featured Negro performers broke downtown box-office records, and nightly throngs of white "tourists" invaded Harlem, drawn to night club and cabaret by colored celebrities of musical and theatrical fame. By the mid-1920's the Negro had become a national pastime.

What had happened to change the intellectual climate from hostility and indifference to sympathetic, if often misguided, interest? For one thing the Jazz Age, which derived its very character from the Negro's music, was in full swing. With "flaming youth" leading the way, a popular uprising was in progress against the stuffiness and artificial restraint of the Victorian era. These were the years of post-war catharsis—of Freud and the sexual revolution, of heavy drinking in defiance of authority, of a wild dance called the Charleston, and of a wilder music which made its way from the bordellos of New Orleans to the night clubs of Chicago and New York. Somewhat to his surprise and not entirely to his liking, the Negro suddenly found himself called upon to uphold a new stereotype: he became a symbol of that freedom from restraint for which the white intellectual longed so ardently.

In the sophisticated art centers of Europe and America, interest in the Negro focused around the cult of the primitive. Insofar as it idealizes simpler cultures, primitivism is a romantic retreat from the complexities of modern life. Reflecting the writings of Sigmund Freud, it exalts instinct over intellect, Id over Super-Ego, and is thus a revolt against the Puritan spirit. For such an artistic movement the Negro had obvious uses: he represented the unspoiled child of nature, the noble savage—carefree, spontaneous, and sexually uninhibited.

The discovery of primitive African sculpture and the ascendancy of jazz reinforced the development of this new stereotype.

Like all previous stereotypes, that of the primitive Negro exercised a coercive effect on the Negro novelist. As in the past, the degree of accommodation was astonishing; with few exceptions the Negro intelligentsia accepted this exotic image of themselves. Perhaps they found in primitivism a useful support for the cultural dualism which they espoused during the Renaissance period. In any event, the younger Negro writers were quite carried away. Langston Hughes wrote ecstatically of jazz as "the tom-tom of revolt," while Countee Cullen discovered "elemental" religion in a Harlem revival meeting. Claude McKay glorified the instinctive Negro in all of his novels, and proudly proclaimed the "primative sexuality" of the Negro race. Jean Toomer, perhaps the most authentic exponent of Renaissance primitivism, wrote in a sophisticated vein of "the zoo-restrictions and keeper-taboos" of modern civilization.

Whatever its excesses, primitivism provided the common ground for a fruitful period of cultural collaboration. Works like Eugene O'Neill's *The Emperor Jones* (1920) and *All God's Chillun Got Wings* (1924), Waldo Frank's *Holiday* (1923), Sherwood Anderson's *Dark Laughter* (1925), Dubose Heyward's *Porgy* (1925) and *Mamba's Daughters* (1927), and Carl Van Vechten's *Nigger Heaven* (1926), acted as a spur to Negro writers and created a sympathetic audience for the serious treatment of Negro subjects. Personal association with white authors meant an end of cultural isolation and provincialism, and an immense gain in technical maturity for the Negro writer. In economic terms alone, considerable patronage and sponsorship occurred, while publishing forts and editorial desks capitulated in the face of a growing market for novels of Negro life. In the forefront of these developments, consciously promoting this cultural exchange, was a white *littérateur* named Carl Van Vechten.

Van Vechten's role in furthering the Negro Renaissance was unique. His literary salons provided a warm atmosphere in which artists and intellectuals of both races could break down their taboos against personal association. His one-man "know the Negro" campaign was eminently successful in overcoming prejudice and awkwardness among his white contemporaries. His efforts on behalf of individual Negro writers and artists were indefatigable, and were amply rewarded in later years when many of his former protégés entrusted their literary effects to his care.

A more questionable contribution, at least in the eyes of some Negro critics, was Van Vechten's *Nigger Heaven*, a novel which appeared in 1926 and quickly ran through several editions. Emphasizing the bawdy and exotic aspects of Harlem life, and heavily influenced by primitivistic conceptions, *Nigger Heaven* shattered the complacency of the Negro intelligentsia by threatening to steal their literary thunder. For most of the Negro middle class the title of the novel was enough. Bitterly attacked in some quarters as a slander against the race, *Nigger Heaven* has been ably defended by James Weldon Johnson, and requires no apologia here. It is sufficient to acknowledge its role in creating an audience for the exotic novel of Harlem life, and its influence on certain members of the so-called Harlem School.

The influence of white intellectuals on the Negro Renaissance ought not to be overestimated. Some Negro critics have charged the New Negro Movement with white domination, but a sober appraisal leaves no doubt of its indigenous character. The New Negro Movement was not a "vogue" initiated by white "literary faddists," but a serious attempt by the Negro artist to interpret his own group life. There were excesses, to be sure, for which the whites must bear their share of responsibility. Insofar as the Negro novelist adopted a pose in response to the "primitive" effusion of the white intellectual, it produced a certain shallowness in his work, and a legitimate suspicion that his novels, like his cabarets, were designed to entertain the white folks. In the long run, however, the Negro novelist outgrew his primitive phase; meanwhile it helped him to discover unsuspected values in his own folk culture.

THE ESSENCE OF THE NEGRO RENAISSANCE

There is a phase in the growth of a derivative literature which corresponds to the adolescent rebellion in an individual—a time when it must cut loose from the parent literature and establish an independent existence. This phase occurred in American literature during the flowering of New England; it was highlighted by Emerson's famous Phi Beta Kappa address, in which he protests, "We have listened too long to the courtly Muses of Europe." The Negro Renaissance represents a similar impulse toward cultural autonomy on the part of the American Negro.

The Negro Renaissance was essentially a period of self-discovery, marked by a sudden growth of interest in things Negro. The Renaissance thus reversed the assimilationist trend of the prewar period, with its conscious imitation of white norms and its deliberate suppression of "racial" elements. The motivation for this sudden reversal was not primarily literary but sociological. The Negro Renaissance, as E. Franklin Frazier has observed, reflects a pattern of adjustment common to all ethnic minorities in America: "At first the group attempts to lose itself in the majority group, disdaining its own characteristics. When this is not possible, there is a new valuation placed upon these very same characteristics, and they are glorified in the eyes of the group."

The discovery of autonomous "racial" values by the Renaissance generation was prompted by a wave of Negro nationalism which swept over the colored community in the wake of World War I. As a direct result of his war experience the American Negro became bitterly disillusioned with the promises of the white majority. Discrimination in the armed forces, brutal attacks on returning veterans, and the bloody riots of the summer of 1919 convinced the Negro that his sacrifices for the nation would be acknowledged only by renewed oppression. With every avenue of assimilation apparently closed, a strongly nationalistic reflex occurred on all levels of Negro society.

Among the Negro masses this reflex took the form of recruitment to Marcus Garvey's "Back to Africa" movement. Garvey's program, in spite of its utterly Utopian content, deserves the closest scrutiny, for it stirred the imagination of the Negro masses as never before or since. Garvey held that the Negro must renounce all hope of assistance or understanding from American whites, leave the country, and build a new civilization in Africa. His secessionist movement preyed upon a dissatisfaction so deep that it amounted to despair of ever achieving a full life in America. His immense popularity stands as a sober warning to all who would underestimate the nationalism of the Negro masses.

Meanwhile the logic of events forced the Negro middle class to adopt what might be called a tactical nationalism. As the fluid patterns of the post-Reconstruction period hardened into a rigid and unyielding color line, it became increasingly clear to the Talented Tenth that they could never hope to breach this caste barrier as a special class of "white" Negroes. The war years in particular convinced them that they could not succeed short of an all-out assault on Jim Crow. Abandoning their former strategy, they turned to the Negro masses for support in the coming struggle.

This *rapprochement* with the black masses could not be consummated without great psychological effort. The habit of emphatically differentiating themselves from the "lower classes" was not easily relinquished by the Talented Tenth. Race leaders perceived at once that they would have to cultivate a mild nationalism in order to achieve a decent show of racial solidarity. One of their number, Jessie Fauset, has preserved this insight for posterity in her novel *Plum Bun*:

> Those of us who have forged forward are not able as yet to go our separate ways apart from the unwashed, untutored herd. We must still look back and render service to our less fortunate, weaker brethren. And the first step toward making this a workable attitude is the acquisition not so much of a racial love as a racial pride. A pride that enables us to find our own beautiful and praiseworthy, an intense chauvinism that is content with its own types, that finds completeness within its own group, that loves its own as the French love their country.

The nationalist reflex of the Negro intelligentsia consisted of a withdrawal of allegiance from the values of the dominant culture, and a search for alternative values within their own tradition. Unlike the nationalism of the masses or of the middle class, that of the intelligentsia was not based on racial considerations alone. It was motivated by factors larger than, but including, race—factors related to the universal revolt of the modern artist from bourgeois civilization. The Negro intellectual of the 1920's shared fully in the spiritual alienation of the Lost Generation. Like the white expatriate, he rejected the chromium plate of American culture. His alienation as an artist caused him in turn to alter his goals as a Negro. Instead of advocating blind assimilation into a hopelessly materialistic culture, he began to think in terms of preserving his racial individuality.

The search for a distinctive tradition led in many directions. The alienated Negro intellectual fell back predominantly on the folk culture, with its antecedents in slavery, its roots in the rural South, and its final flowering on the city pavements. Where the folk culture seemed inadequate to his needs, he turned to the cult of African origins, and to primitivism. At the same time, a new concept of the Negro's manifest destiny arose, to replace the old faith in race progress. Along with a sophisticated critique of (white) European civilization, the thesis was advanced that certain enduring qualities in the racial temperament would redeem the decadent and enervated West. The sum and substance of these explorations was an unequivocal cultural dualism—a conscious attempt to endow Negro literature with a life of its own, apart from the dominant literary tradition.

The frank espousal of cultural dualism by the Negro intelligentsia was viewed with great alarm by the Negro middle class, whose long-range strategy called for eradicating cultural differences. Even at the peak of Renaissance nationalism the middle-class writer could never muster more than token enthusiasm for a distinctive Negro culture. The issues posed by cultural dualism therefore divided the novelists of the period into two schools. The Harlem School, pursuing the nationalist impulse to its logical conclusion, turned to the black masses for literary material. The Old Guard, still intent upon portraying "respectable" Negroes, remained prisoners of the Genteel Tradition.

Those Negro writers of the 1920's who did not shrink from the implications of cultural dualism found that it altered their art in several important respects. To begin with, whatever is distinctively Negro is likely to be of folk, if not of slave, origin. The Harlem School therefore turned to the folk for their major characters and a low-life milieu for their principal setting. Langston Hughes has preserved the flavor of this development: "But then there are the lowdown folks, and they are the majority—may the Lord be praised! The people who have their nip of gin on Saturday nights and are not too important to themselves or the community. Their religion soars to a shout. Work maybe a little today, rest a little tomorrow. Play awhile. Sing awhile. O, let's dance!"

In the second place, whatever is culturally distinctive has been exaggerated to the point of caricature by ignorant and prejudiced whites. Cultural dualism therefore involves characterizations which run dangerously close to the stereotype. The Harlem School faced this issue squarely, by insisting on their artistic prerogatives. It was up to a mature audience, in their view, to distinguish between a dialect farce by Octavus Roy Cohen and a dialect interpretation by a serious writer, designed to achieve a greater literary realism. The Harlem School had simply outgrown what Alain Locke has called "the pathetic over-compensations of a group inferiority complex." Their bold defiance of the stereotype was a refreshing change from the lifeless, "exemplary" characterization of the prewar novel.

Thirdly, the corollary of a distinctive culture is a distinctive language. Beginning with the Harlem School, the linguistic texture of the Negro novel has been greatly influenced by the rhythms and inflections of Negro speech, and especially by jive, the colorful argot of the urban Negro. The certain mark of the Harlem School, for example, are the terms "ofay" (white man) and "dickty" (high-toned Negro). In the early Negro novel a "professor" was a school teacher (inflated achievement); in the Harlem School novel a "professor" is strictly the third party to a rickety piano and a precarious glass of beer. Even in the 1920's jive had developed to a point where one novelist felt compelled to add a "Glossary of Contemporary Harlemese" to his work, in order to make himself intelligible to a mixed audience.

Finally, the Harlem School was more interested in interpreting Negro culture than in pleading the cause of racial justice. Having affirmed the existence of a distinctive Negro culture, they chose to write novels of Negro life rather than novels dealing with relations between the races. Racial tension, though present, is a muted note in the Renaissance novel. Renaissance Harlem is a place of love and laughter, not of struggle and oppression. By insisting that the novel is an art form and not primarily an instrument of racial protest the Harlem School broke cleanly with a long tradition of overt propaganda and moral appeal. This conscious abandonment of "protest" literature freed the Negro novelist from a false conception of racial loyalty which has constantly threatened to strangle his art.

In the last analysis it was a distinctly "racial" atmosphere which gave the Harlem School its revolutionary character. It was not so much that these writers formed a literary coterie in Harlem, nor even that Harlem was a favorite setting for their novels, but rather that a Harlemesque *quality* permeated their work. In the best instances this quality was more than an exotic veneer; it expressed a unique and partially non-Western way of life. The Harlem School, in a word, discovered the advantages of straddling two worlds. These advantages may seem more tangible after a concrete discussion of the novels. . . .

VI: HUNGER: DEPRESSION AND NEW DEAL,

1929–1941

Law and Order

• In 1931 a group of Negro men, nearly all teenagers, were arrested in Alabama and charged with criminal assault. They had allegedly boarded a freight train, forcing several white males to jump off, and then raped two white women who were riding the rails in search of work. During the Depression, when unemployment hit America's youth hardest, freight trains filled with jobless youths were common. The accused blacks, called the Scottsboro Boys after the Alabama town where one of the trials took place, soon learned what "Alabama justice" meant. The case attracted national attention, however, and thus the expected lynching or, what was by then more common, a quick conviction and execution, did not take place. The Communist-dominated International Labor Defense (ILD) became the blacks' legal spokesman, defeating the NAACP's attempt to step in to the case. Although one of the women later repudiated her testimony, Alabama juries returned guilty verdicts that led to years of appeals and litigation. All the while, the Scottsboro Boys remained in prison. Dan Carter's description of the social psychology of white Alabama illuminates graphically and tragically the dual impact of racism, the degradation of the oppressed, and the psychotic instability of the oppressor.

Whether it was the pattern of violence described by Wilbur J. Cash or the "plague of poverty" which plunged one native son into despair, Alabama's eccentricities were those of the entire South, sometimes diminished, more often than not magnified. The state's proud but often unlettered hillbillies of the lower Appalachians little resembled their economic counterparts, the poor white class of the Black Belt, let alone the plantation pseudo-aristocrats. One fixation, however, united

From Dan T. Carter, *Scottsboro: A Tragedy of the American South* (Baton Rouge: Louisiana State University Press, 1969), 104–9, 112–23, 128–36 (footnotes omitted). Reprinted by permission of the publisher.

these people. The Georgia-born historian Ulrich Bonnell Phillips had described it in 1928. Whether expressed with the "frenzy of a demagogue or maintained with a patrician's quietude," he observed, the common resolve of all white Southerners was that the region "shall be and remain a white man's country."

Between 1865 and 1900, white Southerners created an elaborate system of prohibitions for the Negro. However thorough and degrading in their totality, most of these restraints were minor and involved only social conventions which symbolized the subservience of the subordinate caste. There was one restriction far more significant. In 1932 the Winston-Salem, North Carolina, *Journal* noted that "in the South it has been traditional . . . that its white womanhood shall be held inviolate by an 'inferior race.'" And it mattered not whether the woman was a "spotless virgin or a 'nymph de pavé.'" There could be no extenuating circumstances. If a white woman was willing to swear that a Negro either raped or attempted to rape her, "we see to it that the Negro is executed," declared Arkansas poet John Gould Fletcher. For most violations of the color bar, a Southern Negro would be punished by a stern admonition, at most a whipping. For the rape of a white woman, however, there was only one punishment: death.

In 1900 the Scottsboro boys probably would have been removed from their jail cells and summarily hanged on the nearest tree, no matter how firmly the local sheriff protested. Because of their forbearance in allowing the defendants to have their day in court, the citizens of Jackson County "swelled with pride," reported the correspondent of the Chattanooga *Times.* They had "snubbed 'Judge Lynch'" and remained calm when confronted with "the most outrageous crime in the annals of the state." . . .

To the consternation of Alabamians, "outsiders" did not praise their forebearance and calmness. More characteristic was the disgusted outcry of a New York college student. "What kind of a mindless savage are you?" he asked Judge A. E. Hawkins. "Is condemning eight teen-agers to death on the testimony of two white prostitutes your idea of 'enlightened' Alabama justice?" State officials initially dismissed as cranks those who wrote the handful of letters protesting the guilty verdicts. But the amount of mail increased rather than diminished in the days after the trial until Governor Miller reported that he was receiving a half dozen protests a day. . . .

The first public protest that Alabamians read in their newspapers was George Maurer's April 8 telegram to Judge Hawkins and his later message to Governor Miller. It was difficult to tell whether the contents or the tone of the ILD communications most offended Alabamians. White Southerners prided themselves on the fact that they were "raised polite." Rudeness was an egregious social error not to be tolerated by a social equal, and certainly not by an inferior or "outsider." Maurer had written, "We demand that you release the Scottsboro defendants immediately. The masses of black and white workers will hold you personally responsible for the safety of the nine black workers you have ruthlessly railroaded to the electric chair." . . .

Even the Birmingham *News*, Alabama's self-styled advocate of "moderation" on racial issues, joined the resentful chorus. "It is difficult to speak with patience of the attitude of the International Labor Defense toward the trial at Scottsboro . . ." said the *News*. Northerners should be grateful that local officials thwarted mob violence and observed "all the legal forms." . . .

There were exceptions to this reaction. William Terry Couch of the University of North Carolina noted acidly that "every gang of thieves and cut-throats regards the law-abiding citizen as an outsider." But most Southerners, whether avowed liberals or racial demagogues, believed that outsiders could never understand, and therefore should not question, the racial policy of the South. . . .

The main problem with Northerners, noted the dean of Mississippi's Blue Mountain College, was that they seemed unable to understand that the Negro race was an inferior one. No Southern white man, rich or poor, educated or ignorant, doubted this, "because the truth of it is incontestable." Even when the Negro was taught to read and write, he remained a "creature of the jungles." J. M. McCary of Anniston, Alabama, argued that no "native African of unmixed descent was ever educated." Had men like W. E. B. Du Bois, Booker T. Washington, and George Washington Carver been white and made the same achievements, they would have remained obscure. But simply because they had "enough Caucasian brain transmitted to them from white parentage to grasp and maintain a little education they are held up and looked up to as representing their 'race.'" Nor was there any hope for the future. American Negroes had been in contact with European civilization for "hundreds of years and save through infusion of blood, they have not lost a single one of their ape-like characteristics nor developed the slightest shade of mentality." . . .

Should Northerners challenge this interpretation of the Negro's place in Southern society, the region had a perfect historical justification for its attitude: the post-Civil War period. Reconstruction was the alpha and omega of Southerners' attempts to justify their treatment of the Negro. Even nonracists accepted the validity of the Reconstruction totem. . . . According to Alabama historian Frank L. Owsley, Reconstruction in the South "probably had no counterpart in the history of the world." Radical leaders allowed, even encouraged, their black followers "to commit universal pillage, murder and rape." The result was "the most abominable phase barbarism had assumed since the dawn of civilization." . . .

. . . Alabamians and their neighbors saw nothing wrong with the Scottsboro deliberations. Even as the trials ended, P. W. Campbell of the *Jackson County Sentinel* predicted that "over the country there will be many people who . . . will cry that prejudice ruled." He adamantly denied this. The boys were given "every protection and every right of the law for defense. . . ."

Far from being concerned about the precipitous rapidity of the indictment and conviction, the press singled this aspect out for special praise. "Alabama is to be commended upon the dispatch with which this matter was disposed of," said the Chattanooga *Times* at the conclusion of the trials. "If justice were uniformly as swift as it was at Scottsboro, hotheads would take the law into their hands much less frequently." . . .

Part of the difficulty was that the Scottsboro trials, whatever their imperfections, were a genuine step forward. A substantial number of white Southerners believed that the rope was necessary to check the Negro. "The system is a harsh one," observed the Winston-Salem *Journal,* but it was the only way to prevent "racial amalgamation among the lower strata of society." And if Southerners condoned racial degeneration among the lower classes "it may creep upward." A University of Florida professor interviewed ten male students in his classes on their attitudes toward lynching. Nine of them condoned extra-legal execution in the case of Negroes accused of raping white women. . . .

White Southern moderates usually came from the South's upper or upper middle class, and they had a ready explanation for racial injustice. As Clarence Cason argued, "social station" determined the Southerner's attitude toward the Negro. "A warm and personal connection with black retainers is a part of the family tradition of those Southerners who are linked with the ante-bellum squirearchy." Admittedly this did not help the Negro in his more "radical social aims," but it guarded him from "actual cruelty and flagrant injustice." The primary offender was the "poor white." Generations of battling for marginal existence had narrowed his outlook and made him illogically prejudiced. . . .

This explanation conveniently absolved white Southern moderates from ultimate responsibility. In contrast they prided themselves on their efforts on behalf of the Negro. They protested lynching and, to a lesser extent, such inequities as economic persecution and educational inequalities. Occasionally, a particularly courageous Southerner even objected to the political disfranchisement of the Negro. From 1900 to 1930, the number of lynchings gradually decreased from more than a hundred to less than a dozen annually. Beginning in 1930, however, the number rose to an average of almost twenty per year. Even when officials rescued the accused from the mob's vengeance, he seldom obtained impartial justice in the courts. Southerners had earlier discovered that lynchings were untidy and created a bad press. The possibility of a federal antilynching law also acted as a mild restraint. As a result, lynchings were increasingly replaced by situations in which the Southern legal system prostituted itself to the mob's demand. Responsible officials begged would-be lynchers to "let the law take its course," thus tacitly promising that there would be a quick trial and the death penalty. As Arthur F. Raper, author of several works on lynching, observed, such proceedings "retained the essence of mob murder, shedding only its outward forms."

By placing their emphasis on thwarting lynchings and maintaining the legal formalities, Southern leaders created a dilemma. "In the beginning of our [interracial] work, patience and forbearance was urged," declared Mrs. J. F. Hooper, a member of the Alabama Interracial Commission. This had been rewarded by the absence of a lynching Scottsboro. Now the outcry over the results of the legal trial presented a new challenge. "It is a problem that never confronted us before and it is hard to get the proper perspective," she noted. "Just as we adjust our thinking and act on one line of cooperation and justice, something new comes up to confront us."

The Scottsboro Case involved more than the usual question of legal formalities: it went to the heart of the race question in the South and demanded of the white Southern liberal that he take a stand on more fundamental questions than whether the letter of the law had been observed. In the context of Southern social thought in the 1930's, it required a measure of radicalism. And radicalism was the last thing Southern interracial leaders wanted. . . .

Gunnar Myrdal overstated his case when he argued in 1941 that the South was "exceptional in Western nonfascist civilization since the Enlightenment in that *it lacks nearly every trace of radical thought.*" His thesis, however, was essentially correct. On the surface, it would appear that there were relatively large numbers of Southerners who were caustic critics of their region. In the 1920's, for example, three Southern newspaper editors won the Pulitzer Prize for attacks on the Ku Klux Klan. Editorial prizes went to the Charleston *News and Courier* for an editorial on the decline of Southern statesmanship and to the Norfolk *Virginian Pilot* for a campaign against lynching. But without exception, these critics attacked evils from a conservative stance, and none could by any stretch of the imagination be termed radical. A handful of liberals, primarily located around academic institutions such as the University of North Carolina, were tolerated and occasionally respected because of their national prominence. But they remained such a minority that they became, in Myrdal's words, "inclined to stress the need for patience and to exalt the cautious approach, the slow change, the organic nature of social growth." Most remained aloof from direct involvement in Southern social problems. Those who did not saw so little hope for clear-cut victories that they avoided a direct confrontation with controversial issues whenever possible. Their strategy focused around persuading their less advanced white neighbors to accept changes without really understanding what had taken place.

Probably the majority of Southerners involved in interracial work fancied themselves as intellectual descendants of the "old aristocracy." They saw the South's racial problem as an essentially one-to-one (and servant to master) proposition. "If a Negro whose grandfather belonged to your grandfather gets in a jam, he comes to you, tells you about it and ceases to worry," said one Southerner. When forced to grapple with the racial dilemma in its entirety, the Southern moderates differed little from Southerners in general. They refused to accept the view that the conditions they condemned—lynching, economic and educational discrimination—were inevitable results of the South's insistence on complete segregation. . . .

The artificial, elaborately polite and limited contacts between the two races perpetuated the illusion that Southern Negroes were happy with their lot. Southern Negroes (at least those who met occasionally with white leaders) found it expedient to acquiesce in the status quo. When the Alabama Interracial Commission issued a position paper on the Scottsboro case in the summer of 1931, it assured white Alabamians that Negroes "of wide contacts among their people" testified that they had never known more pleasant and harmonious relations between black and white. Interracial leaders of the Deep South had two goals, segregation and justice, and it seldom occurred to most of them that the two might be incompatible. . . .

To the fears of race and sex was added the phobia of communism. Moderate Alabamians repeatedly insisted that most of the animosity aroused by the case was not against the defendants' color, but against their red backers. . . .

It is difficult to judge how much of this resentment was real and how much was feigned. Alabamians had a penchant for using "anti-communism" as a weapon against undesirables. "Whomping the reds" was a more respectable national pastime than "nigger-baiting," noted one cynical observer. Alabama industrial leaders, for example, had early seized upon the "red" issue in order to discredit all unionism just as they earlier had incited racial hostilities in an effort to split Negro and white labor unionists. Even the Alabama AFL, a bitter enemy of the Communists, noted that the "reds" had become convenient scapegoats for all unrest in Alabama during the Depression. The large industrialists had raved about the Communists, declared the *Southern Labor Review*, so that the people of Alabama would overlook the real causes of their trouble.

Alabamians were unanimous, however, in their firm conviction that the Communists had seized the Scottsboro Case for purely mercenary motives. If the reds think they can use the friends of any victim of public or private action, then they begin to "bellow and stink," said the Montgomery *Advertiser*'s Grover Cleveland Hall. "Otherwise, all children under ten in this hated capitalistic republic could be chloroformed like surplus kittens without exciting a murmur of protest from any Communist agitator. . . ." . . .

In the summer of 1931 a series of events confirmed the direst predictions of Alabamians who argued that the Scottsboro Case was a dangerous vehicle of Communist agitation. In late 1930, a young Communist, Donald Burke, had opened an office for the Communist Party, USA, in Birmingham. He organized a few meetings, distributed handbills and leaflets, and sporadically published a newspaper called the *Southern Worker*. Birmingham police periodically raided Burke's office and arrested him, but they were never able to hold him permanently on a vagrancy charge because he could show evidence of employment. Burke concentrated on the Negro district of the city which had been hardest hit by the Depression, but police continuously disrupted Party meetings and intimidated the few Negroes who attended. The Scottsboro Case renewed the Party's hopes that it could organize a significant number of Negroes in the area, and three new assistants joined Burke in his office. Despite repeated threats, ILD representatives distributed leaflets in Scottsboro, Huntsville, Paint Rock, and other areas of Alabama, calling on white and Negro workers to "smash the Scottsboro lynch verdict." . . .

. . . A handful of Communist organizers moved quietly into the rural areas of a few of the Deep South states in the summer of 1931. They made one of their greatest efforts at organizing the "oppressed black peasantry" in Tallapoosa County, Alabama, an impoverished cotton-growing county in central Alabama. Here white and Negro tenants lived in separate but equal squalor. Annually, per capita education expenditures for whites were less than twenty-five dollars, while the budget for Negro education was negligible. Yet the deprivation was not so pronounced as in some of the Black Belt counties such as Dallas, Lowndes, and Greene. And by rural standards of the period, race relations were better than average. Despite the fact that one-third of the county's 31,000 residents were Negroes, there had not been a lynching during the twentieth century. . . .

[*The author then describes the efforts of an integrated team of Communist organizers to form a Negro sharecroppers union, and the violent reactions, physically and in the press, which suppressed the movement. Eds.*]

Not one Alabama newspaper pointed out that, far from being a bloody Negro race riot, it was the whites who formed mobs and terrorized the countryside. The only violence by a Negro was Grey's shooting of the sheriff and deputy, the act of a single individual. Instead, the press and local officials seemed intent on proving to the satisfaction of everyone that the local Negroes were bent on raping and killing the whites of the community. The real crime of the hapless Negroes was simply their effort to organize. Local whites correctly saw this as a threat to the status quo. Any effort to give the Negro tenant a voice in the renting and sharecropping contracts and a role in determining wages was essentially "revolutionary." At heart, Tallapoosa white citizens knew that the movement also threatened the existing biracial relationship. Thus they were unduly concerned about the sharecroppers' stepping "out of their place" in protesting the Scottsboro verdict. This was "white man's business" and of no concern to black tenants. But none of the major Alabama newspapers mentioned in any way the stark deprivation of Tallapoosa Negro tenants which had led them to join the sharecroppers' union in the first place.

The Tallapoosa County furor had scarcely subsided before Alabamians received evidence of further consequences from the infamous Scottsboro Case. Late on the afternoon of August 4 two sisters and a friend from prominent Birmingham families were on their way home after an afternoon movie. As they slowed for a narrow bridge, an armed Negro leaped onto the running board of their car and forced them to follow a narrow winding road to a deserted wooded area just outside the city limits near Leeds, Alabama. The man first raped and then "harangued" the three girls concerning the way in which white people had mistreated his people. When Augusta Williams, one of his victims, distracted him for a moment, her sister, Nell, lunged for the pistol. The assailant began firing wildly and seriously wounded the two Williams girls and killed their young friend, Jennie Wood. Several hours after the shooting, Augusta died, but her pretty younger sister carefully described their attacker from the hospital bed where she lay. He was in his middle thirties, she said, soot black, short and stocky, with a "Charley Chaplin mustache." He appeared to be from "up North" and "very educated," she said, but he apparently knew his way around the area. She was vague about what he had said during the two hours, but she repeatedly described his remarks as a "radical harangue."

. . . One Birmingham newspaper called for "continuous offensive action" until the "negro madman, or fiend incarnate" was arrested and brought to justice. Birmingham citizens responded enthusiastically by bombing a Negro's barber shop and firing upon a group of Negroes as they stood quietly on a sidewalk. Self-styled "deputies" made house-to-house searches of the Negro homes in the area until the News had to call for a moratorium on the "sporadic outbreaks . . . against the persons and property of Negro citizens."

The News believed the tragedy could be traced to the fact that the culprit had been corrupted by outside Communists. "If this is one of the outgrowths of Communism on these shores; if this is the aim of the propaganda of that doctrine, then Southerners and all Americans . . . who understand the inequalities of the races . . . must by every possible means lance out of the social body these infamous and unnatural teachings." Authorities became doubly concerned when several of the unauthorized posses uncovered "radical literature" in the Negro homes they searched. Four days after the attack, Sheriff Hawkins arrested Harry Jackson of Birmingham's Communist Party office and held him on an open charge. Hawkins implied there was some connection between Jackson's propaganda efforts and the shooting and told reporters he had formed a special "anti-red squad" composed of four new deputies. They would spend all their time uncovering Communist cell meetings and "breaking them up." . . .

With public opinion in Alabama already stirred to "fever heat" by the Scottsboro Case and the Camp Hill uprising, the Birmingham shooting produced a "maddening atmosphere," said Howard Kester. In the *New Masses*, Norman MacLeod described white Alabamians' fears of a Negro revolt. Northerners were arrested and searched for literature whenever they passed through the small towns of the state. Whites were tense, worried, almost hysterical. . . .

Other Alabamians were concerned, but their fears only strengthened their resolve to see the Scottsboro boys executed. "I see from the newspapers that you have received a number of threats to release the Scottsboro rapists 'or else,' " said one Alabamian. "I hope that this will not deter you from your duty in seeing that the sentences are carried through." As long as these "black fiends" remained alive, they would be "used by the reds to incite our colored people to riot, rape and kill." . . .

The shooting of the two girls was a chilling dress rehearsal for the problems the Scottsboro boys faced. Approximately two months after the incident Miss Williams, fully recovered, was riding through downtown Birmingham when she excitedly pointed to a Negro man walking quietly down the sidewalk. He was the assailant, she declared. Her brother, Dent Williams, pulled a pistol from the glove compartment and took Willie Peterson into custody. When authorities began a thorough investigation, however, a number of disturbing facts emerged. In the first place, Peterson did not in any way resemble the description of the assailant given by Miss Williams and her sister before she died. He was in his middle thirties, but, far from being short and stocky, he was gaunt and emaciated, his sallow face mirroring a four-year fight with tuberculosis. He had never worn a mustache and his skin color was light chocolate instead of black. Moreover, a half dozen neighbors were willing to swear that they had seen him on the opposite side of town at the time the shootings took place.

In the face of this contradictory evidence, Jefferson County's Sheriff Hawkins tried to dissuade Miss Williams, but once she had decided she had the guilty party, she refused to retract her identification. When it became apparent that Miss Williams had made a mistake, her brother, Dent Williams, asked the sheriff to arrange one further meeting at which his sister might be sure she had the right man. As Williams and his sister entered the interrogation room, county officials searched him; but as soon as Peterson was brought into the room, Williams slipped his hand into his sister's purse, removed a pistol, and shot the thin Negro three times before the deputies could disarm him.

Miraculously, Peterson recovered, but the aftermath of the shooting was a grotesque parody of Southern justice. State officials, knowing full well that Peterson was innocent, went ahead and indicted and tried him as soon as he was able to leave his hospital bed. On the stand, Miss Williams' testimony was so filled with contradictions and inconsistencies that the first jury was unable to reach a verdict after fourty-four hours. The International Labor Defense offered to come to the aid of Peterson, but on the advice of white interracial leaders in Birmingham, he stuck with his local court-appointed attorney. The second time, the jury deliberated only twenty minutes before returning with a guilty verdict. Peterson was sentenced to die in the electric chair. . . .

. . . As one Birmingham attorney said, "Miss Williams has very surely picked the wrong negro. The officials of the state of Alabama know this. The solicitor knows it. . . ." And yet they had gone ahead. This far would Alabamians go in defense of the caste system. Rather than humiliate Miss Williams by contradicting her story, the state of Alabama was willing to convict an innocent man. The "honor" of one white woman was more important than the life's blood of a black man, said the Birmingham *Reporter*. A Negro accused of rape by a white woman had not the "chance of a sheep-killing dog to establish his innocence or to get the benefit of any doubt." Ultimately, through the personal pleas of Alexander and a number of Alabamians (including Sheriff Hawkins) Governor Miller was persuaded to commute the sentence to life imprisonment in Kilby Prison where Peterson died several years later of tuberculosis. Dent Williams was never indicted for the shooting of Peterson.

The Scottsboro boys had one advantage over Peterson. Their accusers were not from Alabama's finest families. Their liabilities, however, far outweighed this one asset. During the summer of 1931, for many Americans, the Scottsboro Case became almost a talisman, a symbol of the daily injustice Southern whites inflicted upon the Negroes of the region. In white Alabama, it also became a symbol of the horrors of communism and the accompanying dreaded "social equality." Most of the concern was groundless. Communist activity in Alabama was ineffectual and extremely limited; the state's news media exaggerated the strength of the movement all out of proportion to its real significance. The Communist press also encouraged these inaccurate estimations because it gave them a facade of strength with which to appeal for further support. Moreover, there was little proof of any connection between the shooting at Leeds and "Communist infiltration," let alone between the attack and the Scottsboro Case. But Carl Carmer captured the attitude of many Alabamians when he talked with an old Harvard classmate from the northern part of the state. "I might have been for acquittin' them at the first trial," his friend declared, "but now after all this stink's been raised, we've got to hang 'em." The friend pointed to the Leeds incident and related how Peterson had talked to the girls "about how white folks oppress the niggers and about Communism." That would not have occurred, he said, "if it hadn't been for this God-damn Scottsboro business and I'm for seeing that it doesn't happen again."

The Croppers' Dilemma

• Neither the Great Migration of the first quarter of this century nor the natural increase of urban Negro population had yet overturned the black demographic balance. Most Negroes still lived on the land when the United States entered the Great Depression of 1929–40, and most of them were poor. Nevertheless the Depression did more than merely make the black cropper poorer. Programs initiated in the 1930's, some of them part of government recovery and relief legislation, undercut the sharecroppers' reason for being. Many black croppers and tenants were thrown off the land. Following the pattern of previous migrants, they flowed into northern cities, woefully unprepared to cope with urban conditions. In a landmark volume on the history and sociology of black America, An American Dilemma, the Swedish scholar Gunnar Myrdal summarized the findings and opinions of a corps of social scientists who studied Negro life under his direction during the late 'thirties and early 'forties. Myrdal's analysis of the changes in southern agricultural society during the New Deal—of what, in effect, became an American enclosure movement—remains pertinent today, since the process by which an uprooted black peasantry moves from countryside to city continues without abatement.

SOUTHERN AGRICULTURE AS A PROBLEM

The main facts of rural Southern poverty and the distress of the rural Negro people in the South have been well-known for a long time. The plantation-tenant system is one of America's "public scandals." . . .

The revolutionary changes within the last decade—and particularly the effects of the A.A.A. on rural Negroes—are less well-known. We

Abridged from Gunnar Myrdal, *An American Dilemma*, pp. 230–34, 237–38, 240–49, 251, 253–54, 256–60, 265–66 (footnotes omitted). Copyright © 1944, 1962 by Harper & Row, Publishers, Incorporated. Reprinted by permission of the publishers.

shall leave those latest developments to be analyzed in the next chapter. In this chapter we want, mainly by way of presenting some illustrative quantitative relations, to give a short survey of the familiar topics: the plight of the rural South and of the Negro farmer.

OVER-POPULATION AND SOIL EROSION

Rural farm areas in the United States in 1940 had a population of about 30,000,000. More than half of this population, or over 16,000,-000, was in the South; and over one-fourth of the Southern farm population (around 4,500,000) was Negro. But the South had only 35 per cent of all land in farms in the country, and the value of this farm land, as well as of the buildings on the land, the farm implements and machinery, constituted but 28 per cent of the national figure. Only 8 per cent of the Southern farm land was operated by Negro owners, tenants, and croppers, and their share in the value of Southern farms, buildings, implements, and machinery was equally small. For the rest, Negroes participated in the Southern agricultural economy only as wage laborers, at low wages and usually without the assurance of year-round employment.

The import of these broad facts is as simple as it is significant. They are behind all the rural poverty of the South. The agricultural South is over-populated, and this over-population affects Negroes much more than whites. This applies particularly to the Old South, including the Delta district, which contains the main concentration of Negroes. In this Black Belt the over-population has—on the whole—been steadily increasing. "Since 1860 the amount of land in southeastern farms has remained stationary, new lands being cleared about as rapidly as old land was exhausted," while the number of male agricultural workers in the same area rose from around 1,132,000 in 1860 to 2,102,000 in 1930.

A cultural heritage from times of pioneering, colonization, and slavery makes the conditions even worse than can be visualized by the ratio of population to land alone. The early colonists and the later land speculators did not have to economize in their use of the land. To the *ante-bellum* plantation owners, it was the slaves that represented the main capital—not the land. This set a pattern also for other Southern farmers. To become rich from the land was to become a plantation owner and a slave owner—not to care for the soil. This tradition has continued until the present time. In the fall of 1938 the writer traveled for two days through a beautiful forest in Tennessee. The woods were burning everywhere. The smoke often made driving difficult. Local newspapers told about small organized forces which were out to fight the fires. From the highways they were nowhere to be seen. There were plenty of people around in several places, but few, if any, seemed to care much about the fires.

Experiences like this make it possible, for even the stranger, to understand the psychology of soil erosion, soil mining, and "selling the soil in annual installments." A sample study made in 1933 suggested that one-third of the Southern land was eroded and that at least half of all eroded land in the country was in the South. . . .

TENANCY, CREDIT AND COTTON

The literature, today as earlier, contains excellent descriptions of how the plantation system, tenancy, and the one-sided cultivation of cotton and corn—and, in some areas, tobacco, rice, or sugar—have contributed to soil erosion; how the credit system, by favoring cash crops, has made it difficult to break away from the vicious circle; how this credit-cotton-tenancy-erosion circle has become loaded downward through some of its own major effects: poverty for most, economic insecurity for all, widespread ignorance, low health standards, relative lack of an enterprising spirit, high birth rates and large families.

The extent to which Southern cash-crop production is based on tenancy is indicated by the following figures. Almost three-fourths of all Southern cotton farms and more than half of the crop-specialty farms (tobacco, potatoes, peanuts, and so on) were, in 1929, operated by tenants. About two-thirds of all tenants in the South, and almost three-fourths of the croppers, worked on cotton farms. Of the full owners, on the other hand, less than one-third had farms where cotton accounted for 40 per cent or more of the gross income. Most of the other two-thirds owned farms which were characterized as crop-specialty, general or self-sufficing.

Negro farmers have always been dependent on the cotton economy to a much greater extent than have been the white farmers in the South. By 1929 three out of four Negro farm operators, as against two out of five white farmers, received at least 40 per cent of their gross income from cotton. Although not more than about one-tenth of the Southern farm land was cultivated by Negro owners, tenants and croppers, almost one-third of the total output in cotton was produced on this Negro-operated land. In addition, an unknown, but probably considerable, quantity of cotton was produced by Negro wage labor on holdings operated by white farmers. The importance of cotton growing for the Negro farmer can thus hardly be over-estimated.

In the main, cotton is cultivated by means of a primitive and labor-consuming agricultural technique which has not changed much since slavery. Cotton is largely responsible for the fact that the Southeast alone had to pay more than half of the national bill for commercial fertilizers. One-third of the national total for all kinds of fertilizer was expended on cotton farms. Cotton growing, as any one-sided agriculture—if it is not lifted up by high techniques to a level where intelligence is constantly used and prosperity secured—has also psychological effects: it "limits interests . . . limits spiritual growth, makes people narrow, single-grooved, helpless." It invites child labor and causes retardation in schools. It favors large families.

The wide fluctuations of the price of cotton—which seem to have become more frequent after 1914, due to wars, inflation, deflation, as well as intensified competition from other countries—make cotton a most hazardous crop, and the farmers who specialize in cotton run extraordinarily heavy risks which are outside their intelligent control. The gambling tradition has been hard to overcome, although almost everybody seems to know that no solid material culture can ever be built on the poor man's speculation. But more fundamentally, the continued cultivation of cotton is called forth—as highly labor-consuming, simple in technique, and easily supervised—by the plantation and tenancy system; or, from another point of view, by over-population and tenancy, and—as a cash crop—by the dependence of Southern agriculture on short-term credit.

The peculiar credit system of the rural South has often been analyzed. It has its historical roots in the slavery economy and, later, in the emergence of the plantation system in the impoverished South after the Civil War. Since then the rural South has been greatly dependent on outside credit both because of the low standards of income and saving in the region and because of the comparatively high requirements on operating capital for cotton growing. The wide fluctuation of cotton prices and farm incomes have added their influence to make lending abnormally risky and, consequently, to make loans expensive. Also, from the point of view of business administration, the organization of banking and credit was most inadequate, and it remained so because of the low plane of political life in the South and the lack of active desire and ability to create large-scale cooperative organizations.

As part of the federal agricultural policy, great improvements have lately been made by the organization of new credit agencies. But still credit is expensive and difficult to get in the rural South, and this is undoubtedly part of the explanation for the insufficient investment in land and buildings and for the slowness of mechanization. To the tenants, credit pressures mean usurious interest rates charged by planters and merchants for advances on food and farming necessities. For the agricultural structure as a whole, credit pressures—themselves partly caused by the dependence on cotton growing—mean a constant stimulus to keep the land in cotton.

THE NEGRO LANDOWNER

The story of the Negro in agriculture would have been a rather different one if the Negro farmer had had greater opportunity to establish himself as an independent owner. In that case he would have become more firmly attached to the soil. He would have known that he worked for his own benefit, that he had a real chance to improve his level of living by his own efforts. "All that is now wanted to make the negro a fixed and conservative element in American society is to give him encouragement to, and facilities for, making himself, by his own exertions, a small landowner," wrote Sir George Campbell in his survey of the South and the Negro problem in the late 'seventies.

There was a time when it really looked as if the rural Negro had some chance of eventually getting established on an ownership basis. True, the development was generally slow, but it seemed to go in the right direction. The number of Negro farm homes in the United States that were owned by their occupants had by 1900 reached a figure of 193,000—constituting about 25 per cent of all Negro farm homes. This percentage marks the peak of the proportion of landowners in the Negro farm population.

The absolute increase continued for some time, but at a slower rate. The absolute number of colored farm owners in the South reached, in 1910, a maximum of about 220,000. After 1920 it gradually declined, and it dropped to 174,000 by 1940. Of all Southern states with any appreciable Negro farm population, only Virginia and Florida showed a majority of owners among the Negro farm operators in 1940. But even in the Virginian stronghold, Negro ownership was weakening, in that the number of colored farm owners had declined by not less than one-third since 1910. And Florida depends relatively less on tenants and relatively more on wage labor than do other states in the South, so that even there but a minority of the Negro farm population resided on their own places.

There are some general factors to be accounted for in this context. On the one hand, the low land values in the South and the low investment in land improvements, houses, and machines should make landownership easier to attain. On the other hand, the inadequate organization of banking and credit, referred to above, works against both the acquiring and the holding of land. Another general factor making landownership, when it is attained, more precarious than it needs to be, is the old-fashioned system of local real estate taxation, which the South shares with the rest of the nation. This means that a landowner does not get a corresponding decrease in his taxation in a year when his crop has failed or his income drops because of a price fall. The dependence on hazardous cotton growing, of course, makes this institutional deficiency more detrimental to the Southern landowners.

More specifically, in interpreting the reversal in the trend of Negro ownership, Southeastern agriculture after 1910, and particularly during the first years of the 'twenties, was hit by the boll weevil and by the general upheaval caused by the War and the post-war depression. The owner group, of course, should have been less affected than the tenant group, as far as living standards are concerned, but the latter had no ownership to lose. The fact that even the number of white owners in the South declined by more than one-tenth between 1920 and 1930 (from almost 1,400,000 to 1,250,000) suggests that conditions in general were unfavorable for the small farm owner. Between 1930 and 1940 (when the number of white owners was 1,384,000), on the other hand, there was a corresponding large increase in the number of white owners, whereas colored ownership continued to decline. This, however, scarcely means that the prospects for economic success in small ownership had become any brighter. As will be shown in the next chapter, it indicates rather that white owners, or those who were able to get into that class, were the ones who had most opportunity to stay on the land, "if, in view of the paucity of migratory outlets, they preferred to do that."

Data on size of farm, acreage values, and farm values give a rather good idea of how marginal the existence of the small owner-operators in the South tends to be. They show, further, that this is particularly true about Negro owners. It seems, finally, that their relative position has become even more unfavorable than it was a couple of decades ago. Land operated by croppers, particularly Negro croppers, has the highest average value per acre. This, as we have said, is due to the fact that plantations, by and large, are located on much of the best land of the South, leaving less of first choice than of second and third choice land to the middle-sized and small owner-operators. Cash tenants and share renters used to take an intermediate position, but are now pretty close to the owner-operators in this respect. White owners showed a higher average acreage value in 1940 ($27.27) than colored owners ($23.89). The decline in acreage value since 1920 was in every tenure group less pronounced for whites than for Negro operators.

Size of farm increases with tenure status. In every case, however, Negroes have much smaller farms than whites. The consequence is that the average size of Negro owner-operated farms (60.4 acres) is about the same as for white sharecroppers (58.9 acres). The mean value of land and buildings of the farm operated by colored owners ($1,443) is lower even than that of the white sharecropper's plot ($1,908). The value of implements and machinery that the colored owner has ($90) is only a fraction of that which the white owner has at his disposal ($322).

HISTORICAL REASONS FOR THE RELATIVE LACK OF NEGRO FARM OWNERS

Even apart from the general economic trends in Southern agriculture, there are several reasons why the Negro has been unable to make a better showing as an independent farm owner.

There is his background in slavery, and the fact that he scarcely ever has been encouraged to show much initiative or been taught that it pays to look after oneself rather than to be dependent. More often he has been given to understand that his racial status provides an excuse for not being able to shift for himself, and that modest acceptance of a low position would rate a reward bigger than that offered for courageous attempts to reach a higher position. In the rural South he has certainly not enjoyed much of that kind of legal security which is a necessary condition for successful entrepreneurship; at any rate, he has had far less of it than the whites with whom he has had to compete. His best security has been to become associated with a white person of some status in the community; and that, in most cases, has presupposed an employer-employee or landlord-tenant relationship. Since his earnings as a farmhand or tenant have always tended to be lower than those of white workers, he has had less chance to save enough money for the purpose of buying land. The belief that he is racially inferior and the social isolation between the two castes have also affected the credit rating even of those individual Negroes who otherwise would have been excellent risks. His educational opportunities in the rural South have been extremely poor.

Although the influence of such general conditions cannot be measured, there is scarcely any doubt about their being highly significant. In addition, however, a number of specific factors have been operative. Some of them have already been touched upon in the preceding chapters. There is, in the first place, the fact that rural Negroes, to a great extent, are concentrated on plantation areas, where comparatively few small holdings are for sale. There was no general land reform, and the Negro did not participate in the development of the West. But even in Kansas, where one of the few noteworthy attempts to organize new *post-bellum* Negro settlements was made, there were not more than a few hundred Negro owner-operators in 1940; and some of these owners probably were the descendants of persons who had been brought to Kansas as slaves. Undoubtedly the attitudes of the white settlers constituted the main cause for this lack of success. In the largely over-populated, white-dominated districts of the South, these attitudes, if anything, were still more pronounced.

There have, however, always been some small holdings for sale in the areas of Negro concentration, and more have been added to this supply as plantations tended to disintegrate. During the years immediately following the Civil War, land values were low, and that was one of the reasons why a few Negroes, along with many poor whites, managed to get into the landowning class. Some ex-slaves bought land from their former masters, and there are places where such Negro properties still constitute a large proportion of all Negro-owned farms. . . .

There has always been an active solidarity among white people to prevent Negroes from acquiring land in white neighborhoods. The visitor finds, therefore, that most often he has to get off the main road and into the backwoods if he wants to see a Negro landowner. The intensity of those attitudes on the side of the whites—which closely correspond to the attitudes behind residential segregation in the cities—seems to have been increasing toward the turn of the century. This was the time when the Jim Crow legislation was built up in the South. There actually were even sporadic attempts in the beginning of the century to institute laws in order to block Negro ownership in white rural districts. It is noteworthy that the trend toward increase of Negro landownership was halted at about the same time.

The last decade, finally, has brought a new competitive advantage to the white owner. Government regulations, which have become of great importance, no doubt have helped the Negro owner along with the white owner. The fact, however, that the local administration of the new agricultural policies is entirely, or almost entirely, in the hands of white people cannot fail to make the Negroes a relatively disfavored group. This problem will be touched upon in the next chapter.

TENANTS AND WAGE LABORERS

In 1880, 64 per cent of the Southern farms were operated by owners. The corresponding figure for 1900 had fallen to 53 per cent. By 1930 it was down to 44 per cent. A majority of the Southern operators were tenants and sharecroppers. There was a similar development in other parts of the country as well. But nowhere else did it go so far. And nowhere else did this trend have quite as serious social implications.

Behind this change are the lagging industrialization, the high rural fertility rates, and the relatively small opportunities for successful ownership in the South. Not only Negroes, but whites also, were affected by these factors. Already by 1900 there were more white than Negro tenants in Southern agriculture, and during the following three decades the number of white tenants increased by more than 400,000, or roughly 60 per cent, where as the corresponding figures for nonwhite tenants were 147,000 and 27 per cent, respectively.

There seems to have been a parallel trend in the case of wage laborers, although much less pronounced. In 1910 more than half of these workers were Negro—in 1930 less than half of them. It should be kept in mind that their status, by and large, is more insecure even than that of the sharecroppers, who, at least, are assured of year-round employment—although not always of a year-round income. This, however, does not reflect on the wage labor institution as such. If all Southern farm labor had been remunerated on a straight wage basis, the conditions would have been entirely different. A greater proportion of the wage laborers would have had year-round jobs, and these year-round employees would have known in advance for what wages they were working—something which is not true about tenants and croppers. At present most Southern agricultural wage laborers are literally "marginal." It is only at seasonal peaks that most of them can count on full employment. This circumstance, more than anything else, accounts for their inferior position.

The fact that nowadays almost two-thirds of the tenants are white has been emphasized time and again in the discussion. It does not follow, however, that white tenancy is more serious than Negro tenancy. Rather it is the other way around. We have seen that Negroes, more than whites, are concentrated in the lower tenure groups, and that in each tenure group Negroes are economically much weaker than whites. In addition, there are certain other significant differences.

It would be a mistake to believe that the plantation system and the tenant system are synonymous concepts. *The majority of all tenants do not work on plantations, but on small holdings.* In 1910, the last time an enumeration of plantations was made, it was found that 39,000 plantations, located in 325 plantation counties, had about 400,000 tenants; whereas, the total number of tenants in the South was over 1,500,000. The ratio of plantation tenants to all tenants must be still lower now, for the number of tenants has increased much more in non-plantation counties than in plantation counties. During the last decade there has even been a decrease in tenancy on the plantations. It may be, therefore, that three out of four tenants in the South today work on small holdings.

While plantation tenancy belongs to the classical subjects in the rural sociology of the South, much less scientific attention has been given to the Southern nonplantation tenant. It is certain, however, that the great majority of these small-holding tenants are white. A large number of them are related to their landlords. For all we know, their conditions, in many cases, may be similar to those of white tenants in other parts of the country, except that, more likely than not, they have to work and live under poorer circumstances, and their general status, to some extent, may have been influenced by the plantation patterns.

The majority of the plantation tenants, on the other hand, are Negro. There has been a "white infiltration" even on this mainstay of Negro tenancy, however. It even happens quite frequently that white and Negro tenants work on the same plantations, although usually not in the same capacity. White workers tend to be relatively more concentrated in the outlying districts, or on the least valuable parts of the plantations where the tenants work more independently and have a higher tenure status; whereas, Negroes more often make up the bulk of the labor force on the main part of the plantations, where they can be closely controlled and supervised by the owners or managers. . . .

THE PLANTATION TENANT

The plight of the plantation tenant has been described so often and so well that there is no need to give more than a short summary here. But a summary we must present. For, despite all scientific and reformistic publicity, these conditions are still news to a great part of the American people; as we see it, they could not otherwise have prevailed in their present form for such a long time. The subject, in a way, is a fascinating one. It is the problem of an antiquated paternalistic labor institution in the midst of modern American capitalistic society.

If we except cash tenants—who usually, but not always, can be regarded as rather independent entrepreneurs, and who make up only about one-tenth of all Negro tenants—plantation tenants are just ordinary laborers, although they are designated as farmers in the census. Their work is usually supervised, more or less regularly, by the landlord or his representative. In some cases they even work by the clock and in gangs. Their wages, however, are not determined according to supply and demand in a free labor market.

Wages are not fixed per week, per month, or per annum. Nor is the sharecropping agreement modeled after the ordinary piece-wage system. The cropper, rather, gets a share of the product. The quantity of the product depends not only on the efforts of the workers but on the conditions of the soil and on the hazards of wind and weather; and it is not the quantity of the output alone but also its price that determines the final reward for the toils of labor. The wages of the sharecroppers and share tenants, in other words, vary in such a way that there is no reason whatever to assume that they, except accidentally and occasionally, would satisfy the supply-and-demand equations of an ordinary free labor market.

While in other parts of our economic system it has been the accepted ideal that risk of investment should be directly correlated with the size of investment, the sharecropper and the share tenant—although nothing but laborers from economic and social viewpoints—have to carry a considerable share of the entrepreneur's risk. It is possible that it is this practice of hedging by spreading the risk over the whole working force which has enabled the planters to carry on the cotton crop gamble much more persistently than otherwise would have been possible. It is true that the share tenant shares in the benefit of a good crop and favorable market conditions with the landowner. It is also true that he does not have much capital of his own. If losses run so high that at the end of the year he finds himself indebted to the landlord, he may often be able—at least nowadays—to get rid of this debt simply by moving to another plantation. But many a time he may find himself having invested a full season's work without having received anything near the wages he would have earned had he been a wage laborer with full employment. On such occasions, at least, he has to face long months of semi-starvation for himself and his family. That certainly is a business risk just as much as any. And should he have any livestock or other assets, the landlord is always free to take them to cover possible debts. In nine cottons states "the landlord has the legal right to sell any and all property the tenant may have to secure payment of rent and furnishings."

Indeed, any study of the concrete details of the system will reveal that the sharecropper or share tenant usually has most of the disadvantages of being an independent entrepreneur without having hardly any of the rights that ordinarily go with such a position. Only in relatively few cases are his rights and obligations set down in a written contract. In most cases he does not sell even his own share in the cotton crop himself. According to the crop lien laws in most states, he has no right to dispose of it until he has paid to the landlord all the rent due and the advances he has received during the season. And since he cannot well do that until the crop has been sold and paid for, the landlord is legally entitled to handle all the marketing as he sees fit. Seldom is the tenant even consulted about how to sell and when.

Worse than that, however, is the general pattern of making all kinds of account-keeping a unilateral affair. The tenant usually has to take the landlord's word for what price has been obtained for the cotton, for what is the total amount of advances received from the landlord, and for what the interest on these advances is, and so on. An attempt on the part of the Negro tenant to check the accounts against his own itemized annotations—if he should have kept any (which is rarely done)—will not accomplish much, in most cases, except possibly to infuriate the landlord. The temptation to cheat the tenants at the final settlement for the year, under such circumstances, must be great. Indeed, Southern plantation owners would be unlike other human beings if they did not sometimes misuse the considerable arbitrary power they have over their tenants.

In several conversations with white planters—as also with employers of Negro labor in cities, particularly of domestics—the writer has noticed the display of a sort of moral double standard. White people of the landowning class who give the impression of being upright and honest in all their other dealings take it for granted and sometimes brag about the fact that they cheat their Negroes. On the other hand, it is equally apparent that there is a strong recognition in the South of the difficulty for a landlord to get and keep good workers if he does not have the reputation of dealing with them on a straight basis. Still, there are too many "settlement jokes" in the Southern folklore and too many statements about the matter in the literature to make a student inclined to dismiss the possibility of outright cheating. There is social significance even in the fact—which every observer will be able to confirm—that "the system leaves the Negro tenant with the *feeling* that he has not been treated justly."

The "advancing" of food, clothing, and other necessities of life is a significant part of the system. Since the tenant is ordinarily without resources—otherwise he would not be a tenant—he cannot usually wait for his wages until the crop has been harvested and sold. He has, therefore, to live on a credit basis at least during a large part of the year. . . .

This should be the place for "balancing the picture" by looking for positive aspects of the paternalistic labor relations on the Southern plantations. The system doubtless has some positive sides. Even the outsider will occasionally find some evidence of them. There are good landlords, who really try to take care of their tenants to some extent. They are the ones who get and hold the good tenants. They are rightly proud of this fact and tell the interviewer about it. Most studies contain some statement from such a plantation owner who has made the discovery that he can get the best out of his Negro tenant just by treating him decently and by appealing to his ambition to get ahead—in other words, by regarding the Negro like any other human being. Since the general standard is so low, it is not expensive to be an exceptionally good planter and have the best tenants.

Yet the fact that planters, too, are ordinary human beings, and that many of them actually are better than the system which they represent, is not high praise of the plantation system as an economic institution. Every social institution, in this way, presents a whole range of cases

—low extremes, normal cases and high extremes. Nevertheless, we can talk about the whole range as being low or high in relation to the corresponding range for alternative institutions. The benevolence of certain landlords certainly is a great help for many individual tenants. But it is, in the final analysis, nothing else than an aspect of the arbitrariness of the whole system.

It is our impression that the predominant feeling among most Negro tenants is that they can get more or less out of the landlord depending upon what kind of landlord he is, and how he is approached. But not often have they been taught to feel that they have definite rights and definite obligations, and that it is up to them to make good. Several local Farm Security officials in the South have informed us of how the inherited paternalistic attitude on the part of the planters and the corresponding attitudes of dependence, carelessness, and lack of ambition on the part of the tenants constitute the toughest problems in their work. The plantation system, in summary, fails flagrantly to meet the standards of social and economic efficiency and justice.

AGRICULTURAL TRENDS DURING THE 'THIRTIES

Of all the calamities that have struck the rural Negro people in the South in recent decades—soil erosion, the infiltration of white tenants into plantation areas, the ravages of the boll weevil, the southwestern shift in cotton cultivation—none has had such grave consequences, or threatens to have such lasting effect, as the combination of world agricultural trends and federal agricultural policy initiated during the 'thirties. These changes are revolutionizing the whole structure of Southern agricultural economy. They have already rooted out a considerable portion of the Negro farmers and made the future of the remaining group extremely problematic. . . .

THE DISAPPEARING SHARECROPPER

Up to the time when the data from the 1940 Census were released, the main emphasis in the discussion was placed upon the increase in tenancy—a trend which had been noticeable ever since the Civil War—and upon the decline in number of farm owners—which became apparent during the 'twenties. The 1940 Census, however, showed that the trends had become reversed. Tenancy was on the decline, for there were 192,000 fewer Negro and 150,000 fewer white tenants in 1940 than in 1930. Ownership, on the other hand, was on the increase in Southern agriculture, except for the Negroes.

Number of Farm Operators in the South, by Tenure and Color:
1930, 1935, and 1940
(in thousands).

Year	Owners and Managers		Tenants Other than Croppers		Croppers	
	Nonwhite	White	Nonwhite	White	Nonwhite	White
1930	183	1,250	306	709	393	383
1935	186	1,404	261	854	368	348
1940	174	1,384	208	700	299	242

The rise in ownership and decline in tenancy did not balance each other, however. The increase in number of owners occurred altogether between 1930 and 1935 and was restricted to the white group. The decrease in the total number of tenants occurred between 1935 and 1940 and was then divided between the two racial groups. Before 1935, however, white cash and share tenants seem to have become much more numerous, whereas all other tenant groups—Negro cash and share tenants as well as Negro and white croppers—had started to decline. The decrease in number of tenants during the following five years became much more pronounced and affected all four color-tenure groups.

The final results, by 1940, of all these changes were that there was a somewhat larger number of white owners than in 1930; a slightly lower number of Negro owners; a much lower number of Negro cash and share tenants, and of Negro and white croppers. The total number of croppers had declined by almost one-third (somewhat more for whites and somewhat less for Negroes), and the decrease in number of Negro cash and share tenants was at least of the same relative size. . . .

The main reason why the Negro lost out, probably, was the fact that he, much more than the white operator and worker, was dependent on the cotton economy which was hit most severely by the depression and by the falling off of foreign markets. Practically all the increase in number of farm operators as well as the total increase in farm population during the period 1930-1935 occurred outside of the cotton regions; and after that period there were no further increases of that kind. Yet, the depression by itself seems to have had much more immediate effects on income conditions than on employment, for the decline in Negro tenancy before 1935 was relatively limited compared with what was to come after that year. It seems, therefore, that *the agricultural policies, and particularly the Agricultural Adjustment program (A.A.A.), which was instituted in May, 1933, was the factor directly responsible for the drastic curtailment in number of Negro and white sharecroppers and Negro cash and share tenants. . . .*

A.A.A. AND THE NEGRO

It is something of a problem, however, that most of the reduction in cotton acreage was carried out before 1935, whereas the decrease in number of Negro and white croppers and of Negro cash and share tenants did not start to become really significant until after that year. Of course, there is nothing unnatural in a certain time-lag between acreage curtailment and effects on employment. The intensification of cultivation of the cotton land not eliminated by the A.A.A., the increase in certain other crops, and the uncertainty about the permanence in the change may have contributed to a certain delay in the reorganization of the labor force. The Supreme Court decision of 1936, invalidating the first A.A.A. program, and the actual occurrence of an all-time peak in cotton production in 1937 justifies, to a degree, the hypothesis that the change may have had the appearance to many planters of being only temporary. By letting the employees share in the reduction of income which had occurred since 1929, and by letting newly instituted rural relief agencies provide supplementary income for part of the labor force during off-seasons, it was possible for the planters to retain most of the tenants for some time.

Furthermore, it was probably not only by the acreage reduction that the A.A.A. later gave inducement to the reduction in number of tenants. Another factor, perhaps equally important, was the A.A.A. benefit payments. During the first years of the A.A.A. system there was a general complaint that landlords simply grabbed the benefit checks which they were supposed to forward to the tenants. Many of these complaints turned out to be justified—even when investigated by county committees which were almost entirely white, and on which landowners were over-represented.

These practices were, in the main, later abolished. In the last few years, benefits are paid direct to the tenants. Although the credit relations between landlord and tenant, the system of unilateral account-keeping, as well as the legal impotence of the Negro tenants, still may enable the landlord to receive a larger share of the benefits than he is supposed to get, the situation certainly has changed. As early as 1935-1936, the Consumer Purchases Study, for instance, showed that even sharecroppers were receiving some A.A.A. payments. The basis for the division of the payments between landlord and tenant, moreover, has been changed, so that the tenant today is to receive a larger share—about equal to his share in the crop—than according to former stipulations. The average benefit per plantation tenant, according to a sample study for some 3,000 plantation tenant families, had increased from $11 per year in 1934 to $27 in 1937. The latter figure constituted almost 10 per cent of the total net cash income of the average tenant family ($300). In all probability there has been a further increase since 1937.

These changes in favor of the tenants, however, must have had the character of a two-edged sword. They gave the landlord a considerable economic interest in decreasing the number of tenants or lowering their status to wage laborers. And it is particularly during the latter part of the 'thirties that this temptation became significant. This may well be the main explanation of why most of the decline in number of sharecroppers and tenants occurred after 1935. Landlords have always tended to change the tenure status of their workers whenever that has been compatible with their own economic interests. There is no reason why they should have behaved otherwise when carrying out the A.A.A. regulations.

It is true that the A.A.A. contracts have included stipulations according to which the landlords were obliged to maintain the normal number of tenants and laborers. Yet such a regulation, even under the best conditions, must be difficult to enforce. Landlords cannot well be asked to keep the same individual tenants and workers as before. When some move away—and they do move often—it can always be claimed that there just are no others good enough to take their jobs and farms. There is another stipulation, however, which should be easier to enforce. It is prescribed that a reduction in the number of tenants and croppers on a farm shall not operate to increase the payment to the landlord. Yet even this safeguard seems to have been insufficient. For Negroes, and tenants generally, have practically no real influence on the local administration of the program. And if a reduction in the number of tenants "is considered justified from the viewpoint of 'sound management,' the stipulation preventing an increase in the amount of payments to the landlords shall not apply." Several observers have noted that landlords actually have substituted wage labor for tenants in order to secure larger A.A.A. payments for themselves. . . .

THE LOCAL ADMINISTRATION OF THE A.A.A.

A few remarks on the local administration of the A.A.A. are pertinent here, as a further explanation of the last point. This administration is in the hands of the Extension Service—that is, the County Farm Demonstration Agents—and the County Agricultural Conservation Committees representing local farmers. It is our impression, based upon a large number of interviews, that the county agents in the plantation South, to a great extent, have an attitude on economic, social, and racial questions which is similar to that of the large landowners. Some of them actually are planters themselves. The committees, at least in plantation counties, are characterized by an overrepresentation of big estate owners. Committee members have often been appointed by the federal administration upon the recommendation of the county agent, which meant that the Extension Service continued to control the local committees. The federal administration has continued attempting to democratize and to decentralize the administration of the A.A.A. An important development is the recent organization of land-use planning committees for the purpose of achieving coordination and local adjustment of the various action programs. The Negro, however, has scarcely profited by these reforms.

It is true that the Negroes commonly vote in A.A.A. referenda for certain decisions, such as the establishment of marketing quotas. Their votes are needed, since a majority of all farmers, including tenants and croppers, must be in favor of the program for it to be adopted. But Negroes are seldom allowed to vote for committeemen. Even when Negroes do exercise some privileges, it seldom means that they have any real influence on the decisions.

Not only Negro tenants and croppers, but Negro farm owners as well, are jeopardized by their relative lack of influence on the decisions of the local A.A.A. administration. The allotment of cotton acreage and benefit payments is a rather complicated affair. There are certain statistical computations involved, and these computations, in part, are based on records concerning previous farm practices on every individual holding. The accuracy of the records and calculations depends on the good-will, conscientiousness, and competence of those in charge of the local control. If they do not adequately represent all local farm groups, it can scarcely be avoided that the rights and interests of under-represented or entirely unrepresented farmers and tenants are overlooked in many individual cases. This is more likely to be the case since such groups, particularly Negroes, include a large proportion of more or less illiterate people who are unable to understand the intricate regulations well enough even to find out whether or not they have been wronged. Indeed even highly educated persons may have to make a special effort in order to check up on their share.

MECHANIZATION

Before we proceed to an evaluation of the A.A.A. program, we must discuss a factor which seems bound to add its influence in displacing Negro labor on Southern plantations: mechanization. We also want to look for tendencies toward concerted defense action on the part of the plantation laborers.

Up to now mechanization has not been important. Cotton cultivation, in the main, is carried on by a technique which has not changed much since slavery. The low degree of mechanization is the reason why cotton growing requires so much labor and keeps this labor down to such low levels of living. At the same time, the cheap labor makes mechanization unprofitable. Otherwise it might be expected that the commercial farming of cotton on the Southern plantations would be more inviting to more efficient production methods than the subsistence production on family farms. But mechanization has actually been slow.

In the last decade, however, there has been a tendency toward a narrowing of the still wide gap between the national and the Southeastern rates of mechanization. That cotton planters in the Southeast would like to buy more machines is evident from a sample inquiry about factors retarding mechanization; half of the informants stressed the difficulty of financing purchases. . . .

Formerly, agricultural machines were not well-adjusted to the rolling terrain in some parts of the South. This is being overcome by newer types of machines constructed to satisfy Southern requirements. As the Southern market for machines increases and, perhaps, other markets contract, the machine manufacturers, no doubt, will direct more of their attention toward the specific needs of the South. The mechanical cotton picker eventually may be perfected to such an extent that it can be used extensively on an economical basis; a mechanical cotton chopper, perhaps, is a nearer possibility. But even without such innovations, there will be more motors running in the agricultural South. The great number of large holdings, in some measure, should facilitate the use of more machine equipment, and Negroes are concentrated in those regions where holdings are large.

The threat against employment opportunities in the rural South is potentially greater, for the very reason that so far there have been but few machines on Southern farms. The displacement of labor which can be brought about by further mechanization is so much greater than anywhere else. Negroes, for several reasons, will feel the effects of this trend more than white workers, in the same way as they have suffered more from the decline in cotton economy. They are more dependent on the cash crop culture. They are more concentrated on plantations. They are objects of prejudice, especially when it comes to handling machinery. To operate an expensive machine is to have a position of responsibility, which, even in the rural South, must draw "white man's pay." Although Negroes have shown that they can acquire the necessary skill for the purpose, there is scarcely any doubt that employers, more often than not, will prefer white labor if farm operations are mechanized. The records show that but a small part of the machine equipment in the South is on farms where there are colored operators. It will always be easier for employers to find workers who know how to run machinery in the white group. More and more the Negro will be reduced to a seasonal worker, and even this opportunity will dwindle if chopping and picking, too, should become mechanized. . . .

ECONOMIC EVALUATION OF THE A.A.A.

. . . From the restricted point of view of production efficiency, the reduction of cotton acreage, and the dismissal of tenants consequent to this and to the special inducement contained in the benefit payments, is all to the good. The Southern plantation has altogether too many workers and tenants; cotton cultivation, as it has been carried on in the South, involves an exploitation of labor that is not compatible with American standards and American economic possibilities. From the same point of view, mechanization also is desirable. Any rise in farm labor standards, through collective bargaining or social legislation, would also, for the same reason, be commendable. In fact, economic progress means that we become able to produce our foodstuffs and agricultural raw materials with less of our available labor.

But there is one important consequence of such a policy which must be taken into account if it is to be deemed rational: *Employment must be found for the agricultural labor dismissed as a consequence of trends or of policy.* Theoretically, there is plenty of place for labor in American industry: the masses of people are in need of many more industrial products. Houses need to be rebuilt; people need more and better furniture and other household gadgets; large sectors of the American population do not enjoy health and educational facilities to an optimal degree. An obvious complement to an agricultural policy of the A.A.A. type would be, therefore, *a large-scale effort to move a part of the agricultural population to industry.* It is an equally obvious inference that this effort should be concentrated upon the younger generation, in which should be invested a vocational training making them fit for industrial work. In regard to Negro education in the South, this policy will require a complete reform of the educational system and, particularly, a reformulation of the aims of vocational education.

In the New Deal's Wake

• Those blacks who fled southern rural improverishment for the northern cities during the 1930's arrived at the worst possible time. Jobs were scarce at best, usually non-existent, and the Depression had all but destroyed the modest advances made in the Negro Community's economic growth in the post-World War I period. The Negro was flattened by the Depression even more than most white Americans. In this connection, the New Deal's national welfare programs, although inadequate and unfairly administered, proved vitally important to Negroes, the group lowest in the economic order: "the last to be hired, the first to be fired." In addition, the New Dealers were "pro-Negro" in ways that went beyond both the performance and the rhetoric of the federal government since Reconstruction. This remained true despite Roosevelt's unwillingness to endorse openly Negro politicians, and despite his strenuous effort to avoid antagonizing southern Democrats. Yet the combination of welfare programs and governmental attitudes (a few crucial symbolic gestures, some recognition of a Negro leadership class within the New Deal bureaucracy, and Mrs. Roosevelt's undisguised pro-Negro activities), helped produce a revolution in black political commitment. Those Negroes who could vote abandoned their traditional patron, the Republican party, and by 1940 a Democratic Negro electorate had become the solidest bloc voting group in American politics.

The rhythm and the tone of the New Deal was set by the man in the White House, since Franklin D. Roosevelt was the spokesman and the master of his administration. His first public statement, the inaugural address of March 4, 1933, pierced the depression-fostered gloom and

From Leslie H. Fishel, Jr., and Benjamin Quarles, *The Negro American: A Documentary History*, pp. 111-21, 126 (footnotes omitted). Copyright © 1967 by Scott, Foresman and Company. Reprinted by permission.

stabbed deftly and surely at the nation's physical and psychological ills. In stark contrast to his predecessor, Roosevelt recognized the prevailing despair, "the dark realities of the moment," and committed himself and his administration to a brighter future. He lashed out in Biblical terms against the profiteers and the selfish among the monied classes and laid down an emphasis which would characterize his administration more than he then realized: "The measure of the restoration lies in the extent to which we apply social values more noble than mere monetary profit." Identifying himself with the unemployed and underprivileged—"our greatest primary task is to put people to work"—he compared the depression to a war emergency and he warned that he was prepared to mobilize the resources of the federal government to fight it.

Like so many of FDR's speeches, including his informal radio fireside chats, the written version of this one paled on paper. His voice exuded warmth and a personal inflection which brought him closer to his listeners. His own physical affliction and the way he bore it earned him deserved admiration and gave encouragement to those who had afflictions of their own, even a darker skin. John Gunther testified to Roosevelt's attraction for people as "concrete and intimate. . . . He set up goals in human terms that the average man could grasp for." The general public responded to his magnetism; one of his secretaries selected a list of salutations which were used on letters addressed to him, and they ran the gamut from "Dear humanitarian friend of the people" to "My Pal!" and "Dear Buddy." Almost all of his callers remarked on his personal charm and persuasiveness.

These characteristics of FDR the man, taken with his consummate ability to personalize his understanding of human exploitation and underprivilege, made him the most attractive President, for Negro citizens, since the Civil War. Robert Vann, publisher of the Negro weekly Pittsburgh *Courier*, who was brought into the 1932 campaign by some of Roosevelt's lieutenants, advised his race to "go home and turn Lincoln's picture to the wall. The debt has been paid in full." Yet, like Lincoln, Roosevelt's actual commitments to the American Negro were slim. He was more a symbol than an activist in his own right. His compassion, though real, was tempered by his own background, by the enormity of the decisions which came up to him, and by political considerations. An enthusiastic politician, he used political weights and measures on a political scale to judge the evidence, and the Negro was often found wanting. When Walter White, the executive secretary of the NAACP, obtained an audience through the good graces of Mrs. Eleanor Roosevelt to plead for the President's public support of the antilynching bill, FDR demurred because he needed Southern votes in Congress on other matters.

Nevertheless, the FDR image eventually became a favorable one; his picture hung in living rooms and infant sons carried his name. At first, though, Negroes waited to be shown. Their publications granted him the benefit of doubt when he spoke about justice and equality, in the hope that he was talking, too, to Negroes. He called lynching murder, remarked W.E.B. Du Bois, and "these things give us hope." His acknowledgment, through his Secretary of Labor, of the National Urban League's survey of economic conditions among Negroes was, in the words of an *Opportunity* editorial, "an evidence of his deep interest in the Negroes' welfare." By midway throught his first term, FDR had captured the admiration and affection of the Negro people and, with that, their votes. During the campaign of 1936, Negroes were outspoken in their support of the Democratic national ticket. Sixteen thousand Harlem residents traveled to Madison Square Garden in September of that year to attend a political rally, and sixty other cities held similar and simultaneous rallies. The New Yorkers mixed a rich fare of music and entertainment with leading New Dealers talking politics, but it was an African Methodist Episcopal Bishop, the Reverend C. Ransome, who symbolized the affair and its meaning by reading a "New Emancipation Proclamation." The vote in November was anticlimactic; the second Roosevelt had weaned the Negro away from the Republican party

Roosevelt did not publicly associate himself with Negro projects or Negro leaders before 1935, but his programs and some of his associates were more aggressive. Early in 1933, he approved of a suggestion that someone in his administration assume the responsibility for fair treatment of the Negroes, and he asked Harold Ickes to make the appointment. A young white Georgian, Clark Foreman, came to Washington at Ickes' request to handle the task, and brought in as his assistant an even younger Negro of great promise, Robert C. Weaver. Foreman successfully made his way through the burgeoning maze of new agencies which were springing up and did a respectable job of calling to the attention of agency heads and their assistants an awareness of the special problems of Negroes. Along with Ickes, Daniel Roper, the Secretary of Commerce; Harry Hopkins, FDR's relief administrator; and Aubrey Williams, a Hopkins deputy, were sympathetic to committing the New Deal to work more generously with and for Negroes.

From the first, the various New Deal agencies carried the major burden of this emphasis, since they translated words into bread and butter, shelter and schooling. For the Negro, the most significant were the Federal Employment Relief Administration (FERA), the National Recovery Administration (NRA), the Works Progress Administration, later called the Work Projects Administration (WPA), the Agricultural Adjustment Administration (AAA), the Tennessee Valley Authority (TVA), the National Youth Administration (NYA), the Civilian Conservation Corps (CCC), and the public housing efforts of several agencies. There were others in the alphabetical jungle which assisted Negroes, as whites, in more specialized ways, such as the Federal Writers' Project and the Office of Education studies. The very number of agencies added credence to the emergent fact that, for the first time, the federal government had engaged and was grappling with some of the fundamental barriers to race progress.

It was one thing to engage and grapple with a problem at the federal level, and another thing to implement it at lower levels. Most of the New Deal agency programs ran afoul of local laws and customs and most of them capitulated on very practical grounds. As a consequence, Negroes vigorously attacked the inequities, even while they appreciated the limited benefits. FERA, the first New Deal agency to work directly to alleviate the plight of the destitute, tried by locally administered dole and work-projects to pump more money into circulation. Until the end of 1935, when it was abolished, it administered most of the direct relief and work relief programs which the New Dealers initiated, distributing about four billion dollars. Its progress was dogged by racial discrimination, since the design of projects and allocation of funds remained in local hands. Jacksonville, Florida, Negro families on relief outnumbered white families three to one, but the money was divided according to proportions of the total city population. Thus 15,000 Negro families received 45 per cent of the funds and 5,000 white families got 55 per cent. Along the Mississippi River, from Natchez to New Orleans, Negroes were passed over for skilled jobs and frequently received less than the stipulated minimum wage. When the state of Georgia squeezed out of the FERA administrator the right to fix hourly wages for Negroes below thirty cents an hour, *Opportunity* mournfully questioned, "Does this presage the end of that heralded concern for the Forgotten Man?"

If the relief program raised questions of discrimination, the NRA brought howls of indignation. In the words of a Negro labor specialist, the NRA administrator, General Hugh A. Johnson, was "a complete failure" for not properly recognizing the Negro. The industrial codes established under NRA deferred to geographic wage and employment consideration so that the Negro worker generally earned less money for equal time and was frozen out of skilled jobs. A young Negro lawyer, John P. Davis, organized the Joint Committee on National Recovery in the fall of 1933 to persuade federal authorities to rectify these policies. "It has filed briefs, made appearances at public hearings," he wrote, and "buttonholed administrative officers relative to the elimination of unfair clauses in the codes," but to little avail. In self-defense, NRA officials explained the difficulty in bucking local customs, pointing out also that the NRA was responsible only for industrial workers. Agricultural laborers, domestic servants, and the service trades were not included, and most of the unskilled workers were exempted by statute from wage and hour minimums. "It is not fair," wrote an NRA administrator in a Negro journal, "to blame the NRA for not curing all these ills, if such they be, within a year." Until the Supreme Court decreed its demise in the spring of 1935, the NRA was a favored whipping boy for Negroes, as well as for others. "The Blue Eagle," a Virginia newspaper observed, "may be [for Negroes] a predatory bird instead of a feathered messenger of happiness."

The TVA and the AAA came under fire in the early years of the New Deal for similar reasons. Negro critics raged at the all-white model towns, such as Norris, Tennessee, which were established in conjunction with TVA. Homes for white workers on the project were substantial, while Negro workers lived in substandard temporary barracks. Skilled jobs went first to whites and most labor crews were segregated. TVA, it appeared to two observers in 1934, "aims to maintain the *status quo.*" A year later, the situation seemed little better. In one sample two-week period, Negroes were 11 per cent of the working force, receiving only 9.5 per cent of the payroll. Under AAA, Negro tenant farmers and sharecroppers, as the most dispensable laborers, suffered first from the crop-reduction policy and found themselves without employment. Concerned about the evolving discriminatory pattern, the NAACP in 1934 devoted a major share of its energy to trying to prevent white landlords from illegally depriving their Negro tenants of crop-reduction bonuses.

Two New Deal programs for young people operated with a minimum of discrimination: the CCC and the NYA. The CCC established segregated camps in the South and in some parts of the North; the great bulk of the integrated camps were in New England. By 1935, its peak year, CCC had over a half million boys in camp. In general, Negroes stayed in CCC camps longer than whites, were not moved up to administrative posts in camps as readily as whites, and were restricted to less than 10 per cent of the total enrollment. Since the proportion of young Negro men in need was substantively higher than this, the quota system was actually inequitable. The NYA, which Mary McLeod Bethune served as administrator of Negro affairs, was shaped to help young men and women in school and with schooling. It grew out of the university and college student relief program established under FERA, and by the end of its first six months, in late 1935, had distributed more than forty million dollars. Conforming to existing state and regional patterns, the NYA still managed to help a critical age group among Negroes.

The debit side of the New Deal's efforts to assist Negroes fell far short of its material and psychological credits. Never before had Negro leaders participated in government affairs as freely and as frequently. The Department of Commerce had E. K. Jones, on leave from the National Urban League; the NYA had Mrs. Bethune; Interior had William H. Hastie and Weaver; the Social Security Board had Ira De A. Reid; Labor had Lawrence W. Oxley; the Office of Education had Ambrose Caliver, to mention a few. Never before had there been so great a stress on improving the education of Negroes. Many relief programs included elementary education and training classes as part of the regimen. Negro colleges and universities received funds for buildings. The Office of Education, along with other agencies, began an important study of the status of Negro education.

Professional opportunities opened up in government, although not at the rate at which Negroes were graduating from college. For the first time, Negroes were employed as architects, lawyers, engineers, economists, statisticians, interviewers, office managers, case aids, and librarians. Nonprofessional white-collar jobs, which had rarely been within reach of the race, now became available to trained stenographers, clerks, and secretaries. While many of these jobs centered around programs for Negroes within the government, such as Negro slum clearance projects, Negro NYA offices, and the like, they broke the dam which had hitherto kept Negroes out of these kinds of positions.

Harold Ickes, a former president of the Chicago chapter of the NAACP, was the first New Dealer to be recognized as a tried friend. He quickly ended discrimination in his department and set the example by placing professionally-trained Negroes in responsible positions.

He first drew FDR's attention to Hastie as a candidate for the federal judge vacancy in the Virgin Islands, and Roosevelt made the appointment in 1937. Ickes appeared at predominantly Negro functions and in 1936, on the occasion of an address at Howard University, even went so far as to wear a University of Alabama hood with his cap and gown because "it seemed to have the best color effect. . . ." While Ickes could not breach established segregation patterns in housing, one-eighth of the federal housing projects planned before the end of 1935 were in mixed neighborhoods. Approximately one-half of them were in Negro slum areas and, thanks to the negotiating skill of Ickes' assistant, Robert C. Weaver, the contracts for a substantial portion of these called for the employment of both skilled and unskilled Negro workers.

Eleanor Roosevelt, the New Deal's conscience, made it her business to reaffirm by word and deed her faith in the equality of opportunity for all. She included Negro and mixed organizations on her itineraries, welcomed mixed groups of adults and children to the White House, and spoke up for the race at critical times. In 1936, as part of a long memo on political strategy in the presidential campaign, she urged party leaders to ask respected Negroes like Mrs. Bethune to participate among Negro groups. The penalty for her unflagging advocacy of the Negro's cause was abuse or occasionally embarrassing questions. As the European war spread after 1939, she confronted questions about the Negro's loyalty. "Rarely," she told a group of New Jersey college women in 1940, "do you come across a case where a Negro has failed to measure up to the standard of loyalty and devotion to his country."

Eleanor Roosevelt was more than a symbol of the New Deal's conscience; she was a vehicle for approaching and influencing the President. She performed this service for Walter White when the anti-lynching bill was before Congress. When the DAR refused to allow Marian Anderson to sing in Constitution Hall, Mrs. Roosevelt was the intermediary who secured permission to use the Lincoln Memorial for the concert. It was useful for the President to have his wife serve in these varying capacities, absorbing some of the criticism, supplying him with information he could get from no other source, and sparking his conscience, when that was needed. This relieved the President from having to punctuate his speeches and press conferences with references to the Negro. Before 1935, these were almost nonexistent; after 1935, they increased in frequence and directness, but Roosevelt did not directly commit himself, as his wife did, until his famous Executive Order 8802 of June, 1941, established a Fair Employment Practice Committee to supervise all defense-contract industries.

In many ways, 1935 seemed to be a pivotal year for the President's public statements to and about the Negro. His annual message to Congress in January asserted that "in spite of our efforts and in spite of our talk, we have not weeded out the overprivileged and we have not effectively lifted up the underprivileged." Uplift and underprivilege were two words which Negroes understood, two words which footnoted their history; yet Roosevelt did not mention the Negro specifically. Shortly after that, he told WPA state administrators that "we cannot discriminate in any of the work we are conducting either because of race or religion or politics," and although he went on to speak of political pressures, the word "race" was there for Negroes to see. In two other public statements later in the year, FDR paid lip service to the accomplishments of the race and by 1936, an election year, he proclaimed his policy that "among American citizens there should be no forgotten men and no forgotten races." The transformation was more one of degree than of conviction; Roosevelt was beginning to speak to the Negro, however rarely, rather than to lump him without identification into massive generalizations. But his eye was ever on the balance of political forces and he never voluntarily came out foursquare for the Negro.

In perspective, Roosevelt's circumspection on some domestic issues was less significant than his New Deal legislative program. Labor unions received substantial encouragement from Section 7a of NRA and from the Wagner Act, although the White House maintained an equivocal position toward both labor and management. The jump in union memberships and the rise of the Committee on Industrial Organization, first within the AF of L and later as the independent Congress of Industrial Organizations (CIO), gained impetus from the newly established right to strike and the newly created federal board to mediate labor disputes. A strengthened labor movement confronted, as one of its problems, the question of Negro members. Older unions such as the United Mine Workers and the International Ladies Garment Workers Union welcomed Negroes without distinction. When the CIO broke from the AF of L, its nucleus of unions including the new and somewhat fragile organizations in the automobile, rubber, and steel industries accepted Negroes on an equal basis, except in those localities where race friction was high. The United Textile Workers attempted to do the same, but the existence of textile plants in southern states made this task more onerous. It was not enough for a union to resolve, as the CIO did, to accept members without regard to race, creed, or color, or even, as the UAW and the organizing committees of the steelworkers did, to offer Negro workers a chance to join up. Negroes still hung back, alternately tempted and frightened by management's offers and threats. The wave of the future was with the industrial unions, and *Opportunity*'s declaration to Negro steelworkers that it would be "the apotheosis of stupidity" for them to stay out of the union battling for recognizance in 1937, was prophetic. The success of the Brotherhood of Sleeping Car Porters, under the leadership of A. Philip Randolph, in gaining recognition as the bargaining agent with the Pullman Company after a twelve-year struggle, marked the beginning of the race's influence in national labor circles and on national labor policy. After his union was recognized, Randolph prodded the AF of L to grant it an international charter, making it an equal with other member unions, and he never eased up his fight to liberalize the AF of L's racial policies. Even though he was not persuasive enough to break down these craft and railway-union prejudices, Randolph emerged before World War II as a dominant voice in Negro circles and a power to be reckoned with in American unionism.

Of the many voices which spoke out for and against the race, none was more deceptive than that of the Communists. Before 1935, their ideology committed their followers to support a separate slate for Negroes, the so-called Black Republic, and insisted that they work independent of all other groups toward this end. When the NAACP unsucessfully defended the Scottsboro boys—nine young Negroes accused of rape on an Alabama freight train in 1931—the Communists abusively blamed the NAACP for the failure. With shrill bravado, they muscled the NAACP out of the picture and took over the defense. They were unsuccessful in court, but they publicized the case all over the world as an example of capitalistic exploitation and milked the American public for uncounted (and unaccountable) thousands of dollars. In 1935, the Communist ideology swung over to a united-front tactic, and they abandoned their attacks on existing non-Communist organizations and held out the carrot of co-operation. Their purpose was to mix with these organizations and either subvert them directly or gain control behind the scenes. The National Urban League and the NAACP quickly recognized the move for what it was and co-operated at a chilly distance. The League had to dissolve some of its worker's Councils, established in northern cities, because the Communists took them over. The NAACP agreed to work with Communist support on the Scottsboro case, but continued to warn against close co-operation.

Failing to engage the two dominant Negro organizations, the Communists jumped at the chance to work with these and other Negro groups through the newly formed National Negro Congress. The brain-child of New Deal critic John P. Davis, it was organized under the co-sponsorship of almost forty Negro organizations and met in Chicago in 1936 with close to 900 delegates. The Communists stayed in the background—Davis was sympathetic—and the resolutions were non-Stalinist, but Davis was elected executive secretary and maintained close touch with Communist leaders. The 1937 Congress met in Phila-delphia with even larger crowds. But soon after that the more conser-vative organizations and individuals withdrew their sponsorship and the Congress, handicapped by lack of funds, began to crumble. Some local councils established by the Congress were active in Western cities, but after 1937 the Congress as a national group dwindled into impotence and in 1940 became an openly controlled Communist organization. This take-over followed the Stalin-Hitler pact and sig-nalized the 180-degree pivot which American Communists were forced to execute, exploding the united front movement. Organizations like the NAACP which had worked with Communists at a distance sud-denly found themselves subject to vituperative and irrational attack, but the vast majority of Negroes merely continued to ignore Commu-nism as a method of achieving their goals.

With the exception of the church, the major Negro organizations felt the sting of mass apathy. "We recognize our lack of skill at mass appeal," NAACP's Roy Wilkins admitted in 1941. The national office of NAACP attracted men and women of an intellectual bent whose convictions on race matters had not changed with the seasons, since the organization was still dedicated to the abolition of segregation and discrimination. But the spark which had sent John Shillady, Walter White, and James Weldon Johnson into race-hatred areas, North and South, burned low. On the national level, the NAACP fought its battles in court, in Congress, and in the press, but not in communi-ties where racism flourished. At local levels, it depended upon its branches, many of which were woefully weak in finances and leader-ship, to seek out and rectify racial problems of every description. Its base was too narrow for its superstructure, and its bones creaked from inaction at the community level; yet it thrived because it learned to speak the language of influence in political circles and because it chose wisely the cases of discrimination and segregation which it pursued through the courts. Indeed, the road to the 1954 desegregation de-cisions was charted, bulldozed, paved, and landscaped by the NAACP.

The National Urban League was tested during the depression and not found wanting. Its leadership was similar to that of the NAACP, except that to the extent that its goals were more specific, framed in terms of employment, family welfare, health, and education, it was accused of being more timid, dominated by white liberals, and hostile to trade unionism. Its chief executive, E. K. Jones, replied to these criticisms in a private memo in 1941. The League, he said, was not a Negro but "truly an interracial movement. . . . Any movement of this character which advocates understanding through conference and discussion must necessarily refrain from advocating mass action of one race calculated to force the other group to make concessions." Gunnar Myrdal, the Swedish sociologist whose monumental study of the Negro in America was published during World War II, found that the League worked actively with unions and held "the lead as a pro-union force among the Negro people." Urban League branches were beginning to receive local support from Community Funds, which gave them greater strength and a source for independent leadership. Taken together, these two Negro organizations, in spite of their lack of popular support, moved together in harmony along parallel paths to the great good of the race.

The Negro's church maintained its grip on the masses during these years as it had for centuries, but its hold was loosening. Strong in numbers and appeal, the church had inherent weaknesses which gradually reduced its potency in modern America. It was not one church but many, from the strong African Methodist Episcopal (AME) and African Methodist Episcopal Zion (AMEZ) to the independent colored branches of the Baptist denomination. To these were added smaller denominations and sects and store-front evangelical churches which dissipated the religious energies of the race. The differences were more personal than ideological; in fact, except for the split between the liberal and the fundamentalist churches—a split matched in white denominations—there was no basic theological difference. The churches' hierarchies stood in the way of closer co-operation. The Negro church was all-Negro and proudly so, a self-perpetuating, segregated institution which made no effort to reach across race barriers, individually or institutionally. In the North, this would have been troublesome for white churches, whose precepts were in advance of practice. Negro preachers generally stayed in Negro pulpits. In the South this would have been almost impossible. The Northern Negro church bred isolation; the Southern Negro church fostered accommodation. Fettered by a strain of fundamentalism and emotionalism, and weakened by the diffusion of denominations, the Negro church had little appeal for the younger generation. In the 1930's and 1940's it struggled without success to find a vehicle for its latent power, but its leadership had lost touch with the material and moral issues of the day. It failed to see its obligation as a participant in the fight for equal rights. "We are the policemen of the Negroes," a Southern colored preacher observed in 1941. "If we did not keep down their ambitions and divert them into religion, there would be upheaval in the South." For the second third of the twentieth century, this message was anachronistic.

It would be simplistic to suggest as have some recent novelists, such as James Baldwin in *Go Tell It on the Mountain*, that the church's withdrawal for fear of upheaval led directly to upheaval, but there is a trace of truth in it. When Harlem rioted in 1935, *The Crisis* explained that only the patience of the Negro had delayed it that long. Patience was not enough to counter the "sneers, impertinence, and personal opinions of smart-aleck investigators, supervisors and personnel directors." Unemployment, rent gouging, and the belief that Harlem had not received its share of relief money snapped the uneasy calm; the riot erupted with a frenzied attack on whites and the purposeful looting of food and clothing stores. The prompt on-the-scene appearance of New York City's popular mayor, Fiorello H. La Guardia, helped restore rationality. When the United States entered World War II, Harlem still seethed from overcrowding, white insolence, and price gouging, and again rioting broke out, followed by riots in other cities, most notably Detroit. The hands of the clock had swung half circle and the Negro had learned from the white how to use violence and lawlessness when order and the law were not sufficient.

Toward the end of the 1930's the federal government turned more and more of its attention to the European conflict, the economy flourished as the industrial bastion of the embattled Allies, and the Negro had committed himself to the New Deal and to President Roosevelt. Polls in 1940 showed that Negro voters overwhelmingly supported Roosevelt for a third term, and the polls were right. The reason for this support was not difficult to surmise. Outside of what the Democratic Administration had tried to do directly and indirectly, the decade itself was marked with identifiable milestones of progress. In athletics, Jesse Owens was an Olympic champion, and Negro football players starred on many of the major college teams. Professional baseball still resisted, but its time was not far off. In interracial activities, conferences on a variety of subjects began to meet with overbearing regularity and, though self-consciously interracial, the pattern developed almost irrevocably. College students and adults met to talk about education, religion, economic matters, and, of course, civil rights. Even in the South, the indomitable Mrs. Bethune organized an interracial conference at the college she founded, and the white University of Florida tentatively sent delegates. In the deep South, interracial conferences were held on a segregated basis; Eleanor Roosevelt told of attending one in Birmingham and inadvertently sitting in the colored section. "At once the police appeared to remind us of the rules and regulations on segregation. . . . Rather than give in I asked that chairs be placed for us with the speakers facing the whole group." White Southerners began to speak up for the Negro. They were still a small minority, but the mere fact that a white state supervisor of schools in Georgia would admit to the inequalities of segregated schools, or a white North Carolina legislator would question a decreased appropriation for a Negro college, was a sign of change. The rise of Huey Long in Louisiana brought a different attitude, one of ignoring race differences without changing race relationships. The all-white Mississippi Education Association established a committee in 1938 to recommend ways in which students might study Negro life, and several Northern newspapers in 1940 editorially acknowledged the importance of Negro History Week. The tide had turned, and Negroes credited the turning to the New Deal.

The sudden shock of the surprise attack which drew the United States into World War II served more to expose sore spots than to blanket them in loyalty. In the First World War, the protests against unequal treatment were slow to develop and not widely heard, but the Second World War was different. Even before Pearl Harbor, clamors arose from the South warning that the Negro was not going to "come out of this war on top of the heap as he did in the last one." However distorted the comparison, the attitude was clear, and it influenced the government's decision to extend pre-Pearl Harbor patterns into the war period.

The Negro soldier remained separate in the armed services, and not always welcome. Judge William L. Hastie resigned as civilian aide to the Secretary of War in protest against the dissembling tactics of the Army Air Corps to keep the Negro on the ground. *The Crisis*, returning to a World War I cry, criticized the appointment of Southern white officers for Negro troops and the explanation that they could handle them better. When FDR queried Walter White about the carelessness of the Negro press and the consistency of its attack on the war effort, White replied that better treatment for Negroes in the armed services and the invitation of Negro editors to presidential press conferences and top briefings would clear up the problem.

White became an important man in the war effort and was finally sent overseas as a war correspondent in early 1944. He toured every major front in Europe and the Pacific and his reports did not make soothing reading. Wherever he went, he later wrote, "there was a minority of bigots who were more determined to force their bigotry on others than they were to win the war." This was particularly true of officers, both Northern and Southern. Separation, he found, bred this spirit, especially when key officers were "prejudiced or weak, or both." When Negroes and whites actually fought together, as they did during the Battle of the Bulge in December of 1944, attitudes changed, according to polls among white officers and men. "After the first day," a white South Carolinian admitted, "when we saw how they fought, I changed my mind." The top combat brass, such as General Dwight Eisenhower and Admiral Chester Nimitz, were willing to co-operate, but they were hemmed in by Washington orders and junior officer reluctance. . . .

The twenty years between the inauguration of Franklin D. Roosevelt and the eve of the Supreme Court desegregation decision were the most revolutionary two decades in the history of the American Negro up to that time. In part, the elemental movements had little to do with race matters; depression, war, prosperity—these were not issues of black and white. Yet they determined a basic posture change: that whites and Negroes would work closely together on matters of national and international importance which had nothing to do with race. Perhaps the most startling development to emerge from these decades was that prominent Negroes began to assume responsibilities in government, business, labor, athletics, education, and the social services which had no connection with race. Negroes, finally, were working in critical jobs because they were needed, and not simply because they were Negroes. Ralph Bunche of the United Nations, Jackie Robinson of the Brooklyn Dodgers, Ira De A. Reid of Haverford College, to name just a sampling, were men who were doing their jobs—and who happened to be Negroes.

While this was the wedge, slowly to be driven into the grain of American society, pressures which mounted throughout these two decades supplied the hammer to drive it home. Some of these pressures were cumulative, like the development of substantial numbers of highly skilled and highly educated Negroes, and the steady flow of

Negroes from farm to city, from South to North. Other pressures were selective, like the magnetism of FDR and the dogged determination of Harry S Truman. There were economic forces, like the dawning awareness by retailers of the Negro market and the sudden realization by most unions that integration meant greater strength. Then, too, there were such forces as the quiet efforts of Southern liberals to make integration in higher education successful.

The Negro himself was a pressure on the wedge. Still smarting as a second-class citizen, more ready than ever to step up to equal citizenship, he used every resource available. Some were peaceful and passive, like the continuing desire for education and the calculated use of votes. Some were peaceful and active, like the push to break down labor union and employment barriers and the play to get more national publicity. Some were outside the law and violent. These efforts were not concerted and not always effective, but the total impact was pervasive. American society could no longer sit back, consoled by the thought that the Negro was not yet prepared. By the end of these two decades, he was ready, and in the decade to come, the young men and women of his race would make this clear.

VII: HOPE: THE FOUR FREEDOMS

AND THE BLACK MAN,

1941–1954

Stirrings of Revolt

• *Disappointment awaited those New Deal Democrats who hoped that token-ism in lower level appointments and wel-fare-ism for Negroes would produce a contented and com-placent black constituency. Instead, the Negro began to speak more stridently and self-confidently in the late 1930's, when international crisis and ultimately the United States' entry into World War II in 1941 propelled blacks into the war effort and forced the government to respond more fre-quently to their demands. Characteristically, initial white reactions to Negro soldiers and Negro workers in defense plants were discouraging. Meaningful black participation and advances in both areas required constant struggle. Richard Dalfiume's essay highlights the importance of the war years in black history, when increased militancy played a vital role in the Negro's post-Depression ascent.*

A recent president of the American Sociological Society addressed himself to a puzzling question about what we know as the Civil Rights Revolution: "Why did social scientists—and sociologists in particular —not foresee the explosion of collective action of Negro Americans toward full integration into American society?" He pointed out that "it is the vigor and urgency of the Negro demand that is new, not its direction or supporting ideas." Without arguing the point further, the lack of knowledge can be attributed to two groups—the ahistorical social scientists, and the historians who, until recently, have neglected modern Negro history.

The search for a "watershed" in recent Negro history ends at the years that comprised World War II, 1939-1945. James Baldwin has written of this period: "The treatment accorded the Negro during the Second World War marks, for me, a turning point in the Negro's rela-tion to America. To put it briefly, and somewhat too simply, a certain

From Richard M. Dalfiume, "The 'Forgotten Years' of the Negro Revolution," *The Journal of American History*, LV (June 1968), 90–106 (footnotes omitted). Reprinted by permission.

hope died, a certain respect for white Americans faded." Writing during World War II, Gunnar Myrdal predicted that the war would act as a "stimulant" to Negro protest, and he felt that "There is bound to be a redefinition of the Negro's status in America as a result of this War." The Negro sociologist E. Franklin Frazier states that World War II marked the point where "The Negro was no longer willing to accept discrimination in employment and in housing without protest." Charles E. Silberman writes that the war was a "turning point" in American race relations, in which "the seeds of the protest movements of the 1950s and 1960s were sown." While a few writers have indicated the importance of these years in the recent Negro protest movement, the majority have failed to do so. Overlooking what went before, most recent books on the subject claim that a Negro "revolution" or "revolt" occurred in 1954, 1955, 1960, or 1963. Because of the neglect of the war period, these years of transition in American race relations comprise the "forgotten years" of the Negro revolution.

To understand how the American Negro reacted to World War II, it is necessary to have some idea of the discrimination he faced. The defense build-up begun by the United States in 1940 was welcomed by Negroes who were disproportionately represented among the unemployed. Employment discrimination in the revived industries, however, was rampant. When Negroes sought jobs at aircraft factories where employers begged for workers, they were informed that "the Negro will be considered only as janitors and in other similar capacities. . . ." Government financed training programs to overcome the shortages of skilled workers discriminated against Negro trainees. When government agencies issued orders against such discrimination, they were ignored.

Increasing defense preparations also meant an expansion of the armed forces. Here, as in industry, however, Negroes faced restrictions. Black Americans were assigned a minimal role and rigidly segregated. In the navy, Negroes could enlist only in the all-Negro messman's branch. The marine and air corps excluded Negroes entirely. In the army, black Americans were prevented from enlisting, except for a few vacancies in the four regular army Negro units that had been created shortly after the Civil War; and the strength of these had been reduced drastically in the 1920s and 1930s.

Although the most important bread-and-butter issue for Negroes in this period was employment discrimination, their position in the armed forces was an important symbol. If one could not participate fully in the defense of his country, he could not lay claim to the rights of a full-fledged citizen. The NAACP organ, the *Crisis*, expressed this idea in its demand for unrestricted participation in the armed forces: "this is no fight merely to wear a uniform. This is a struggle for status, a struggle to take democracy off of parchment and give it life." Herbert Garfinkel, a student of Negro protest during this period, points out that "in many respects, the discriminatory practices against Negroes which characterized the military programs . . . cut deeper into Negro feelings than did employment discrimination."

Added to the rebuffs from industry and the armed services were a hundred others. Negroes, anxious to contribute to the Red Cross blood program, were turned away. Despite the fact that white and Negro blood is the same biologically, it was deemed inadvisable "to collect and mix caucasian and Negro blood indiscriminately." When Negro citizens called upon the governor of Tennessee to appoint some black members to the state's draft boards, he told them: "This is a white man's country. . . . The Negro had nothing to do with the settling of America." At a time when the United States claimed to be the last bulwark of democracy in a war-torn world, the legislature of Mississippi passed a law requiring different textbooks for Negro schools: all references to voting, elections, and democracy were to be excluded from the black student's books.

The Negro's morale at the beginning of World War II is also partly explained by his experience in World War I. Black America had gone into that war with high morale, generated by the belief that the democratic slogans literally meant what they said. Most Negroes succumbed to the "close ranks" strategy announced by the crusading NAACP editor, W. E. B. Du Bois, who advocated subduing racial grievances in order to give full support to winning the war. But the image of a new democratic order was smashed by the race riots, lynchings, and continued rigid discrimination. The result was a mass trauma and a series of movements among Negroes in the 1920s which were characterized by a desire to withdraw from a white society which wanted little to do with them. When the war crisis of the 1940s came along, the bitter memories of World War I were recalled with the result that there was a built-in cynicism among Negroes toward the democratic slogans of the new war.

Nevertheless, Negroes were part of the general population being stimulated to come to the defense of democracy in the world. When they responded and attempted to do their share, they were turned away. The result was a widespread feeling of frustration and a general decline of the Negro's morale toward the war effort, as compared with the rest of American society. But paradoxically, the Negro's general morale was both low and high.

While the morale of the Negro, as an American, was low in regard to the war effort, the Negro, as a member of a minority group, had high morale in his heightened race consciousness and determination to fight for a better position in American society. The same slogans which caused the Negro to react cynically also served to emphasize the disparity between the creed and the practice of democracy as far as the Negro in America was concerned. Because of his position in society, the Negro reacted to the war both as an American and as a Negro. Discrimination against him had given rise to "a sickly, negative attitude toward national goals, but at the same time a vibrantly positive attitude toward racial aims and aspirations."

When war broke out in Europe in 1939, many black Americans tended to adopt an isolationist attitude. Those taking this position viewed the war as a "white man's war." George Schuyler, the iconoclastic columnist, was a typical spokesman for this view: "So far as the colored peoples of the earth are concerned," Schuyler wrote, "it is a toss-up between the 'democracies' and the dictatiorships. . . . [W]hat is there to choose between the rule of the British in Africa and the role of the Germans in Austria?" Another Negro columnist claimed that it was a blessing to have war so that whites could "mow one another down" rather than "have them quietly murder hundreds of thousands of Africans, East Indians and Chinese. . . ." This kind of isolationism took the form of anti-colonialism, particularly against the British. There was some sympathy for France, however, because of its more liberal treatment of black citizens.

Another spur to isolationist sentiment was the obvious hypocrisy of calling for the defense of democracy abroad while it was not a reality at home. The NAACP bitterly expressed this point:

> THE CRISIS is sorry for brutality, blood, and death among the peoples of Europe, just as we were sorry for China and Ethiopia. But the hysterical cries of the preachers of democracy for Europe leave us cold. We want democracy in Alabama and Arkansas, in Mississippi and Michigan, in the District of Columbia—*in the Senate of the United States.*

The editor of the Pittsburgh *Courier* proclaimed that Negroes had their "own war" at home "against oppression and exploitation from without and against disorganization and lack of confidence within";

and the Chicago *Defender* thought that "peace at home" should be the main concern of black Americans.

Many Negroes agreed with columnist Schuyler that "Our war is not against Hitler in Europe, but against the Hitlers in America." The isolationist view of the war in Europe and the antagonism toward Great Britain led to an attitude that was rather neutral toward the Nazis and the Japanese, or, in some extreme cases, pro-Axis. Appealing to this latent feeling, isolationist periodicals tried to gain Negro support in their struggle against American entrance into the war. By 1940 there were also Negro cults such as the Ethiopian Pacific Movement, the World Wide Friends of Africa, the Brotherhood of Liberty for the Black People of America, and many others, which preached unity among the world's darker people, including Japanese. Many of these groups exploited the latent anti-semitism common among Negroes in the urban ghettos by claiming that the racial policies of Germany were correct.

Reports reached the public that some black Americans were expressing a vicarious pleasure over successes by the "yellow" Japanese and by Germany. In a quarrel with her employer in North Carolina, a Negro woman retorted: "I hope Hitler does come, because if he does he will get you first!" A Negro truck driver in Philadelphia was held on charges of treason after he was accused of telling a Negro soldier that he should not be in uniform and that "This is a white man's government and war and it's no damned good." After Pearl Harbor, a Negro share cropper told his landlord: "By the way, Captain, I hear the Japs done declared war on you white folks." Another Negro declared that he was going to get his eyes slanted so that the next time a white man shoved him around he could fight back.

It is impossible to determine the extent of this kind of pro-Axis sentiment among Negroes, but it was widespread enough for the Negro press to make rather frequent mention of it. In 1942 and 1943 the federal government did arrest the members of several pro-Japanese Negro cults in Chicago, New York, Newark, New Jersey, and East St. Louis, Illinois. Although the numbers involved were small, the evidence indicated that Japanese agents had been at work among these groups and had capitalized on Negro grievances.

By the time of the Pearl Harbor attack, certain fundamental changes were taking place among American Negroes. Nowhere is this more evident than in a comparison of Negroes' reactions to World Wars I and II. The dominant opinion among them toward World War

I was expressed by Du Bois. In World War II, most Negroes looked upon the earlier stand as a great mistake. The dominant attitude during World War II was that the Negro must fight for democracy on two fronts—at home as well as abroad. This opinion had first appeared in reaction to the discriminatory treatment of Negro soldiers; but with the attack on Pearl Harbor, this idea, stated in many different ways, became the slogan of black America.

American Negroes took advantage of the war to tie their racial demands to the ideology for which the war was being fought. Before Pearl Harbor, the Negro press frequently pointed out the similarity of American treatment of Negroes and Nazi Germany's treatment of minorities. In 1940, the Chicago *Defender* featured a mock invasion of the United States by Germany in which the Nazis were victorious because a fifth column of southern senators and other racists aided them. Later the *Crisis* printed an editorial which compared the white supremacy doctrine in America to the Nazi plan for Negroes, a comparison which indicated a marked similarity. Even the periodical of the conservative Urban League made such comparisons.

Many Negroes adopted a paradoxical stand on the meaning of the war. At the same time that it was labeled a "white man's war," Negroes often stated that they were bound to benefit from it. For example, Schuyler could argue that the war was not for democracy, but "Peace means . . . a continuation of the status quo . . . which must be ended if the Negro is to get free." And accordingly, the longer the war the better: "Perhaps in the shuffle we who have been on the bottom of the deck for so long will find ourselves at the top."

Cynicism and hope existed side by side in the Negro mind. Cynicism was often the attitude expressed after some outrageous example of discrimination. After Pearl Harbor, however, a mixture of hope and certainty—great changes favorable to the Negro would result from the war and things would never be the same again—became the dominant attitude. Hope was evident in the growing realization that the war provided the Negro with an excellent opportunity to prick the conscience of white America. "What an opportunity the crisis has been . . . for one to persuade, embarrass, compel and shame our government and our nation . . . into a more enlightened attitude toward a tenth of its people!" the Pittsburgh *Courier* proclaimed. Certainty that a better life would result from the war was based on the belief that revolutionary forces had been released throughout the world. It was no longer a "white man's world," and the "myth of white invincibility" had been shattered for good.

There was a growing protest against the racial status quo by black Americans; this was evidenced by the reevaluation of segregation in all sections of the country. In the North there was self-criticism of past acceptance of certain forms of segregation. Southern Negroes became bolder in openly questioning the sacredness of segregation. In October 1942, a group of southern Negro leaders met in Durham, North Carolina, and issued a statement on race relations. In addition to endorsing the idea that the Negro should fight for democracy at home as well as abroad, these leaders called for complete equality for the Negro in American life. While recognizing the "strength and age" of the South's racial customs, the Durham meeting was "fundamentally opposed to the principle and practice of compulsory segregation in our American society." In addition, there were reports of deep discontent among southern Negro college students and evidence that political activity among the blacks of the South, particularly on the local level, was increasing.

The American Negro, stimulated by the democratic ideology of the war, was reexamining his position in American society. "It cannot be doubted that the spirit of American Negroes in all classes is different today from what it was a generation ago," Myrdal observed. Part of this new spirit was an increased militancy, a readiness to protest loud and strong against grievances. The crisis gave Negroes more reason and opportunity to protest. Representative of all of the trends of black thought and action—the cynicism, the hope, the heightened race consciousness, the militancy—was the March on Washington Movement (MOWM).

The general idea of exerting mass pressure upon the government to end defense discrimination did not originate with A. Philip Randolph's call for a march on Washington, D.C., in early 1941. Agitation for mass pressure had grown since the failure of a group of Negro leaders to gain any major concessions from President Franklin D. Roosevelt in September 1940. Various organizations, such as the NAACP, the Committee for Participation of Negroes in the National Defense, and the Allied Committees on National Defense, held mass protest meetings around the country in late 1940 and early 1941. The weeks passed and these efforts did not seem to have any appreciable impact on the government; Walter White, Randolph, and other Negro leaders could not even secure an appointment to see the President. "Bitterness grew at an alarming pace throughout the country," White recalled.

It remained, however, for Randolph to consolidate this protest. In January 1941, he wrote an article for the Negro press which pointed out the failure of committees and individuals to achieve action against defense discrimination. "Only power can effect the enforcement and adoption of a given policy," Randolph noted; and "Power is the active principle of only the organized masses, the masses united for a definite purpose." To focus the weight of the black masses, he suggested that 10,000 Negroes march on Washington, D.C., with the slogan: "We loyal Negro-American citizens demand the right to work and fight for our country."

This march appeal led to the formation of one of the most significant—though today almost forgotten—Negro protest movements. The MOWM pioneered what has become the common denominator of today's Negro revolt—"the spontaneous involvement of large masses of Negroes in a political protest." Furthermore, as August Meier and Elliott Rudwick have recently pointed out, the MOWM clearly foreshadowed "the goals, tactics, and strategy of the mid-twentieth-century civil rights movement." Whites were excluded purposely to make it an all-Negro movement; its main weapon was direct action on the part of the black masses. Furthermore, the MOWM took as its major concern the economic problems of urban slumdwellers.

Randolph's tactic of mass pressure through a demonstration of black power struck a response among the Negro masses. The number to march on Washington on July 1, 1941, was increased to 50,000, and only Roosevelt's agreement to issue an executive order establishing a President's Committee on Fair Employment Practices led to a cancellation of the march. Negroes then, and scholars later, generally interpreted this as a great victory. But the magnitude of the victory is diminished when one examines the original MOWM demands: an executive order forbidding government contracts to be awarded to a firm which practiced discrimination in hiring, an executive order abolishing discrimination in government defense training courses, an executive order requiring the United States Employment Service to supply workers without regard to race, an executive order abolishing segregation in the armed forces, an executive order abolishing discrimination and segregation on account of race in all departments of the federal government, and a request from the President to Congress to pass a law forbidding benefits of the National Labor Relations Act to unions denying Negroes membership. Regardless of the extent of the success of the MOWM, however, it represented something different in black protest. Unlike the older Negro movements, the MOWM had captured the imagination of the masses.

Although overlooked by most recent writers on civil rights, a mass militancy became characteristic of the American Negro in World War II. This was symbolized by the MOWM and was the reason for its wide appeal. Furthermore, older Negro organizations found themselves pushed into militant stands. For example, the NAACP underwent a tremendous growth in its membership and became representative of the Negro masses for the first time in its history. From 355 branches and a membership of 50,556 in 1940, the NAACP grew to 1,073 branches with a membership of slightly less than 450,000 in 1946. The editors of the Pittsburgh *Courier* recognized that a new spirit was present in black America. In the past, Negroes

> made the mistake of relying entirely upon the gratitude and sense of fair play of the American people. Now we are disillusioned. We have neither faith in promises, nor a high opinion of the integrity of the American people, where race is involved. Experience has taught us that we must rely primarily upon our own efforts. . . . That is why we protest, agitate, and demand that all forms of color prejudice be blotted out. . . .

By the time of the Japanese attack on Pearl Harbor, many in America, both inside and outside of the government, were worried over the state of Negro morale. There was fear that the Negro would be disloyal. The depth of white ignorance about the causes for the Negro's cynicism and low morale is obvious from the fact that the black press was blamed for the widespread discontent. The double victory attitude constantly displayed in Negro newspapers throughout the war, and supported by most black Americans, was considered as verging on disloyalty by most whites. White America, ignorant of the American Negroes' reaction to World War I, thought that black citizens should subdue their grievances for the duration.

During World War II, there was pressure upon the White House and the justice department from within the federal government to indict some Negro editors for sedition and interference with the war effort. President Roosevelt refused to sanction this, however. There was also an attempt to deny newsprint to the more militant Negro newspapers, but the President put an end to this when the matter was brought to his attention. The restriction of Negro newspapers from military installations became so widespread that the war department had to call a halt to this practice in 1943. These critics failed to realize that, although serving to unify black opinion, the Negro press simply reflected the Negro mind.

One of the most widely publicized attacks on the Negro press was made by the southern white liberal, Virginius Dabney, editor of the Richmond *Times Dispatch*. He charged that "extremist" Negro newspapers and Negro leaders were "demanding an overnight revolution in race relations," and as a consequence they were "stirring up interracial hate." Dabney concluded his indictment by warning that "it is a foregone conclusion that if an attempt is made forcibly to abolish segregation throughout the South, violence and bloodshed will result." The Negro press reacted vigorously to such charges. Admitting that there were "all-or-nothing" Negro leaders, the Norfolk *Journal and Guide* claimed they were created by the "nothing-at-all" attitude of whites. The Chicago *Defender* and Baltimore *Afro-American* took the position that they were only pointing out the shortcomings of American democracy, and this was certainly not disloyal. The NAACP and the Urban League claimed that it was patriotic for Negroes to protest against undemocratic practices, and those who sought to stifle this protest were the unpatriotic ones.

The Negro masses simply did not support a strategy of moderating their grievances for the duration of the war. After attending an Office of Facts and Figures conference for Negro leaders in March 1942, Roy Wilkins of the NAACP wrote:

> . . . it is a plain fact that no Negro leader with a constituency can face his members today and ask full support for the war in the light of the atmosphere the government has created. Some Negro educators who are responsible only to their boards or trustees might do so, but the heads of no organized groups would dare do so.

By 1942, the federal government began investigating Negro morale in order to find out what could be done to improve it. This project was undertaken by the Office of Facts and Figures and its successor, the Office of War Information. Surveys by these agencies indicated that the great amount of national publicity given the defense program only served to increase the Negro's awareness that he was not participating fully in that program. Black Americans found it increasingly difficult to reconcile their treatment with the announced war aims. Urban Negroes were the most resentful over defense discrimination, particularly against the treatment accorded black members of the armed forces. Never before had Negroes been so united behind a cause: the war had served to focus their attention on their unequal status in American society. Black Americans were almost unanimous in wanting a show of good intention from the federal government that changes would be made in the racial status quo.

The government's inclination to take steps to improve Negro morale, and the Negro's desire for change, were frustrated by the general attitude of white Americans. In 1942, after two years of militant agitation by Negroes, six out of ten white Americans felt that black Americans were satisfied with things the way they were and that Negroes were receiving all of the opportunities they deserved. More than half of all whites interviewed in the Northeast and West believed that there should be separate schools, separate restaurants, and separate neighborhoods for the races. A majority of whites in all parts of the country believed that the Negro would not be treated any better after the war than in 1942 and that the Negro's lesser role in society was due to his own shortcomings rather than anything the whites had done. The white opposition to racial change may have provided the rationale for governmental inactivity. Furthermore, the white obstinance must have added to the bitterness of black Americans.

Although few people recognized it, the war was working a revolution in American race relations. Sociologist Robert E. Park felt that the racial structure of society was "cracking," and the equilibrium reached after the Civil War seemed "to be under attack at a time and under conditions when it is particularly difficult to defend it." Sociologist Howard W. Odum wrote from the South that there was "an unmeasurable and unbridgeable distance between the white South and the reasonable expectation of the Negro." White southerners opposed to change in the racial mores sensed changes occurring among "their" Negroes. "Outsiders" from the North, Mrs. Franklin Roosevelt, and the Roosevelt Administration were all accused of attempting to undermine segregation under the pretense of wartime necessity.

Racial tensions were common in all sections of the country during the war. There were riots in 1943. Tensions were high because Negro Americans were challenging the status quo. When fourteen prominent Negroes, conservatives and liberals, southerners and northerners, were asked in 1944 what they thought the black American wanted, their responses were almost unanimous. Twelve of the fourteen said they thought that Negroes wanted full political equality, economic equality, equality of opportunity, and full social equality with the abolition of legal segregation. The war had stimulated the race consciousness and the desire for change among Negroes.

Most American Negroes and their leaders wanted the government to institute a revolutionary change in its race policy. Whereas the policy had been acquiescence in segregation since the end of Reconstruction, the government was now asked to set the example for the rest of the nation by supporting integration. This was the demand voiced by the great majority of the Negro leaders called together in March 1942 by the Office of Facts and Figures. *Crisis* magazine summarized the feelings of many black Americans: Negroes have "waited thus far in vain for some sharp and dramatic notice that this war is not to maintain the status quo here."

The White House, and it was not alone, failed to respond to the revolutionary changes occurring among the nation's largest minority. When the Fraternal Council of Negro Churches called upon President Roosevelt to end discrimination in the defense industries and armed forces, the position taken was that "it would be very bad to give encouragement beyond the point where actual results can be accomplished." Roosevelt did bestir himself over particularly outrageous incidents. When Roland Hayes, a noted Negro singer, was beaten and jailed in a Georgia town, the President dashed off a note to his attorney general: "Will you have someone go down and check up . . . and see if any law was violated. I suggest you send a northerner."

Roosevelt was not enthusiastic about major steps in the race relations field proposed by interested individuals within and without the government. In February 1942 Edwin R. Embree of the Julius Rosenwald Fund, acutely aware of the growing crisis in American race relations, urged Roosevelt to create a commission of experts on race relations to advise him on what steps the government should take to improve matters. FDR's answer to this proposal indicates that he felt race relations was one of the reform areas that had to be sacrificed for the present in order to prosecute the war. He thought such a commission was "premature" and that "we must start winning the war . . . before we do much general planning for the future." The President believed that "there is a danger of such long-range planning becoming projects of wide influence in escape from the realities of war. I am not convinced that we can be realists about the war and planners for the future at this critical time."

After the race riots of 1943, numerous proposals for a national committee on race relations were put forward; but FDR refused to change his position. Instead, the President simply appointed Jonathan Daniels to gather information from all government departments on current race tensions and what they were doing to combat them. This suggestion for what would eventually become a President's Committee on

Civil Rights would have to wait until a President recognized that a revolution in race relations was occurring and that action by the government could no longer be put off. In the interim, many would share the shallow reasoning of Secretary of War Stimson that the cause of racial tension was "the deliberate effort . . . on the part of certain radical leaders of the colored race to use the war for obtaining . . . race equality and interracial marriages. . . ."

The hypocrisy and paradox involved in fighting a world war for the four freedoms and against aggression by an enemy preaching a master race ideology, while at the same time upholding racial segregation and white supremacy, were too obvious. The war crisis provided American Negroes with a unique opportunity to point out, for all to see, the difference between the American creed and practice. The democratic ideology and rhetoric with which the war was fought stimulated a sense of hope and certainty in black Americans that the old race structure was destroyed forever. In part, this confidence was also the result of the mass militancy and race consciousness that developed in these years. When the expected white acquiescence in a new racial order did not occur, the ground was prepared for the civil rights revolution of the 1950s and 1960s; the seeds were indeed sown in the World War II years.

The Black Vote

• The history of universal suffrage in the United States has seldom been a history of black suffrage. Before the Civil War few northern states allowed free Negroes to vote, while southern states, of course, barred all blacks from the polls. During Reconstruction, Negro voting, although heavy, proved short-lived. Restoration of white rule in the South brought Negro disfranchisement by century's end and only when large numbers of blacks began migrating to northern states in this century could they command appreciable voting power. A previous essay described the shift in political alignment among Negroes from the Republican party to the Democratic party during the 1930's. In the following article a political scientist, Oscar Glantz, analyzes black voting behavior in the decade after World War II. His data indicate that although commitment to the Democrats remained strong, the full Negro voting potential had barely emerged, not surprising since all lower-income ethnic groups vote less regularly than middle- and upper-income groups. Nevertheless the crucial importance to the Democratic party of Negro bloc voting emerges clearly from Glantz's figures. The author correctly forecast a close election in the 1960, Kennedy-Nixon contest, but his belief that Negro commitment to the Democrats would wane in the 'sixties proved incorrect. Both Kennedy and Johnson were extremely popular among Negroes, and even the lackluster Democratic candidate, Hubert Humphrey, retained the overwhelming allegiance of black voters in 1968.

The political role of Negro citizens in northern industrial cities has been described and discussed in numerous reports and commentaries on Negro political behavior, particularly in reference to presidential

From Oscar Glantz, "The Negro Voter in Northern Industrial Cities," *Western Political Quarterly*, XIII (December 1960), 999–1010 (footnotes omitted). Reprinted by permission of the University of Utah, copyright owners.

and gubernatorial elections. In presidential elections, for example, the best available data indicate that Negro voters have been supporting the Democratic party since 1936, by contrast to a history of strong allegiance to the Republican party in the seventeen elections from Reconstruction through 1932. Moreover, it is evident that the northward migration of southern Negroes, plus the accelerated migration to California, has served to enlarge the numerical force of the Negro body politic. In the single decade from 1940 to 1950, for example, Negro migrants accounted for more than 50 per cent of the increase in potential Negro voters in various northern cities (Table 1). In several outstanding cases, Negro migrants accounted for no less than 80 per cent of the increment.

Table 1

Contribution of Net Negro Migration, 1940–1950, to the Increase in Potential Negro Voters, 1940–1950.

			Net Migrants, 21+, 1940–1950	
	Number of potential voters, 1950*	Increase in potential voters, 1940–1950	Number†	As percentage of increase in potential voters, 1940–1950
Chicago	331,825	140,107	110,500	78.9
Cincinnati	52,491	15,235	13,100	86.3
Cleveland	97,757	41,811	24,500	58.7
Detroit	202,101	102,231	89,700	87.8
Kansas City	39,722	9,062	4,200	46.9
New York City	511,538	194,183	160,700	82.8
Pittsburgh	53,508	12,842	9,200	71.9
St. Louis	101,911	26,761	10,900	40.9

* With the exception of New York City, the number of Negroes in the non-citizen category is a fraction of one per cent. In New York, it is approximately two or three per cent. No adjustment was made for this factor.

† To estimate the net intercensal migration of Negroes in the eight cities, the writer utilized statewide data available in Everett S. Lee, *et al*, *Population Redistribution and Economic Growth* (Philadelphia: The American Philosophical Society, 1957), Vol. I, Table 1.14, pp. 87–90. For the task at hand, the "census survival" estimate for a given state (e.g., Illinois: 215,300) was divided proportionately according to the percentage of Negroes in the state who were

As a consequence of such increments, Negro voters in northern and western industrial cities have achieved a balance-of-power position in local, state and national elections. On the national level, this position was notably effective in contributing to Mr. Truman's dramatic victory in the presidential election of 1948. When one recalls that his victory would not have been possible without the electoral votes of California, Illinois, and Ohio, and that he managed to carry those states by narrow margins of 17,000, 33,000, and 7,000 votes respectively, it is readily apparent that the overwhelming pro-Truman preference of Negro voters was indispensable in placing the three states in the Democratic column. One political commentator has suggested that "less than a fifteen per cent switch in the Negro vote would have delivered all three of those states to Dewey, enough to have slipped him into the White House and made Korea a 'Republican War.'"

This is not to say that the Negro vote is sufficient in itself to assure political success to this or that candidate in any given election. For example, various cursory estimates of the Negro vote in 1952 and 1956 indicate that northern Negroes continued to return varying majorities to the Democratic party, thereby playing a negative role in the two elections. In the event of a close election, however, it is evident that a large turnout of Negro voters and a substantial proportion of ballots for one of the candidates can lead to the margin of victory in at least nine important states. It must be said, of course, that such margins are meaningful only when one compares the Negro vote with the white vote taken collectively. Obviously, certain sub-groups within the white group (e.g., organized labor) are capable of contributing heavily to one particular candidate or the other, but when the white group is treated as a single group, these sub-group contributions may be counterbalancing, an effect which creates a close election.

Yet it should be noted that a close election is not an *automatic* condition whereby Negro voters gain the balance of power.

> In addition to a close election, this would require the overwhelming majority of all potential Negro voters to be registered, highly organized and flexible. This is a large order, requiring most sharply

resident in the city under review (e.g., Chicago: 215,300 × 76.2 = 164,058). The number allocated to the given city was then multiplied by an age standard for that city (percentage of Negroes in the 21+ age-group in 1950) in order to estimate the number of potential voters gained through net migration (e.g., Chicago: 164,058 × 67.4 = 110,575). Some refinement in this procedure was possible, of course, but the purpose of the current study did not warrant it.

drawn issues. Cohesiveness of the Negro vote increases greatly where his rights and aspirations are at issue. However, even though there is an unusually high feeling of group identity among Negroes, there are strong class differentiations and complete political solidarity is quite unlikely where both parties make any real effort to secure their support.

PURPOSE OF THE CURRENT STUDY

In view of the possibility of an exceedingly close presidential election in 1960, and in view of the increasingly important role of Negro voters in such elections, it was the purpose of the current study to gain a precise measure of developments in Negro political participation and preference in eight industrial cities, namely the ones which are listed in Table 1. Stated as questions which can be answered on the level of empirical observation: (1) to what extent, if any, has the Negro body politic altered its pattern of political participation in the last three presidential elections, and (2) to what extent, if any, has the Negro body politic altered its pattern of political preference in the last three presidential elections?

The data on political participation will refer to the percentage of registrants who excercised their political franchise by voting for a presidential candidate. The data on political preference will refer to the percentage of voters who voted for the candidate of the Democratic party. To sharpen the focus of the report, the participation and preference data for Negroes will be compared to similar data for the total population of each city. Unfortunately, it was impossible to distinguish between the total population and the white population within it. Thus, in examining the comparative data in Tables 4 and 5, one should recall that the differences would always be larger if Negro and white behavior had been compared directly. Nonetheless, by placing the trends of Negro participation and preference within the context of general trends, it will be possible to draw additional inferences from the data.

PROCEDURES

The measurement of Negro political behavior was accomplished by utilizing official data for rigorously selected sample areas in each city. On the basis of a severe "90 plus" criterion, these areas were located according to the following procedures:

1. (a) For Chicago, Cleveland, Detroit, Kansas City, Pittsburgh, and St. Louis, the writer selected all census tracts in which the Negro population exceeded 90 per cent of the total population in 1950. This approach yielded a total of 134 tracts for the six cities, ranging from 4 tracts in Kansas City to 77 in Chicago.

1. (b) In the case of New York City, the selection was limited to Manhattan (New York County) so as to reduce the burden of collecting the necessary political data. Moreover, the selection was limited to all census tracts in which the Negro population exceeded 90 per cent of the total population in 1940 as well as in 1950. Nonetheless, there were 14 tracts which met the double "90 plus" criterion, with approximately 157,000 Negroes in 1950.

1. (c) In Cincinnati, the sample was limited to the 16th Ward, where the Negro proportion of the total population was 92.1 per cent in 1940 and 94.5 per cent in 1950.

2. (a) For the seven cities other than Cincinnati, the census tracts were plotted on maps containing political subdivisions. All precincts which fell within the census tracts *at the time of each election* were taken as the basic political units for the study. Inasmuch as precinct boundaries are changed from time to time, it should be noted that the number of precincts in each sample area varied from one election to the next.

2. (b) The same procedure was not necessary for Cincinnati, where the sample area and the basic political unit were coterminous.

One last note concerns the procedure which was employed to collect the necessary political data. They were assembled from official records in the offices of registration and election commissioners in each city.

ADEQUACY AND REPRESENTATIVENESS OF THE SAMPLE AREAS

In Table 2, it can be observed that the number of Negroes in each sample area accounted for an adequate proportion of the total Negro population. The lowest figures are for New York City (21.1 per cent) and Cincinnati (23.7 per cent). The remaining percentages vary from 31.3 in Pittsburgh to 67.7 in Chicago.

To test the representativeness of each sample area, the non-white labor force, by sex, in the non-white population of each sample area was compared to the non-white labor force, by sex, in the city-wide non-white population. It was impossible to make a comparison of this sort for the Cincinnati sample, but in the other seven cities the sample areas appear to be representative (Table 3).

Table 2

Population Composition of Sample Areas, 1950*

| | Sample Area | | | |
	Total	Negro	Per cent Negro	Negroes in S.A. as percentage of Negroes in city
Chicago	339,854	333,488	98.1	67.7
Cincinnati†	19,625	18,547	94.5	23.7
Cleveland	76,355	73,135	95.8	49.5
Detroit	110,267	106,013	96.1	35.3
Kansas City	21,259	20,028	94.2	36.0
New York City	159,311	157,828	99.1	21.1
Pittsburgh	27,866	25,841	92.7	31.3
St. Louis	85,693	80,202	93.6	52.2

* Source: U. S. Bureau of the Census, *Seventeenth Census of the United States*, 1950, Volume III, Census Tract Statistics, Table 1, P-D Bulletins 10, 12, 17, 27, 37, 43 and 47; selected tracts.
† Collins, *op. cit.*, Table 2, p. 133.

In 10 of the 14 available comparisons, it can be seen that the difference is one per cent or less. The other four comparisons point to differences of −2.2 per cent for males in the Cleveland sample, −3.2 per cent for males and −4.0 per cent for females in the Detroit sample, and +4.7 per cent for females in the New York sample. The minus signs indicate underrepresentation of male workers in the Cleveland sample and both male and female workers in the Detroit sample, while the plus sign indicates overrepresentation of female workers in the New York sample. To the extent that workers and non-workers differ in political behavior, the accuracy of the political data for Cleveland, Detroit, and New York may be slightly impaired.

POLITICAL PARTICIPATION IN 1948, 1952, AND 1956

Although presidential elections fail to involve large percentages of the adult population in any region of the United States, they tend to attract relatively large percentages of the registered population, par-

Table 3

Representativeness of Sample Areas*. Non-white persons in the labor force, 14 years old and over, as percentage of all non-white persons 14 years old and over.

	Males		Females	
	City	Sample Area	City	Sample Area
Chicago	79.1	78.7	40.6	39.9
Cincinnati†	—	—	—	—
Cleveland	80.2	78.0	37.0	36.6
Detroit	81.9	78.7	29.4	25.4
Kansas City	76.2	75.4	42.7	42.8
New York City	76.6	77.0	47.6	52.3
Pittsburgh	75.4	74.4	28.7	28.5
St. Louis	72.5	73.2	37.7	37.7

* Source: U. S. Bureau of the Census, *Seventeenth Census of the United States*, 1950, Volume II, Characteristics of the Population, Chapter C, Parts 13, 22, 25, 32, 35 and 38 (city-wide data) and Volume III, Census Tract Statistics, Table 4, P-D Bulletins 10, 12, 17, 27, 37, 43 and 47 (S.A. data, selected tracts).

† Sample area is 16th Ward. Labor force data unavailable.

Table 4

Percentage of Registrants Who Voted for a Presidential Candidate.

	Of All Registrants*			Of Negro Registrants†		
	1948	1952	1956	1948	1952	1956
Chicago	84.6	84.8	83.3	72.8	71.5	72.5
Cincinnati	77.9	82.9	83.6	61.4	66.4	63.1
Cleveland	70.9	83.2	85.0	66.0	71.0	77.5
Detroit	76.7	82.3	81.7	68.7	73.4	78.2
Kansas City	87.2	93.5	87.4	81.7	83.5	78.2
New York City‡	—	—	—	—	—	—
Pittsburgh	78.7	85.7	83.3	71.3	80.4	73.7
St. Louis	84.4	89.8	83.8	73.7	80.9	78.3

* City-wide data.

† Based on data for sample areas.

‡ Registration data unavailable for New York City.

ticularly in urban places. The latter point is evident from the data in the three columns on the left-hand side of Table 4, where the reader may note that the turnout of all registrants was typically in the range from 75 to 85 per cent in 1948 and from 80 to 90 per cent in 1952 and 1956. Thus, an individual's intention to vote in a presidential election is initially a function of his earlier motivation to get on or remain on the registration roster. In the registration-to-participation nexus, however, it is obvious that the first event is a necessary legal antecedent to the second event,. so that the question of final motivation for the turnout of registrants still goes unanswered in the current study. Fortunately, several interview-studies have provided reasonable answers to the latter question by utilizing the panel technique, i.e., by conducting pre- and post-election interviews. One writer, for example, has reported recently that "the greater the feeling of involvement in the election campaign, the more likely the voter will fulfill a positive intention to vote."

It would be injudicious to assume that a given turnout rate is likewise a measure of group-wide psychological involvement in a given election campaign, inasmuch as numerous uninvolved persons manage nonetheless to vote on election day. However, to the extent that *differential turnout* is a reflection of *differential involvement*, comparative turnout rates can be taken as rough measures of group-wide *differences* in psychological involvement. Indeed, differential turnout can be attributed to differences in various psychological factors which are related presumably to political participation, e.g., the "interest complex" and the "sense of political efficacy" and that old-fashioned tag known as "political apathy." In these terms, differential turnout rates for two cities, e.g., 84.6 percent for all registrants in Chicago (1948) and 77.9 per cent for all registrants in Cincinnati (1948), or differential turnout rates for two population groups, e.g., 84.6 per cent for all registrants in Chicago (1948) and 72.8 per cent for Negro registrants in Chicago (1948), or differential turnout rates for a single population group in two elections, e.g., 72.8 per cent for Negro registrants in Chicago (1948) and 71.5 per cent for Negro registrants in Chicago (1952), can be taken as indications of a higher feeling of involvement, higher interest, a higher sense of political efficacy, less political apathy, and so on. In the current study, the writer will exercise the option of favoring the concept of political efficacy.

Along this line, a consistently lower group-wide sense of political efficacy on the part of Negro registrants, by contrast with the registered population in general, can be inferred from the comparative data in Table 4. Although the level of Negro participation varied from city to city and from one election to the next, it never matched the level of total participation in any of the city-by-city comparisons in any of the three presidential elections under review. On a more generalized basis, it can be noted that the turnout of Negro registrants was typically in the range from 65 to 75 per cent in 1948 and from 70 to 80 per cent in 1952 and 1956. When one recalls that the turnout of all registrants was typically in the range from 75 to 85 per cent in 1948 and from 80 to 90 per cent in 1952 and 1956, a continuous discrepancy of approximately ten percentage points is evident. Thus, by failing to match the turnout of the total population, Negro registrants fail to enhance their position as a balance of power.

In connection with the 1952 election, however, it is appropriate to emphasize the upward trend in the level of Negro participation at the ballot box. With the exception of the turnout in Chicago (where there was a small decrease of 1.3 percentage points), the activity of Negro registrants increased by approximately two points in Kansas City (where the rate was relatively high in 1948), five points in three additional cities (Cincinnati, Cleveland, and Detroit), seven points in St. Louis and nine points in Pittsburgh. The upturn continued into the 1956 election in Cleveland and Detroit, but it was not sustained in the other cities. Nonetheless, there is some suggestion in the data for 1952 that Negro registrants are approaching a new level of political consciousness, and in these terms, a new sense of political efficacy. Under certain circumstances, of course, there is always the possibility that a significant portion of the Negro body politic may decide to boycott both parties in a given presidential election, but it is much more plausible to suggest that the concomitants of urbanization, such as educational and re-educational opportunities, intensified communications, machine politics and convenient polling places, will tend eventually to maximize political participation on the part of the Negro people. This is not to say that the aforementioned discrepancy between the total body politic and the Negro body politic will be narrowed in the immediate future. As it happens, there were parallel increments in political activity on the part of the total registered population in each of the cities which have been examined here.

POLITICAL PREFERENCE IN 1948, 1952, AND 1956

It is not uncommon, particularly in the popular literature, for publicists and political analysts to describe the Negro vote in terms which imply racial solidarity, e.g., "en masse voting" and "en bloc voting." In such terms, various writers have claimed that "Negroes must be appealed to en masse," that "Negroes, on the sole issue of civil rights, voted almost en masse [in 1948]," and that "Negroes have in fact tended to vote en bloc, as a few simple statistics will testify." It is not the purpose here to question these claims, but it should be said that there are some logical objections concerning the applicability and utility of this notion of bloc voting as a means of characterizing the Negro vote or the vote of any other single group. For example, in a specific reference to the Negro vote, one commentator posed the issue as follows: "In what degree . . . [is it] a function not of racial-bloc voting but of socio-economic status?" Moreover, in a generalized reference to the voting behavior of any group, a leading pollster suggested recently that "there is no such thing as bloc voting," a term which is "too often used to describe what is just a tendency on the part of a particular group to vote more unilaterally than does the general public."

With these objections in mind, the analysis of Negro voting behavior in the current study will be phrased in terms of voting strength rather than racial solidarity. From the balance-of-power standpoint, such strength can be measured in terms of two calculations, the first of which is based on four factors which determine the size of a given candidate's margin of victory among Negro voters. These factors are (1) the number of potential Negro voters in a given city or state; (2) the level of registration; (3) the level of participation at the polls; and (4) the level of support for the candidate in question. The second calculation is simply the size of the candidate's margin of victory among all voters. If the first figure is larger than the second, it can be said that the Negro body politic had sufficient strength to play a decisive role in the election.

To use the Negro vote in Chicago as an example (1948), the first calculation can be obtained on the assumption that the number of potential Negro voters was approximately 303,000 in 1948 (note in Table 1 that the number was 331,000 in 1950, with an average increase of 14,000 each year from 1940 to 1950), that the level of registration was approximately 70 per cent, that the level of participation at the polls was 73 per cent (see Table 4), and that the level of support for Mr. Truman was 70 per cent (see Table 5). Thus, the number of registrants was 303,000 × .70 = 212,000; the number of voters was 212,000 × .73 = 154,833 (say 154,000); the number of votes for Truman was 154,000 × .70 = 107,800 (say 107,000); the number of votes for Dewey was 154,000 −107,000 = 47,000; and the margin of victory for Truman was 107,000 −47,000 = 60,000. In the entire state of Ilinois, Mr. Truman's margin among all voters was 33,000, indicating clearly that the Negro vote in Chicago (to say nothing of the Negro vote in other districts of Illinois) was responsible for the statewide victory, at least when the white vote is viewed collectively. An additional example of decisive voting strength in 1948 is provided by the data for two cities in Ohio, a state where Mr. Truman's margin among all voters was only 7,000. Among Negro voters, however, his margin was approximely 10,000 in Cincinnati and 18,000 in Cleveland, more than enough in either city to change the statewide decision in an election which was otherwise closely contested.

This is not to say that Mr. Truman received his strongest support from Negro voters in Chicago (70 per cent), Cincinnati (75 per cent) and Cleveland (71 per cent), but rather to indicate that these levels were crucial in the sense that they served to tip the balance in favor of a given candidate. As the reader may observe in Table 5, the level of pro-Truman support among Negro voters in the other cities under review was roughly as high in St. Louis (68 per cent) and New York (72 per cent) and higher in Kansas City (77 per cent), Pittsburgh (77 per cent) and Detroit (84 per cent). Insofar as political cohesiveness influences the general drift of social and economic decisions in various branches of government, each of these levels was significant. However, they were not crucial from the balance-of-power standpoint.

On the assumption that the 1960 presidential election will be closely contested, thereby providing the Negro body politic with another opportunity to exercise the balance of power in a number of states, it is the further task of this paper to examine the extent to which Negro voters have altered their pattern of political preference since 1948. Specifically, to what extent did Negro voters endorse Mr. Stevenson's candidacy in 1952? To what extent was this endorsement withdrawn in 1956? And of greatest importance, to what extent and in which direction did the pattern in 1956 differ from the pattern in 1948?

From the data in Table 5, it can be seen that the peak of Negro allegiance to the Democratic party was reached in 1952, which is to say that Mr. Stevenson polled a larger percentage of Negro ballots in 1952 than Mr. Truman had polled in 1948, and probably a larger percentage than Mr. Roosevelt had polled in any of the previous four elections. The level of support for Mr. Stevenson was 75 per cent in Chicago, from 78 to 83 per cent in six additional cities, and one-

Table 5

Percentage of Voters Who Voted for the Presidential Candidate of the Democratic Party.

	Of All Voters*			Of Negro Voters†		
	1948	1952	1956	1948	1952	1956
Chicago	58.2	54.2	48.6	70.4	74.7	62.6
Cincinnati	48.3	43.4	37.5	75.0	81.2	72.2
Cleveland	64.5	59.9	54.6	71.3	78.8	62.7
Detroit	59.3	60.2	61.7	83.9	89.9	84.4
Kansas City	61.1	51.6	53.1	77.3	81.8	70.0
New York City‡	51.5	58.4	55.7	71.8	83.2	68.9
Pittsburgh	59.6	55.7	52.2	77.6	82.0	76.9
St. Louis	64.2	62.1	61.1	68.4	79.6	74.8

  * City-wide data.

  † Based on data for sample areas.

  ‡ Limited to Manhattan (New York County). Data include Liberal vote for Democratic candidate.

tenth of one percentage-point short of 90 per cent in Detroit. In a year which marked the end of the New and Fair Deals for thousands of white voters, this pro-Democratic increment on the part of the Negro body politic can be taken as an outstanding example of political fidelity. As a consequence, the pro-Democratic gap between the Negro vote and the general vote ranged from 17 percentage points in St. Louis to 38 in Cincinnati.

However, when Mr. Stevenson altered his political posture in 1956, he lost some of the ardent support which had developed among Negro voters in his first campaign. Although there was less alienation than one might have expected in three of the cities (a decrease of approximately five percentage points in Detroit, Pittsburgh, and St. Louis), the downturn was significant in a majority of cases. There was a loss of 9 points in Cincinnati, 12 points in Chicago and Kansas City, 14 points in New York, and 16 points in Cleveland. Moreover, when the data for 1956 are compared with the data for 1948, it can be seen in Table 5 that Negro voters in six of the eight cities gave Mr. Stevenson less support in 1956 than they had given Mr. Truman in 1948. The largest downturns are evident in the comparative data for Chicago (-7.8), Cleveland (-8.6) and Kansas City (-7.3), while downturns of less significance are recorded for Cincinnati (−2.8), New York (−2.9) and Pittsburgh (−0.7).

From the balance-of-power standpoint, these developments suggest that the Democratic candidate in 1960 will have only a slim chance of gaining the electoral votes of Illinois and Ohio if the current level of Negro support in Chicago, Cleveland, and Cincinnati remains unaltered or continues downward, assuming of course that the next election will be as closely contested as was the one in 1948. With the exception of Michigan, where the current level of Democratic preference on the part of Negro voters in Detroit is extremely high, a similar conclusion can be reached for Missouri (given contradictory trends in St. Louis and Kansas City) and possibly New York and Pennsylvania. It should be noted, however, that this conclusion presupposes a relatively static situation from 1948 to 1960. In the event that the Negro body politic in these places has been augmented considerably by continuing in-migration, and in the event that this body politic manages to raise its level of participation at the polls, the current pro-Democratic level, even if it continues downward to a small extent, may be sufficient nonetheless to tip the balance in favor of the Democratic candidate. By way of illustration, if it is necessary to obtain 70 per cent of the ballots of 150,000 Negro voters in order to overcome a lead of 59,000 votes among all other voters, the same lead of 59,000 can be overcome by 60 per cent of 300,000 Negro ballots.

In summary, the leading observations and inferences from the current study are as follows: (1) There was a consistently lower group-wide sense of political efficacy on the part of Negro registrants, by contrast with the registered population in general. Although the level of Negro participation at the polls varied from city to city and from one election to the next, it never matched the level of total participation in any of the city-by-city comparisons in any of the three presidential elections under review. (2) At the same time, the participation data for 1952 indicate that there was an increase in Negro activity at the polls in seven of the eight cities examined here. These increments suggest that Negro registrants are approaching a new level of political consciousness, and in these terms, a new sense of political efficacy. (3) From the balance-of-power standpoint, Negro voters in Illinois (represented here by Chicago) and Ohio (Cleveland and Cincinnati) played a decisive role in tipping the balance in favor of Mr. Truman in 1948. (4) The peak of Negro allegiance to the Democratic party in each of the eight cities was reached in 1952, when Mr. Stevenson polled a larger percentage of Negro ballots than Mr. Truman had polled in

1948. In a year which marked the end of the New and Fair Deals for thousands of white voters, such allegiance on the part of the Negro body politic serves as an outstanding example of political fidelity, comparable perhaps to the high level of Negro allegiance to Mr. Hoover in 1932. (5) When Mr. Stevenson posed as a moderate in 1956, he lost varying amounts of support among Negro voters in each of the eight cities. These losses were within a range from five percentage points in three of the cities to 16 points in Cleveland. (6) Moreover, Negro voters in six of the eight cities gave Mr. Stevenson less support in 1956 than they had given Mr. Truman in 1948. The largest downturns occurred in Chicago, Cleveland, and Kansas City. (7) From the balance-of-power standpoint, these downturns suggest that the Democratic candidate in 1960 will have only a slim chance of gaining the electoral votes of Illinois, Ohio and Missouri (and possibly New York and Pennsylvania) if the current level of Democratic preference remains unaltered or continues downward, assuming of course that the next election is closely contested. (8) However, to the extent that the Negro body politic has been augmented to any substantial degree by continuing northward-migration, and to the extent that Negro registrants participate in greater force in the next election, the current level of Democratic preference, even if it turns downward slightly, may be sufficient to change the verdict of a closely contested election. In any event, neither party can afford to ignore the numerical weight of the Negro vote. In the next campaign, the Democratic candidate will have the responsibility of reversing the changing-image of the Democratic party, while the Republican candidate will have the responsibility of enlarging the social and economic appeal of the Republican party.

Education: Parallel Inequality

⌐ • When the U. S. Supreme Court declared racial segregation
in public schools unconstitutional in 1954, many white southerners attacked the decision as "sociological law." Whatever
the phrase meant to segregationists, the Court did consider
the social setting of Negro education in reaching its decision,
displaying remarkable foresight considering the slight interest
demonstrated by most white Americans in the subject of the
black schools. The precise nature of racially segregated education's inherent inequality is treated in the following sensitive
essay by Henry Allen Bullock. He shows that the commitment to racial segregation fundamentally altered the thrust
of Negro education. Original ideas of industrial or vocational
training for the freedmen yielded to more academic curricula
since the segregated blacks had to develop their own professional elite. Although this leadership group duly emerged,
in the twentieth century, it did so often at the expense of
the mass of blacks whose education remained inadequate or
non-existent. The socially destructive costs of this dual-gauge
educational system are still being paid by both races. ⌐

By the close of the nineteenth century, the future of the Negro in
American life had been settled for the next fifty years. It was clear that
the black ballot would be virtually silent; that the two races would
constitute distinct castes, neither crossing over into the domain reserved for the other; that white and black children would be trained
in two different kinds of schools—indeed, in two distinct sociocultural worlds; and that whites and Negroes, though obligated to the
same flag, would become two different kinds of peoples.

It must always be said that the settlement was not one of vengeance but one of compromise. Negroes had responded to their

From Henry Allen Bullock, A History of Negro Education in the South (Cambridge: Harvard University Press, 1967), pp. 147–66 (footnotes omitted).
Copyright 1967 by the President and Fellows of Harvard College. Reprinted
by permission of the publishers.

disfranchisement with verbal protests, but had accepted inferior educational and social opportunities as a consolation prize. They had agreed to gear their educational aims to standards defined in terms of their own limited life sphere rather than to aspire to become the white man's equal. Having lost their fight to become like all other Americans, they had settled for a chance to become different. In a successful attempt to save the Negro schools, Northern whites had designed educational opportunities for the Negro people which were directly in line with the conditions prescribed by the segregated order. These Northerners had gained substantial financial support from private philanthropy and had influenced the South to give public support to Negro schools under these compromise conditions.

It was this great detour that gave special education such a special place in the Negroes' long struggle to gain educational opportunities. Special education was more than a series of public schools and colleges. It was even more than the system of industrial education to which most of the public schools were turning at that time. It was a way of life to which Negroes were exposed for the purpose of perpetuating their caste condition, and the schools were to serve merely as the formal channel of this educative process.

Therefore, it was planned that the maintenance of Southern traditions as related to Negroes would come through a neat biracial arrangement of peoples and expectations. Negroes were to be kept socially isolated from whites by means of a rigid system of residential segregation; they were to be limited to special occupational pursuits by means of job restrictions; they were to be tailored in "Negro ways" through a rigid code of interracial etiquette; and they were to be reinforced in their obedience to caste rules through formal schooling. The point at which this biracial society began forming a way of life for Negroes, tailoring them into a particular social type, and utilizing the schools to serve the ends of segregation marks the real beginning of Negro education as a traditional American institution.

A PRIVATE WORLD OF COLOR AND A LIMITED WORLD OF WORK

First, there was the creation of a new and very effective sociocultural setting through which the basic elements of Negro education could be informally transmitted and logically justified. This was a private world of color within which the life of every Negro was to be rigidly regulated and to whose limitations the Negro schools were to be firmly anchored. It was a world in which the races were to be symbiotically organized in all things economic but, as Booker T. Washington had proposed, kept as separate as the fingers on the hand in all things social.

The rise of this type of setting was a logical consequence of a Southern economy that had changed little in its use of Negro workers. The plantation economy had been dependent primarily upon cotton, sugar cane, rice, tobacco, and Negro labor. Wherever these crops had shifted, as when the cotton patches flowed west, a full complement of Negro labor had shifted with them. Not even freedom had been able to break this ecological affinity between the plantation and the Negroes. So firmly were the relationships rooted in the past that scarcely any change in the geographical distribution of the Negro population occurred between 1860 and 1910. Consequently the first decade of the current century found most Negroes concentrated in a very small area of the United States. Of the 9,827,763 Negroes in the entire nation at that time, 90 percent were living in the South. Over 60 percent of these were living in Georgia, Mississippi, Alabama, the Carolinas, and Louisiana. The census of 1910 showed the largest proportion to be located in an area composed of a band of counties extending from eastern Virginia and North Carolina, across Alabama, to the lower portions of the Mississippi River Valley. Over half the population of these counties was Negro. This area formed the South's Black Belt and became the birthplace of the Negro subculture.

This Negro world was more than a mere geographical distribution of people. It was quickly shaped into a series of community structures whose respective populations were composed almost totally of Negroes. Paramount in the entire scheme were the small rural communities that exercised so much influence in shaping Southern Negroes into a particular kind of folk. Here one could find close-set rows of cabins on the edges of vast stretches of cotton fields. Since the presence of a few whites in these settlements was not a violation of caste rules, the home of a white planter, overseer, or commissary owner often stood in the midst of a cluster of Negro cabins.

Parts of the respective communities were bound together over a wide area by crooked little footpaths—threads of neighborliness. The main paths and roadways led eventually to the white-washed church and the cabin school, which composed the focal points of rural community life. Some roadways stretched beyond, functionally uniting the neighborhoods with the villages they surrounded. Wagons, and eventually automobiles, carried families to town, where purchases were made from service institutions not available in the plantation settlement. Nevertheless many of the Negroes seldom got to town. Their supplies were purchased from the plantation commissary on credit and at rates that were almost certain to keep the purchaser in debt.

In similar fashion the small towns and cities of the South developed their Negro settlements too. Like those of the rural area, these communities were composed totally of Negroes who, by tradition, were contained in a small amount of living space. Negro communities were basically peripheral, located on the edges of the larger villages. Seldom were white residential areas beyond them. Nevertheless they were separated from each other within the same corporate area by white neighborhoods whose paved streets, electric lights, running water, and sewerage connections seemed to run out before reaching the Negro homes.

As residential segregation spilled over into the larger cities of the South, Negroes began concentrating in relatively fixed positions near the central business districts of these cities, in areas that had already begun to deteriorate under the force of urban growth. For example, the free Negroes of Virginia who migrated to the cities of that state occupied huts along the docks and around the marketplaces since their presence was tolerated only in such areas. Sommerville, one of the first areas of Atlanta to be occupied by Negroes, was once a city dumping ground. Even where a highly diffused pattern of Negro settlement developed, as in Charleston, historic practices dictated the fact: Negro servants had been able to find living space in backyards of their wealthy employers. Beginning, therefore, under the effective control of a rigid code of racial segregation, Negro communities of the larger Southern cities developed into some of the most colorful areas of the urban South. They became basically characterized by main streets that served as traditional symbols of all urban Negro communities and their ghetto-like qualities. There were Beal Street of Memphis, Rampart of New Orleans, Second and Leigh of Richmond, Dowling and Lyons of Houston, and Auburn Avenue of Atlanta. As early as 1900 the process of residential segregation had created a series of black islands in a great white urban sea.

Paralleling the Negro's private world of color was the limited world of work which constituted the basic economic dimension of his community life. This work-a-day world supplied him with job opportunities but only at the lower end of the occupational ladder. Whenever he worked at a higher level, it was mainly for the purpose of rendering some function to his own community and his own people.

The rigidity of the Southern policy of job restriction for Negroes may be seen in the proportion of workers who were employed in the various industries during the days when the special educational movement was being shaped. In 1890, six out of every ten in the Negro American labor force were engaged in agriculture. Three fourths of these were sharecroppers, holding the land by paying a share of their harvest as rent. Approximately three out of every ten were in some form of domestic and personal service, and the others were found working as laborers in manufacturing and mechanical industries or serving as professionals in the segregated Negro community.

Once again tradition had set the pattern of racial confinement. Agriculture continued to dominate the Negro's economic life because it offered him immediate employment. Immediately after emancipation, the cotton economy had provided him with a readily available and familiar means of earning a living in a free labor market. Nevertheless, there were particular changes which helped to foster more racial restrictions in the employment field. Many of the slaves who held high positions in the building trades prior to emancipation found it difficult to capitalize upon their experiences because of certain changes in building methods which the South experienced during its period of economic reconstruction. Plumbing, steam fitting, and electrical work became associated with these trades, and the training the former slaves had received did not encompass the skills required by this new kind of work. Since emancipation meant the entrance of Negro workers into the free labor market, some hostility was naturally directed against them. Urged to protect their interests, whites of the laboring class debarred most qualified Negro craftsmen from trade unions and refused to accept them as apprentices. Also the Southern image of work changed. The tendency to judge certain types of jobs as "nigger work" melted away under the shock of the economic revolution, and Negroes were eventually displaced in many of the jobs to which they had been assigned by tradition.

Since it was upon the agricultural industry of the South that the Negro's economic destiny most heavily depended, it was through it that his economic relations with whites were most dominantly shaped. Gripped as he was by the evils of the tenant system, the Negro farmer and his family experienced all the insecurities and depressions that regularly haunted those who fell victims of this type of land-tenure arrangement. The cropper who worked under the tenant system lived on a credit arrangement that consisted of purchasing against his future harvest at a special store usually operated by his landlord. The average credit for him and his family was about $88 per year in the 1920s, and the interest rate was usually a flat 10 per cent. Since the duration of the credit was only for a few months, the actual rate was approximately 37 percent. Commissary prices were often marked up considerably, and the interest plus the markup placed a severe strain upon the tenant family and virtually prohibited their rising above the sharecropper level. These arrangements often led to perpetual indebtedness and forced servitude.

Enforcement of this state of perennial indebtedness rested with a constituted legal authority that accepted the protection of caste regulations as its moral obligation. As Ray Stannard Baker followed the "color line" through the South during the first decade of this century, he sketched this picture of the Negro sharecropper who struggled to escape the plight of peonage:

> If he [sharecropper] attempts to leave, he is arrested and taken before a friendly justice of the peace and fined or threatened with imprisonment. If he is in debt, it sometimes happens that the landlord will have him arrested on the charge of stealing a bridle or a few potatoes . . . and he is brought into court. On appearing in court . . . the white man is there and offers as a special favor to take him back and let him work out the fine. . . . In this way, Negroes are kept in debt . . . year after year, they and their whole family.

Some statutes provided for the punishment of any laborer, renter, or sharecropper who would leave without the consent of his employer and before the expiration of his contract. These laws, however, were declared unconstitutional in the peonage cases of 1903 and by a Mississippi court in 1912. Nevertheless these judicial decisions failed to give adequate protection to Negro farmers who sought to escape the tentacles of the cruel credit system. It was too easy for landlords to secure criminal convictions of Negroes on the slightest accusation of theft. Because of this fact many Negro croppers became imprisoned by the very land they tilled.

As the Negro's inferior position in the Southern social order crystallized in terms of residential segregation and job restrictions, certain sociological mechanisms designed to shape his mind went into operation. The caste system was brutal in its power to make every Negro think of himself as a "colored person." One mechanism through which this power operated effectively was social isolation, for through it the complete assimilation of the Negro race was blocked. Negro children tended to grow up almost completely within their restricted living space. The only sustained contacts they experienced across racial lines were those involving black and white children at play. But even here, maturity usually brought a clean break, causing those of each race to acquire a sharper image of their respective places than if the contacts had never been made. Since the main channels of personal communication with the larger society were closed to them, Negro children had no models except those of their own race. Teachers of the Negro schools most often originated in the same sociocultural setting as their pupils. Consequently, they tended to teach their pupils to grow up as they had done. Only occasionally did either teacher or pupil catch a glimpse beyond the horizon of his colored world and escape its tyranny. Nevertheless, the escape was often final. Few ever returned to pour nontypical traits into the closed world of the Negro community.

Social isolation also functioned at the adult level, for highly personal contacts between whites and Negroes at this level were kept to a bare minimum. Where these contacts did exist, they occurred underground in clandestine attachments or incidental to master-servant relations. Some cross-cultural exchange did occur this way, as when mulatto children inherited some of the prestige of their white parentage or when domestic servants acquired some of the more expensive tastes of their white employers. But the frustrations that often resulted from restrictions in the use of the ideas gained in this way rendered the goods seldom worth the cost.

There was still another mechanism operating to shape the Southern Negro into a particular folk type. This was a system of interracial etiquette that defined so clearly the Negro's inferior position in the general society. It was a series of codes of social usage required by custom and tradition in all contacts between the races. The codes regulated ceremonial relations involving greetings, salutations, and conversations. They controlled contacts and situations in which reference was made to persons of either race; they directed conventions involving business relations in which economic obligations were at stake; and, in short, they shaped behavior patterns for most of the circumstances under which the two races met.

The caste badge was made prominent in all instances of greetings, salutations, and conversations. Negroes normally greeted white men with the title of "Mister." Occasionally, the title "Cap'n" or "Cap" was used where more persistent contact had bred some degree of familiarity. Familiarity also permitted them to address whites by their first name, as "Mr. John" or "Miss Mary." But in speaking of white women generally, Negroes were expected invariably to refer to them as "white ladies." On the other hand, white persons were not expected to address Negroes as "Mister," although "boy" was a good usage. Titles usually assigned to whites were seldom, if ever, assigned to Negroes. The title "Mrs." for Negro women was especially taboo. Newspapers referring to colored women of note would avoid using the title. Mrs. Booker T. Washington was referred to as "the widow of Booker T. Washington" or as a noted "negress." The lower-case n was usually used in reference to Negroes. There were times when the attainment and position of Negro men obviously required respect. Nevertheless, the ritual of greeting and reference firmly preserved the caste position of each race. Such Negroes were addressed as "Parson," "Reverend," "Professor," or even "Doctor," but never "Mister."

Wherever members of the two races met in public places, fixed rituals went into operation. In hotels, offices, restaurants, or other public places reserved for whites, the Negro was expected to remove his hat whether others had done so or not. On the other hand, it was apparently not proper for a white man to remove his hat in either public or private places reserved for Negroes. Insurance and installment collectors who frequented Negro homes never violated this caste requirement. No matter how low his class, a white person was not expected to show this courtesy to Negroes. Bertram Doyle who depicted these requirements of interracial etiquette so well, added these cogent words: "Probably the only place where white men did remove their hats, though they were seldom there, was in the Negro church."

Business relations between the races were never definite and contractual. They were so arranged that blacks had few demands that whites were obligated to meet. Trading arrangements involving credit were always settled on the basis of the white man's bookkeeping. If arguments about these obligations did arise, the Negro seldom won. Inherent in these relations, too, were arrangements between white employers and Negro workers. The arrangements made the Negro almost completely dependent upon the white man's mercy and most conclusively resigned to an inferior state.

Caste regulations constituted a most powerful force in the South's special educational program for Negroes. The methods of informal education inherent in the enforcement of these regulations *did* teach. They created within the minds of both whites and Negroes patterns of self-perception which were highly appropriate for the segregated order. As a natural outcome of the juxtaposition of two divergent ethnic groups, white and black people learned to distinguish themselves from each other as distinct kinds of persons, and both races eventually perceived the Negro as a contrasting conception. Black and white were constantly presented as antipodes, negative and positive poles on a continuum of goodness. In the minds of whites, Negroes stood as the antithesis of the character and properties of white people. This psychology of self-debasement soon matured, and Negroes began to see themselves as whites did. Negro children learned to offend each other by calling each other "black." Negro business enterprises that did not seem to measure up to segregated standards were referred to as "nigger business" by Negroes themselves. Booker T. Washington, in speaking of his youth, recalled that it was assumed that everything white was good and everything black was bad. Once the system of differential expectations was really set, the conduct of whites and Negroes came to be judged on different value scales, and there came into being a black and white code of morality.

It was logical that the greatest force in depressing the Negro's self-image should be found in the rural South, where so many Negroes lived under the constant threat of the tenant system. Here is where many of them tottered between dependency and utter despair, for there were times when the system kept both tenant and landlord poor. Statements made by sharecroppers of Macon County, Alabama, illustrate well the manner in which the character of the rural Negro eroded under the influence of the South's tenant system. When asked of his relationship with his landlord, one of the croppers reported, "I asked landlord to 'vance me er pair of overalls, he say he need overalls hisself." Another, unwittingly expressing the depressing effect of sharecropping upon human aspirations, summarized his hopes when he said, "Ain't make nothin', do'n spec nothin' 'till I die." And in obvious defeat, a cropper confessed, "Dis ole mule lak me—he ain't much good no more."

The sharecropper's imprisonment was not confined to the land. It extended to an enslavement of his mind, for the system was a good teacher. It taught the cropper to mine the soil, use the fence rails for firewood, to make no repairs, to practice no economy of self-help through animal husbandry or family gardening. With the cotton rows running to his cabin door, he could hardly have instituted this practice even if the system had not robbed him of the will.

Conditions like these—social isolation, occupational immobility, and the rigid enforcement of interracial etiquette—generated within Negroes the personality inclinations that now form the basis for the various negative stereotypes so often used against them. Negroes and whites became different because they were kept apart. White Southerners insisted that they be 'kept apart' because they were different. Segregation begat segregation.

Nevertheless, this type of program of informal education did not influence all Negroes in the same way. Every Negro had some feeling of protest against the caste system, and each had some sort of conflict with the white world. But these represented various degrees of deviancy from the norm of caste acceptance and were met with sanctions consistent with the extent of rebellion. For most Negroes, no overt expression of rebellion came at all; in fact, some of these were aggressively cooperative in defending the prevailing customs. Whites thought of these as "safe" Negroes, the type who could be counted upon to employ their influence in the task of keeping other Negroes satisfied with the existing caste requirements. The "safe" Negroes developed their influence over the others of their race not because the others respected them but because they feared them. There developed also the "sycophant," the Negro who knew better but acted in his own personal interest. He worked with whites as Br'er Rabbit worked with Br'er Fox. He learned to gain community influence and to satisfy his own limited aspirations by flattering white people into serving his own ends. At the other end of the continuum developed the "uppity" Negro who, by training and ambition, mirrored a constant challenge to the caste line. He was often ignored by the Negro masses but was most usually feared by whites. The fear was logical, for the "uppity" Negro was eventually to become the white man's nemesis and the David who would eventually slay the South's Goliath.

A SCHOOL SYSTEM IN CAPTIVITY

Strategically located in the Negro's private world of color and skillfully designed to inculcate those values which would adequately adjust the Negro people to their caste conditions were the Negro schools, public and private. By the first decade of the twentieth century, these schools had found their way into the heart of the Negro South.

Despite some degree of public indifference and because of the generosity of philanthropic agencies, every Negro community of the rural or urban South could boast of some type of organized educational institution.

Setting the pace and characterizing the entire Negro educational structure at the public school level were the county training schools that were organized through the generosity of the John F. Slater Fund. Beginning with four of these schools in 1911, the Southern states, under the leadership and financial support of the fund, had developed 355 by 1928. By this time, 14,092 Negro children living in the various counties of the South were receiving secondary education from 2,379 teachers in these schools. There was hardly a Southern Negro community in which a county training school was not operating when the 1933–1934 school year started.

Another look at the influence of John F. Slater will show that the trustees of the fund he established virtually captured the Negro public schools of the South. They facilitated the establishment of public high schools for Negro children by financially cooperating with all local agencies willing to share the initial expenditures and continue the support. They took the larger elementary schools of rural areas where the Negro population was dense and combined them in the largest consolidation movement the South had ever experienced. They designed a curriculum that placed emphasis on rural life and established "Smith-Hughes teachers" as principals. Characteristically located in the open country of a Southern county whose population was predominantly Negro, the county training school developed a community-centered program aimed directly at the task of helping rural Negroes improve their living conditions within the framework of segregated living. No attack was made on the tenant system, but an occasional diplomatic move was made to secure the permission of a landlord to involve his tenants. Caste regulations were intentionally left undisturbed, and influential whites who had some fear that the program would threaten the *status quo* were encouraged to cooperate through an appeal to their self-interest. Local and philanthropic agents occasionally succeeded in getting them to believe that the school's program would make the Negroes more economically useful to them. As the white South gained confidence in the movement, the schools moved firmly under the captivity of the segregated order.

Industrial education was the core of the county training school's program. Farmers were encouraged to buy equipment collectively;

the schools served as custodians of this equipment, and the students used it in their studies. In 1929 farmers who came under the school's influence were encouraged to drop cash crops like cotton and tobacco and to turn to food products like wheat, vegetables, and livestock. The agents whom the various state departments of education had supplied for the Negro rural communities furnished the leadership in efforts designed to train the Negroes to live at home and like it. Following the methods that had been created earlier by the Jeanes teachers, these agricultural leaders taught the people to can fruits and vegetables, to butcher livestock, plant gardens, whitewash cabins, and even make household furniture out of discarded apple boxes and orange crates. Most of this was adult education, but some attempt was made to integrate it with the students' courses just as the Jeanes Plan had specified. Abstract mathematics was replaced by exercises in bookkeeping related to farming and farm products. World geography and history were replaced by a study of the local environment. So far as intentions were concerned, the pupils were to know a great deal about where they lived though little about the living conditions of other people.

Long before the county training schools were conceived, a thread of Negro colleges and universities was woven into the fabric of the South's Black Belt. These, too, were the product of philanthropic generosity and inevitably became captives of the South's program to educate Negroes for their caste assignments. Thirty of these institutions were established during the first decade after the Civil War, and others appeared gradually after that time until, by the middle of this century, 112 such institutions had been established for Negroes in the South.

Like the public schools, the colleges were strategically located. There was hardly a Negro community in the South that did not come under the influence of one or more of them. Organized originally for liberal arts purposes, the Negro college slowly instituted industrial education as one of its basic functions. Shops, kitchens, and sewing rooms were added as laboratories for the students, and some of the institutions that had been most dedicated to the liberal arts program advertised rather freely the emphasis they were professing to place upon the manual arts. Hampton and Tuskegee had set the pattern, and those colleges that showed the most vivid signs of following this pattern were given the greatest share of the money which had begun to flow South and into the Negro schools at the opening of our century. A system of Negro land-grant colleges grew out of some of the older normal schools, and teaching the manual arts became a public compulsion with this group.

The South's system of Negro education was completed by 1933. The Slater Fund and other philanthropic agencies like it had inspired the development of secondary schools for Negroes, and practically any Negro child in the South could get at least two years of high school training at public expense without walking too far for it. Higher education had been made available to the Negroes, and the "colored South" had begun to feel the effects of its influence. Although they did not attack the caste problem directly and with dedicated intentions, the private colleges, with their greater freedom, did venture in this direction. They worked to elevate the Negroes by pressing against the extreme end of the range of tolerance set by the agencies that gave them support and by the state officials who gave them their rating.

A SCHOOL SYSTEM IN UNCONSCIOUS REBELLION

Despite all the planning that had been put into the Negro educational movement, it was quite evident, even at the start, that some of its byproducts would contradict its aims and rise to threaten the social system it was engineered to preserve. There were signs that neither the Restoration that followed the collapse of congressional Reconstruction nor the marriage between North and South that was consummated at Capon Springs would be able to survive the long pull of history. These signs appeared particularly in the public schools and colleges themselves. Apparently neither the schools nor the segregated communities were to serve the caste order without creating some dissatisfaction with it. Both were to vacillate between two different kinds of services to two different kinds of masters.

During the early days of the 1870s, when the South's public school movement was in its infancy, the signs of vacillation were subtle and obviously unconscious. Nevertheless, the seed of growing dissatisfaction with caste were there, first planted by the public compulsion to make the curriculum of the Negro schools basically similar to that of other schools. Those who administered the public school system could not escape the magnetic pull toward the literary. Therefore, at the base of every Negro child's educational opportunity was a literary training that took precedence over the industrial. The classical academic tradition that Americans inherited from England proved to be extremely viable. It was considered to be the required foundation for all kinds of formal education. When the people thought of schools, whether for Negroes or for whites, literary subjects invariably came to their minds. Consequently, superintendents of the various systems looked for literary training in the teachers they sought to employ, and lamented the absence of this orientation in many who applied.

In 1870 the school examiners of Jones County, North Carolina, complained that both white and colored applicants for teaching certificates were so wanting in fitness that some regard for efficiency had to be sacrificed. Nevertheless, no certificate was issued to any applicant of either race until each had "passed" a tolerably fair examination in arithmetic. Reporting later on the qualities that he looked for in teachers, Josiah H. Shinn, superintendent of public instruction for Arkansas, listed good scholarship as his first requirement. He expected his teachers of geography, for example, not only to treat the earth as a home for man but also to correlate the instruction with subject matter drawn from "the allied branches of botany, geology, and mineralogy." In all the examinations given Negroes who sought to qualify for a teaching position, competency in English, mathematics, geography, and spelling was given close scrutiny. No test of the teacher's skill in industrial arts was ever recorded. This does not mean that caste regulations failed to function in the selection of Negro teachers, for seldom were the qualifications for teaching in the Negro schools as high as those required for teaching in the white schools. Neither does it mean that the curricula of the two school systems were absolutely the same. Caste limitations lowered the standards of the Negro schools, including schools for Negro teachers, but they failed to stem the imitative tide that was rising within the Negro community and causing Negroes to want the same curriculum as whites.

Throughout the South, as for the rest of the nation, the three R's, geography, and a bit of history composed the basic character of the region's graded school curriculum. The Negro school was no exception to this rule, and Negro children were constantly exposed to this kind of curriculum as they progressed to the higher branches, the normal school, and the college level. In an attempt to keep faith with the industrial education movement, some courses in the manual arts were offered, but these were basically supplementary, acting in no important sense as a focal point of the curriculum. By 1903 there were 13,797 Negro children receiving some kind of industrial training at the high school level in the South. Nevertheless, 8,055 of these were taking "classical, scientific, English, and business courses as the hard core of their curriculum."

Different educational movements came later in an attempt to revive the industrial emphasis, but these were directed more toward the larger community than toward the school and its pupils. The Jeanes teachers made heroic attempts to get local teachers, particularly those in rural areas, to organize their courses of study around the everyday life and "practical" needs of the Negro communities in which the schools were located. Despite all their ingenuity and dedication, the more classical curriculum of even the rural schools remained unshaken, and the rural cabins from which the masses of Negroes were later to depart remained characteristically unpainted. The girls were exposed to some domestic science, and boys were given some carpentry, blacksmithing, and agronomy. However, this became merely window dressing, like singing Negro spirituals when white people came to visit the schools. It was merely a way of making favorable impressions upon some visiting school officials whose influence with philanthropic agencies could stimulate more money for the school.

Another force that inclined the colored schools away from the industrial and nearer the conventional curriculum was the Negro community in which each school was so tightly anchored. Since these communities constituted a separate part of a biracial society, the Negroes found it necessary to provide for themselves those institutions whose services were not available to them through the larger community complex. Therefore the importance which these institutions assumed in Negro community life spotlighted the need to make certain types of professional training available to the population. The Negro schools had to be staffed with teachers, and these teachers had to be trained. The summer institutes held for Negro teachers did not prove capable of meeting the demand. Gradually and with the help of philanthropic foundations the Negro colleges organized normal departments. By the 1920s practically all these colleges were in the business of training teachers.

The pulpits of churches had to be filled with intelligent leadership, for the Negro people, finding themselves surrounded by a hostile world, once again turned to a religious faith. Their churches multiplied rapidly and with the schools became the most powerful influence in Negro community life. The revival around the turn of the century was motivated not solely by emotional needs, although these needs still prevailed in all their dynamic force; it was also a result of the necessity to provide some source of mutual aid for the depressed Negro population. Not all the churches were involved, and most of those that were tended to center in the larger urban areas. But as early as 1897 Negro churches in nine Southern cities had accumulated 30,000 active members and $1,542,460 in real estate value. They had aggregated an annual income of $157,678 by that time and were putting forth some effort to protect the Negroes against their many deprivations. Twenty-seven of these churches were spending $8,907 annually for charitable purposes and had established mission units in the slums of these cities. Several were working with homes for the aged, orphanages, and other welfare institutions at that time, and some had even ventured to extend help to needy families through a system of home visits.

Although it has been reported that the Negro church functioned in the interest of the caste system for many years, there is no denying that it nourished some serious threats against the system. It cried out for and elicited a leadership whose training exceeded the limits of industrial education. Almost all the private colleges for Negroes had theological departments by 1890 and had produced 512 ministers who were trained in divinity before the close of the century. What the South did not know at that time was that out of one of these colleges would come the minister, Martin Luther King, whose leadership would spark a new kind of American revolution.

The demand for business enterprises within the Negro communities did not falter despite the unfortunate experiences which accumulated around the banks and fraternal orders that Negroes tried to operate. As time passed the need for these kinds of service institution grew larger, causing a rather complete set to come into existence. There first appeared eating, drinking, tonsorial, medical, recreational, and other places which offered services to a highly personal nature. They grew up along the main streets that pierced the Negro areas. They were seldom attractive or well run, but their monopolistic power to draw patronage encouraged the development of other kinds of institutions. Financial enterprises, insurance companies, and even newspaper establishments eventually won sufficient support to maintain a strong position in such Southern cities as Durham, Richmond, and Atlanta. Although these enterprises shared minutely in the Negro's total purchasing power, they were profitable enough to sustain a small proprietary class within the race. Gradually, physicians, dentists, preachers, teachers, and undertakers developed into a small professional class. These two classes—proprietary and professional—constituted the upper crust of a world that had turned black. It was the children of this class who were to demand higher and professional education; it was this class that was to gain power steadily and supply the force of discontent out of which the protest movements of later years were to grow.

Therefore, the many daily needs of the segregated Negro community justified giving young Negroes higher and professional training. Southern whites realized that if the segregated system was to work, the Negro schools, particularly the colleges, would have to teach courses in business, economics, journalism, medicine, teacher training, and theology. Some educators, both white and Negro, had anticipated this possibility when they contended as did William T. Harris in 1890, that Negroes needed a more classical education, which would provide them with trained leadership.

Responding to this growing need with greater realism, the Negro colleges more speedily inclined their programs toward literary and professional fields. Hampton, Arkansas A. and M., Prairie View Normal and Industrial, and Alabama Agricultural and Mechanical College were founded especially for the purpose of giving industrial training. Along with eight other institutions that appeared in 1897, they helped to form a core around which the land-grant college system for Negroes was built. Nevertheless these agricultural and mechanical colleges very quickly became teacher-training institutions whose actual curricular emphasis was far more literary than industrial.

During the school year 1899–1900, Tuskegee offered six different curricula to 1,231 students. These curricula were liberal arts, industrial, agricultural, biblical, nursing, and musical. Courses composing these departments were taught by 80 teachers, but half of these instructors were assigned to literary courses. It was through these courses that Tuskegee hoped to correlate the literary and the industrial to furnish young men and women for leadership in the various phases of Negro community life. What Tuskegee had actually begun to do at that time, as later trends indicated, was to train teachers for the Negro public schools. Of the 321 students who were graduated from the Institute from 1885 to 1889, 255 were teaching at the close of the period.

North Carolina's Agricultural and Mechanical College for the Colored Race showed a similar inclination toward the literary and teacher-training functions. During the 1903–1904 school year this institution taught four different curricula: agriculture and chemistry, mechanics, industrial, and liberal arts. These courses were taught to

163 students by seven teachers. Although only two of these teachers were instructing in the liberal arts department, this department, along with its teacher-training functions, seemed to have been the core of the college. The college graduated 72 students between 1899 and 1901, and two thirds of those graduates whose occupations were known to the officials of the school were engaged in teaching.

Some of the Negro colleges got ahead in the literary field by accepting a teacher-training and liberal arts responsibility early. These are best represented by the many normal institutes established for Negro teachers by North Carolina and several other Southern states, and by the several liberal arts colleges that operated within the tradition of Talladega, Fisk, or the Atlanta University group. Beginning mainly as preparatory schools, these institutions were to evolve into four-year colleges, which would supply public school teachers, doctors, lawyers, businessmen, and even college teachers for the Negro society. While the theological departments of several of these colleges had turned toward the production of a formally trained Negro clergy by the opening of the twentieth century, Shaw University at Raleigh, Walden University at Nashville, and Howard University at Washington, D.C., had begun to produce a corps of doctors and nurses.

And so it happened that Negro education, instead of being specialized along industrial lines, became somewhat of a duplication of the education which was offered to white children. It was separate; it was judged in terms of the value scale held for Negroes; and it symbolized America's dual standard of academic competency. Nevertheless, it was to be the stuff out of which revolutions are made.

Very Deliberate Speed

• The supposed equality of the parallel system of racially segregated schools, including those in many northern and western states, as well as in the South, fooled no one. But white America seemed not to care until recently, while black America remained too weak to force a change in the system. Nevertheless black economic and political advances, especially after World War II, ensured the end of the educational status quo, though not the equality promised by the Constitution. All-white higher education fell first, and the NAACP's push against segregated primary schools produced the Brown v. Board of Education decision of 1954. Loren Miller's study of the desegregation decisions puts proper emphasis not on the case alone, but on the subsequent and less known "enforcement" decision of 1955, in which the Warren Court left the door open to massive delay and resistance. "All deliberate speed" turned into "every possible delay," as Justice Black recently acknowledged ruefully. Although resistance to desegregation did not in itself produce the Black Revolution of the 1960's, it undeniably contributed to those events and helped erode black faith in the legal-political process.

. . . A dozen years elapsed between the decisions in the Gaines and Sweatt cases,* but events moved much faster in the 1950's. Less than four short years after the Sweatt case had been decided, the Supreme Court was ready to announce its sweeping decision in cases involving segregation in elementary and secondary schools. The quickened tempo was due to the fact that the NAACP was better organized and better equipped to press its litigation, that restless Negroes were less

From Loren Miller, *The Petitioners: The Supreme Court and the Negro* (New York: Pantheon Books, 1966), pp. 342–54, 356, 359–60, 364 (footnotes omitted). Copyright © 1966 by Loren Miller, Jr. Reprinted by permission of Pantheon Books, a Division of Random House, Inc.
* Cases involving Negroes barred from graduate and professional training by southern universities and decided in 1938 and 1950.

inclined to wait for vindication of their claimed civil rights, and that the Supreme Court's decisions favorable to the exercise of those rights had brightened the national climate of public opinion and pricked the conscience of the American people. An increasing number of Americans had looked through the separate-but-equal rule and had seen it for what it was: a device to stigmatize Negroes and fix a brand of inferiority on them. Troubled and troublesome international events played their part; the nation had assumed a stance as the defender of the free world, and all over the globe other people looked askance at the manifestations of racism in the United States.

A year after Herman Sweatt entered the University of Texas law school, cases were on file in four states and the District of Columbia asking four federal and one state court to apply the qualitative test of the Sweatt case to elementary and secondary schools, and declare that the separate-but-equal rule had no validity in the area of public education. The four states involved were Kansas, South Carolina, Virginia, and Delaware. Ultimately, the four state cases were grouped together and decided as *Brown v. Board of Education of Topeka*, and the District of Columbia litigation was decided in a separate case, *Bolling v. Sharpe*. All were decided on May 17, 1954.

The first of the cases to actually reach the Supreme Court was a suit by Harry Briggs, Jr., and 66 other Negro children, who sued the Clarendon County, South Carolina, School Board No. 22, in a case known as *Harry Briggs, Jr., v. R. W. Elliott*, charging that Clarendon County's Negro schools were far inferior to its schools for white children. They asked a three-judge federal court to hold that South Carolina's separate school laws and constitutional provisions were invalid under the equal-protection clause of the Fourteenth Amendment. The federal judges agreed that the schools for Negroes were inferior to those maintained for white children, and ordered the board to equalize the school systems and report back in six months as to the progress it had made. The judges also ruled that they were bound by *Plessy v. Ferguson* and that South Carolina's separate school laws were valid. The Supreme Court agreed to review the case in June, 1951, but on January 28, 1952, sent it back to the three-judge court with instructions to report on what progress had been made toward equalization. Justices Black and Douglas dissented on the ground that the report was "wholly irrelevant to the constitutional questions presented" and urged that the case be set for argument. In March, 1952, the three-judge district court found that the Clarendon County board had complied with the equalization order, praised it for its compliance, and again upheld South Carolina segregation laws as valid under the Plessy case. The Supreme Court then restored the case to its docket.

Meanwhile, Oliver Brown had sued the Topeka, Kansas, Board of Education because his eight-year-old daughter was denied entrance to a white school only 5 blocks from her home and forced to travel 21 blocks to a Negro school. Kansas laws permitted but did not require cities of more than 15,000 to impose school segregation. Topeka imposed segregation in its grade schools but not in high school. On August 3, 1951, a three-judge federal court held that Topeka's Negro and white schools were substantially equal, criticized the separate-but-equal rule but decided it was bound by *Plessy v. Ferguson* and refused to invalidate Kansas laws. Mr. Brown lost his case and promptly appealed. When his appeal reached the Supreme Court in October, 1951, the South Carolina case had been sent back to the district court for the report on equalization plans. The Court agreed to review Brown's case, and thus it became number one on the list of school segregation cases set for hearing and decision. Brown won immortality of a sort by securing top billing: the school segregation cases would be forever known as *Brown v. Board of Education*.

The Virginia case was heard in still another three-judge federal court in that state on March 7, 1952. Dorothy E. Davis and other high-school students sued the county school board of Prince Edward County asking that Virginia's constitutional and statutory provisions imposing segregation be declared invalid or that the county's Negro and white high schools be ordered equalized. The court granted the equalization request but also fell back on the Plessy case to deny the plea for invalidation of the segregation requirements of Virginia's constitution and laws. The case was appealed to the Supreme Court as *Davis v. County School Board of Prince Edward County*.

The Delaware case was filed in the courts of that state, and on April 1, 1952, Delaware Chancellor Collins J. Seitz found the Negro schools inferior to white schools and enjoined Deleware from enforcing segregation laws because of that inequality. The chancellor expressed his opinion that the "separate but equal doctrine in education should be rejected," but added that rejection must come from the Supreme Court. Delaware's supreme court upheld the injunction on August 28, 1952, but seemed to say that the order should be dissolved as soon as Negro schools were equalized. On November 24, 1952, the Supreme Court added the case, *Gebhart, v. Bolton*, to the list of school cases which it was willing to decide.

Brown v. Board of Education now encompassed the four state cases, each of which presented the question of the application of the separate-but-equal rule to public schools. Each of them rested on the contention that the equal-protection-of-the-laws clause of the Fourteenth Amendment prohibited state-imposed segregation in tax-supported schools. Obviously, they could be argued together and decided together. The Court made such an order.

The Fourteenth Amendment does not apply to the District of Columbia but only to the states. Consequently, there is no equal-protection clause for the District; however, the Fifth Amendment like the Fourteenth, forbids denial of the due process of law. Spottswood Bolling, who sued for admission to a Washington high school, claimed that the due-process-of-law clause of the Fifth Amendment was broad enough to forbid segregation in public schools, and he asked the federal courts, which exercise jurisdiction in the District, to invalidate congressional legislation requiring separate schools. His suit was dismissed, and on November 10, 1952, the Supreme Court granted review in his case, known as *Bolling v. Sharpe,* and set it down for argument at the same time as the four state cases.

There was more to this carefully stage-managed selection of cases for review than meets the naked eye. The Kansas case concerned grade-school children in a northern state with a permissive segregation statute; the Virginia case involved high-school students in a state having compulsory laws and located in the upper tier of southern states; South Carolina represented the Deep South, and Delaware the border states. The state cases all presented the issue of the application of the equal-protection-of-law clause of the Fourteenth Amendment, and the Court could have reached and decided that question in any one of them, but the wide geographical range gave the anticipated decision a national flavor and would blunt any claim that the South was being made a whipping boy. Moreover, the combination of cases included Kansas with its permissive statute, while other cases concerned state constitutional provisions as well as statutes with mandatory segregation requirements. Grade-school students were involved in the Kansas case; high-school students in the Virginia case, and all elementary and secondary students in the Delaware and South Carolina cases. The District of Columbia case drew due process of law into the cases as an issue, in distinction to the equal-protection-of-law clause, and also presented an opportunity for inquiry into the congressional power to impose racial segregation. The NAACP had touched all bases.

Initial arguments were made on December 9, 1952, two-and-a-half years after the Sweatt decision. But the Court reached no decision on the basis of the first briefs and arguments. On June 8, 1953, it issued an order setting the case for reargument that fall, submitting a series of questions to the litigants, and inviting the United States Attorney General to participate in the arguments.

The Court's first question asked what evidence there was that the Congress which submitted and the states which ratified the Fourteenth Amendment contemplated that the amendment would abolish school segregation. It then asked whether Congress had the power to abolish all school segregation, regardless of whether the framers or ratifying states believed that the amendment required its immediate abolition, and what was the reach of the Court's power under those circumstances. Its third inquiry was the extent of the Court's power to abolish school segregation in the event that the answers to the first two questions were inconclusive. The fourth question was that of whether a decree favoring the Negro plaintiffs would carry with it an order directing their immediate admission to state-supported schools or whether the Court could devise a gradualistic scheme for their enrollment—a very obvious and very curious, inquiry as to whether the rights of Negro grade-school students to attend public schools were *personal and present* (as all constitutional rights are) or whether their exercise could be delayed until a more propitious time. The fifth question concerned the form the decree should take, if the Court decided on a gradualistic abolition of segregation.

Thurgood Marshall, counsel and director of the NAACP Legal Defense & Educational Fund, convoked sessions of lawyers, law school professors, and historians from all over the nation to help find answers to the Court's questions and to fashion briefs and arguments. The hard-pressed states hired John W. Davis, one-time Democratic candidate for the presidency of the United States and one of the nation's leading constitutional lawyers, to head an imposing array of counsel.

Reargument began on December 8, 1953 and continued for three days. Then the Court took all of the cases under submission for later decision.

The showdown had come; judgment day was near for *Plessy v. Ferguson* in the field of public education. . . .

Chief Justice Earl Warren was almost through reading his opinion for a unanimous Court in the case of *Brown v. Board of Education* before he pronounced the fateful words: "We conclude that in the field of public education the doctrine of 'separate but equal' has no place. Therefore, we hold that the plaintiffs and others similarly situated for whom the actions have been brought are, by reason of the segregation complained of, deprived of the equal protection of the laws guaranteed by the Fourteenth Amendment." The date was May 17, 1954. That Great Gettin' Up Morning storied in the old Negro spiritual had arrived.

The Chief Justice had picked a careful path toward that conclusion. He began by referring to the history of the amendment in reference to schools, in an effort to ascertain the understanding of its framers, and found the evidence inconclusive at best. "The most avid proponents of the post-War Amendments undoubtedly intended them to remove all legal distinctions among 'all persons born or naturalized in the United States,'" he said. "Their opponents . . . were antagonistic to both the letter and spirit of the Amendments. . . ." He thought that the low estate of public education, particularly in the South, also contributed to the inconclusiveness of sentiment in both Congress and the ratifying states in respect of separate schools.

The separate-but-equal rule, Chief Justice Warren reminded the nation, "did not make its appearance in [the Supreme] Court until 1896 in the case of Plessy v. Ferguson, not involving education but transportation." But, he pointed out, the Supreme "Court construing the Fourteenth Amendment [in cases] decided shortly after its adoption . . . construed it as proscribing all state-imposed discrimination against the Negro race." He then reviewed the fifty-year-old history of the application of the Plessy rule in education, beginning with the Cummings case in 1899 and ending with the Sweatt case in 1950. "In none of these cases," he said, "was it necessary to examine the [Plessy] doctrine to grant relief to the Negro plaintiff."

Lower courts in cases under review in 1954, however, had either found Negro schools equal to their white counterparts or had ordered their physical equalization, and the Chief Justice remarked: "Our decision, therefore, cannot turn on merely a comparison of these tangible factors in the Negro and white schools involved. . . . We must look instead to the effect of segregation itself on public education." H insisted that in doing so the Court could not "turn the clock back to 1868 when the Amendment was adopted, or even to 1896 when Plessy v. Ferguson was written."

The Chief Justice then stressed the importance of public education in a democratic society. He posed the crucial question: "Does segregation of children in public schools solely on the basis of race, even though the facilities be equal, deprive children of the minority group of equal educational opportunity?" His answer was yes. He found support for his affirmative view in the findings of the Kansas and Delaware courts and made footnote references to sociological, historical, and educational data to the same effect. It was then that he pronounced the judgment of the Court.

What he had said was that the command of the Fourteenth Amendment was a command for equality and that when state laws subverted that command, they were unconstitutional and must be stricken down by the Supreme Court, even though such laws had been tolerated at some earlier historical times when their effect was not apparent. Plainly he had in mind Chief Justice Marshall's more than a century-old admonition that "ours is a constitution intended to endure for ages to come, and consequently to be adapted to the various crises in human affairs."

The May 17 decision did not dispose of the cases. The Court renewed its previously made request for submission of briefs and arguments on the issues of whether invalidation of segregation statutes permitted it to devise a gradualistic formula for admission of Negro children to state-supported schools and, if so, what kind of a decree it should fashion to achieve that end. The Attorney General of the United States and attorneys general of states requiring or permitting segregation were invited to express their points of view. Hearing on those issues was set for the October, 1954, term of the Court. The Brown decision settled the segregation question for the four state cases which had come to the Court from Kansas, Delaware, South Carolina, and Virginia and which involved the Fourteenth Amendment.

Chief Justice Warren then turned to *Bolling v. Sharpe*, which had arisen in the District of Columbia. "The legal problem in the District," he said, "is somewhat different. . . . The Fifth Amendment which is applicable to the District of Columbia, does not contain an equal protection clause [as does the Fourteenth] which applies only to the States." But he found that the concepts of due process of law and equal protection of the law both stemmed from "our American ideal of fairness" and that while they were not interchangeable, it was true that "discrimination may be so unjustifiable as to be a violation of due process."

He reiterated the constitutional doctrine that "Classification based solely upon race must be scrutinized with particular care" and arrived at the conclusion that "segregation in public education . . . imposes on Negro children of the District of Columbia an arbitrary

deprivation of their liberty in violation of the Due Process clause."
Moreover, he said, "in view of our decision that the Constitution
prohibits the states from maintaining separate schools it would be
unthinkable that the same Constitution would impose a lesser duty
on the Federal Government." The Bolling case was also put on the
October, 1954, docket for further consideration of the proper remedy
and decrees.

Reargument on the issues of gradualism and proper decrees began
on April 11 and ended on April 14, 1955. Lawyers for the plaintiffs,
the states directly involved, the District of Columbia, the Attorney
General of the United States and attorneys general for Florida, North
Carolina, Arkansas, Oklahoma, Maryland, and Texas filed briefs and
participated in the arguments. Chief Justice Warren again spoke for a
unanimous Court on May 31, 1955. He explained that "Full implementation of . . . constitutional principles may require solution of
varied local school problems. School authorities have the primary
responsibility for . . . solving these problems; courts will have to
consider whether the action of school authorities constitutes good
faith implementation of the governing constitutional principles. Because of their proximity to local conditions and the possible need for
further hearings, the courts which originally heard these cases can
best perform this judicial appraisal. Accordingly, we believe it appropriate to remand the cases to those courts."

The courts to which the cases were remanded were admonished
to apply equitable principles that would be fair to both the Negro
children and school authorities, but, he said, "it should go without
saying that the vitality of these constitutional principles cannot be
allowed to yield simply because of disagreement with them." The
courts were also told to "require that the defendants make a prompt
and reasonable start toward full compliance with our May 17, 1954
decision. . . . Once such a start has been made, the courts may
find that additional time is necessary to carry out the ruling in an
effective manner."

The ideal toward which the defendants were ordered to move was
"good faith compliance at the earliest practicable date." The burden
was put on the defendants to establish the need for additional time.
"To that end," the Chief Justice said, "the courts may consider
problems related to administration, arising from the physical condition of the school plant, the school transportation system, personnel,
revision of school districts and attendance areas into compact units
to achieve a system of determining admission to the public schools
on a non-racial basis, and revision of local laws and regulations which

may be necessary in solving the foregoing problems." The courts were ordered to enter "such orders and decrees consistent with this opinion as are necessary and proper to admit to public schools on a racially non-discriminatory basis with all deliberate speed the parties to these cases."

If the Court's order seems in the retrospect of ten years to be steeped in judical naïveté, in light of the fact that in 1965 Negro children had been admitted to so-called white schools in less than 25 per cent of southern school districts and that not a single Negro child involved in the cases ever attended integrated schools in Clarendon County, South Carolina, or Prince Edward County, Virginia, it must be borne in mind that the Court was carried away by its own optimism in 1955. Chief Justice Warren noted with transparent pride in the second Brown decision that "substantial steps to eliminate racial discrimination in public schools have already been taken, not only in some of the communities in which these cases arose but in some of the states appearing as [friends of the Court] as well. Substantial progress has been made in the District of Columbia and in the communities in Kansas and Delaware involved in this litigation." The ink was hardly dry on the second decision before the states of the old Confederacy embarked on a program of massive resistance to the Boston decision. Compliance was orderly and meaningful only in the border states and in northern and western states with permissive segregation statutes.

The harsh truth is that the first Brown decision was a great decision; the second Brown decision was a great mistake. In the 1954 case, the Court said unequivocally that segregation of Negro children in public schools deprived them "of the equal protection of the laws guaranteed by the Fourteenth Amendment." As it had said so many times and with so much emphasis, a constitutional right is always *personal and present*. It inheres in the individual, in the *person* in constitutional language. But in the 1955 case, the Court held that a *person and present* constitutional right could be deferred and extended gradually to those who were entitled to exercise it by virtue of a constitutional amendment. There was no constitutional warrant for such a ruling.

The notion that a Negro could be required to defer his exercise of a constitutional right was a by-product of the earlier attempts of southern states to hold fast to segregation in graduate and professional schools until they had time to construct separate-but-equal facilities. In its proper turn, the concept that a special rule could be applied to Negroes traced back to the Dred Scott dogma that freeborn Negroes constituted an intermediate class of beings within the constitutional scheme who were not endowed by birth with the rights of free white persons. In the first cases construing them, the Court held that the all-pervading purpose of the Civil War Amendments was to abolish all racial distinction and put Negroes on a plane of absolute equality with white Americans. Whatever rights white men had, Negroes had; all were citizens of the nation and of their states; all were free men.

The great vice of the Plessy case lay in the fact that the Court was induced to rule that the Constitution as amended recognized racial distinctions; the corollary was that the Negro could exercise commonplace rights and privileges, vouchsafed by birth to white persons, such as using *public* parks, playgrounds, and libraries, attending *public* schools or enjoying full use of *public* utilities such as trains or boats at the *sufferance* of the white majority. The Negro was not a *free man*; he was a *freedman*, to whom rights could be doled out by those who had set him free. (The vulgar expression of this notion is reflected in commonly heard complaints that the Negro is "moving too fast" or "demanding too much" when he seeks to exercise the same rights enjoyed as a matter of course by the white complainant.)

The Court readily saw the incongruity of requests that it defer exercise of the constitutional rights if found existent in the graduate and professional school cases, and rejected those requests out of hand by reiterating the truism that a constitutional right is always *personal and present*. No American lawyer anywhere had ever supposed that the Supreme Court, or any other organ of government, could suspend the exercise of a peacetime constitutional right for a single day. The reason is simple: a constitutional right which is not exercised at the moment of the possessor's desire is forever lost. Even Southern lawyers who argued for delay in the graduate and professional school cases were not really asking for the suspension of a constitutional right; their argument boiled down to the contention that the request for such instruction was so suddenly made that the states should have time to provide the facilities within the context of valid separate-but-equal statutes. Once the separate-but-equal rule was disavowed, there was no constitutional basis for delay in the exercise of constitutional rights.

When the Court temporized in the 1955 Brown decision and devised the deliberate-speed formula, it did so out of the best of motives. It was acting out its traditional role as the guardian of Negro rights and was moved by the triple belief—hope may be a better word—that a prompt start would be made toward compliance, that the federal district courts would act with firmness and dispatch, and that the entire process would take only a short time. No doubt it wanted to assuage the white South. It was wrong on all scores; it only succeeded in opening a Pandora's box of troubles.

The deliberate-speed formula was not only a constitutional blunder but also a practical mistake of the first order. It armed the recalcitrant states with a built-in device for delay and resistance, and actually suggested delay in some quarters. The disposition of the four state cases after the Court had devised the formula was prophetic. In the Delaware case, *Gebhart v. Bolton,* the state courts had ordered admission of the Negro plaintiffs prior to the 1954 decision and that order was not disturbed. In another case, arising after the 1954 case and when it was apparent that the Court was going to issue a gradualistic order of some kind, the Delaware supreme court refused to order immediate admission of Negro pupils saying that it would delay action because the Brown opinion did not require "immediate desegregation of public schools." The 1955 Brown opinion actually delayed desegregation in that instance.

The three-judge Kansas federal court that had scored separate schools as discriminatory in its original opinion accepted the 1955 decision as an invitation for delay. When the plaintiffs requested a decree directing immediate desegregation, the judges responded by holding a hearing on the admittedly incomplete desegregation plan of the Topeka School Board. The Topeka superintendent admitted that the plan did not accomplish desegregation for the 1955–56 school year, but the judges were satisfied merely because a "good faith" start had been made.

The Virginia and South Carolina federal courts contented themselves with the issuance of meaningless decrees enjoining the boards of education from "refusing on account of race or color to admit . . . any child to enter" their schools. But the injunctions were to go into effect only after the boards had made "necessary arrangements . . . with all deliberate speed." Because their rights were not declared to be personal and present, Prince Edward and Clarendon County plaintiffs had won nothing except a semantic victory. They would never attend, or have an opportunity to attend, desegregated schools.

Only in the special case of the District of Columbia were the schools quickly desegregated. Fortunately, the District acted prior to the 1955 decision.

Of course, the Brown cases were binding only on the litigants before the Court. That is true in any case, but men of good judgment do not wait until their own conduct is condemned when they live under a government of laws and the course they have been pursuing is identical with that proscribed by the courts in another case. They put their own houses in order and thus ward off litigation. The border states of Oklahoma, Missouri, Kentucky, West Virginia, and Maryland did just that, as did the western states where segregation was permissive. But . . . the states of the old Confederacy have never pursued any such policy in the area of civil rights. They have always depended on obstruction and defiance to preserve their old ways. They clung to that course as far as schools were concerned and waited for lawsuits, district by district, while they devised obstructionist laws and procedures. As a first step, Negroes had to apply for admission to public schools and, when refused, had to appeal to school boards for desegregation plans. If the boards refused to act, as many did, or drew up inadequate plans which were little more than legal jests, as many were, the offended Negroes had to file suit either to force the boards to act or to submit desegregation plans that were meaningful. The tragic inadequacies of the deliberate-speed formula were soon apparent. . . .

In shying away from declaring the rights sought in the Brown case to be personal and present, the Court was also undoubtedly moved by the belief that the gradualistic approach would be less offensive and more readily acceptable to the South. The sober truth is that change would have been gradual in any event. Negroes habituated to segregation would have moved slowly. As the chosen instrument of Negroes seeking change, the NAACP lacked financial resources and manpower to proceed in any other than a gradual manner, district by district, where boards of education did not act on application of Negroes. It could have, and undoubtedly would have, acted with as much dispatch as possible, but it could not have wrought a revolution. Armed, as they should have been, with a declaration that the right imbedded in the Fourteenth Amendment was personal and present, Negroes could have secured the claimed right at a much faster pace for the good of Negro children—and for the nation. . . .

The slow pace of desegregation in southern schools had reached the proportions of a public scandal by the 1960's; it was apparent that the deliberate-speed formula was being used to maintain segregation. The Supreme Court voiced its impatience in three cases and issued what was in effect a public reprimand to school boards which proposed, and district courts which approved, slow-moving desegregation plans. In *Goss v. Board of Education,* decided in 1963, it said: "We are not unmindful of the deep rooted problems involved. Indeed it was consideration for the multifarious local difficulties and 'variety of obstacles' which might arise in this transition that led this Court eight years ago to frame its mandate in *Brown* in such language as 'good faith compliance at the earliest practicable date' and 'all deliberate speed.' Now, however, eight years after this decree was rendered and over nine years after the first *Brown* decision, the context in which we must interpret and apply this language to plans for desegregation has been significantly altered." A similar warning had been sounded in *Watson v. City of Memphis,* also decided in 1963, and was re-issued in *Calhoun v. Latimer,* decided in 1964 by quoting the language of the Goss case. The Court spelled out what it meant in *Griffin v. County School Board* in 1964, when it said in waspish language that "There has been entirely too much deliberation and not enough speed in enforcing the constitutional rights which we held in *Brown v. Board of Education* had been denied. . . ." Plainly, the Court was tiring of evasion and delay.

The Griffin case, in which the Court found "too much deliberation and not enough speed," was the same case under a new name that had been considered as one of the four state cases in the first Brown decision. It was originally filed as *Allen v. County School Board* in 1951, and thirteen years after its filing, Prince Edward County, Virginia, had not budged an inch: there had been no desegregation and the high-school children involved had long since been graduated. Some of them had school-age children themselves. All public schools in the county had been closed since 1959, in order to forestall desegregation. It was back in the Court to test the issue of whether or not a state could close its public schools when desegregation was ordered and educate white children at "private" schools through tuition grants and rebatement of taxes. . . .

Whatever its shortcomings as regards the deliberate-speed formula, *Brown v. Board of Education* is a great landmark case in American constitutional law. The Court did turn the clock back—back toward the bright promise of 1868, when the Fourteenth Amendment was ratified and when the nation wrote into its fundamental law the proposition that there is no color and there is no caste here, as the first Justice John Marshall Harlan had seen so clearly and said so eloquently. The Court's long backward step in *Plessy v. Ferguson* disrupted but did not destroy that principle. When the Supreme Court restored that principle in the Brown case, it broke down a blockade of law and custom and reopened the road toward equality, a road beset with many obstacles—obstacles growing out of slavery and out of the institutionalization of racial discrimination created by the separate-but-equal rule and by other cases in which the Court restricted constitutional rights.

As for the deliberate-speed formula, it has nearly run its course. The Court's increasing dissatisfaction with and criticism of the application of the rule presages the day when it will declare its end and restore the constitutional doctrine that a right imbedded in the Constitution is always personal and present. Meanwhile the 1964 Civil Rights Act has provided additional leverage for desegregation through provisions that the federal government may withhold school funds where no adequate desegregation plan has been undertaken by a school board. That provision hastened desegregation in the fall of 1965 and will become an increasingly important device to disestablish separate schools. . . .

A Selected Modern Bibliography

GENERAL WORKS

Monroe N. Work, A Bibliography of the Negro in Africa and America (New York, 1928)
Erwin K. Welsch, The Negro in the United States: A Research Guide (Bloomington, Ind., 1965)
Elizabeth W. Miller, The Negro in America: A Bibliography (Cambridge, Mass., 1966)

Herbert Aptheker (ed.), A Documentary History of the Negro People in the United States, 2 vols. (New York, 1951)
W. E. B. Du Bois, Black Folk, Then and Now: An Essay in the History and Sociology of the Negro Race (New York, 1939)
Carter G. Woodson and Charles H. Wesley, The Negro in Our Society (10th edition, Washington, 1968)
J. Saunders Redding, They Came in Chains (Philadelphia, 1950)
John Hope Franklin, From Slavery to Freedom: A History of Negro Americans (3rd edition, New York, 1969)
August Meier and Elliott M. Rudwick, From Plantation to Ghetto (New York, 1966)
E. Franklin Frazier, The Negro in the United States (rev. edition, New York, 1957)
Thomas F. Gossett, Race: The History of an Idea in America (Dallas, 1963)

E. Franklin Frazier, The Negro Family in the United States (Chicago, 1939)
Carter G. Woodson, History of the Negro Church (Washington, 1921)
E. Franklin Frazier, The Negro Church in America (New York, 1963)
Joseph R. Washington, Jr., Black Religion: The Negro and Christianity in the United States (Boston, 1964)
Andrew E. Murray, Presbyterians and the Negro: A History (Philadelphia, 1966)
Horace M. Bond, The Education of the Negro in the American Social Order (New York, 1934)
Dwight O. W. Holmes, The Evolution of the Negro College (New York, 1934)
Henry Allen Bullock, A History of Negro Education in the South from 1619 to the Present (Cambridge, Mass., 1967)
Rayford W. Logan, Howard University: The First Hundred Years, 1867–1967 (New York, 1969)
Frederick G. Detweiler, The Negro Press in the United States (Chicago, 1922)

Earl E. Thorpe, *The Mind of the Negro: An Intellectual History of Afro-Americans* (Baton Rouge, 1961)

I: THE CIVIL WAR AND THE BLACKS, 1863–1865

Benjamin Quarles, *Lincoln and the Negro* (New York, 1962)
John Hope Franklin, *The Emancipation Proclamation* (New York, 1963)
Mark M. Krug, "The Republican Party and the Emancipation Proclamation," *Journal of Negro History*, XLVIII (April 1963)
Charles L. Wagandt, *The Mighty Revolution: Negro Emancipation in Maryland, 1862–1864* (Baltimore, 1964)
Harold D. Moser, "Reaction in North Carolina to the Emancipation Proclamation," *North Carolina Historical Review*, XLIV (Winter 1967)

James M. McPherson, *The Struggle for Liberty: Abolitionists and the Negro in the Civil War and Reconstruction* (Princeton, 1964)
Willie Lee Rose, *Rehearsal for Reconstruction: The Port Royal Experiment* (Indianapolis, 1964)
Laura W. Roper, "Frederick Law Olmstead and the Port Royal Experiment," *Journal of Southern History*, XXXI (August 1965)
W. Harrison Daniel, "Southern Protestantism and the Negro, 1860–1865," *North Carolina Historical Review*, XLI (Summer 1964)

V. Jacques Voegeli, *Free But Not Equal: The Midwest and the Negro During the Civil War* (Chicago, 1967)
Forrest G. Wood, *Black Scare: The Racist Response to Emancipation and Reconstruction* (Berkeley, 1968)
Albon P. Man, Jr., "Labor Competition and the New York Draft Riots of 1863," *Journal of Negro History*, XXXVI (October 1951)

Herbert Aptheker, *The Negro in the Civil War* (New York, 1938)
Benjamin Quarles, *The Negro in the Civil War* (Boston, 1953)
Dudley T. Cornish, *The Sable Arm: Negro Troops in the Union Army, 1861–1865* (New York, 1956)
Fred A. Shannon, "The Federal Government and the Negro Soldier, 1861–1865," *Journal of Negro History*, XI (October 1926)
John W. Blassingame, "The Union Army as an Educational Institution for Negros, 1862–1865," *Journal of Negro Education*, XXXIV (Spring 1965)
Wallace E. Davies, "The Problem of Race Segregation in the Grand Army of the Republic," *Journal of Southern History*, XIII (August 1947)
Peter Burchard, *One Gallant Rush: Robert Gould Shaw and His Brave Black Regiment* (New York, 1965)
Tilden G. Edelstein, *Strange Enthusiasm: The Life of Thomas Wentworth Higginson* (New Haven, 1968)
Richard H. Abbott, "Massachusetts and the Recruitment of Southern Negroes, 1863–1865," *Civil War History*, XIV (September 1968)
Brainerd Dyer, "The Treatment of Colored Union Troops by the Confederates, 1861–1865," *Journal of Negro History*, XX (July 1935)

Bell I. Wiley, *Southern Negroes, 1861–1865* (New Haven, Conn., 1938)
Harvey Wish, "Slave Disloyalty Under the Confederacy," *Journal of Negro History*, XXIII (October 1938)
Bernard H. Nelson, "Legislative Control of the Southern Free Negro, 1861–1865," *Catholic Historical Review*, XXXII (April 1946)
Charles H. Wesley, "The Employment of Negroes as Soldiers in the Confederate Army," *Journal of Negro History*, IV (July 1919)

II: RECONSTRUCTION, 1865–1877

W. E. B. Du Bois, "Reconstruction and Its Benefits," *American Historical Review*, XV (July 1910)
W. E. B. Du Bois, *Black Reconstruction in America, 1860–1880* (New York, 1935)
John Hope Franklin, *Reconstruction After the Civil War* (Chicago, 1961)
Kenneth M. Stampp, *The Era of Reconstruction, 1865–1877* (New York, 1965)
Lerone Bennett, Jr., *Black Power U. S. A.: The Human Side of Reconstruction, 1867–1877* (Chicago, 1967)
Robert Cruden, *The Negro in Reconstruction* (Englewood Cliffs, 1969)

Alrutheus A. Taylor, *The Negro in the Reconstruction of Virginia* (Washington, 1926)
Richard L. Morton, *The Negro in Virginia Politics, 1865–1902* (Charlottesville, Va., 1919)
Alrutheus A. Taylor, *The Negro in South Carolina During Reconstruction* (Washington, 1924)
Joel Williamson, *After Slavery: The Negro in South Carolina During Reconstruction, 1861–1877* (Chapel Hill, 1965)
Elizabeth Studley Nathans, *Losing the Peace: Georgia Republicans and Reconstruction, 1865–1871* (Baton Rouge, 1968)
Joe M. Richardson, *The Negro in the Reconstruction of Florida, 1865–1877* (Tallahassee, 1965)
Horace M. Bond, "Social and Economic Forces in Alabama Reconstruction," *Journal of Negro History*, XXIII (July 1938)
Vernon Lane Wharton, *The Negro in Mississippi, 1865–1877* (Chapel Hill, 1947)
Alrutheus A. Taylor, *The Negro in Tennessee, 1865–1880* (Washington, 1944)

LaWanda and John Cox, *Politics, Principle and Prejudice: The Dilemma of Reconstruction America, 1865–1866* (Glencoe, Ill., 1963)
Theodore B. Wilson, *The Black Codes of the South* (University, Ala., 1965)
Joe M. Richardson, "Florida Black Codes," *Florida Historical Quarterly*, XLVII (April 1969)
Thomas Wagstaff, "Call Your Old Master—'Master': Southern Political Leaders and Negro Labor During Presidential Reconstruction," *Labor History*, X (Summer 1969)

Donald E. Reynolds, "The New Orleans Riot of 1866, Reconsidered," *Louisiana History*, V (Winter 1964)

Jacobus TenBroek, *Antislavery Origins of the Fourteenth Amendment* (Berkeley, 1951)
Joseph B. James, *The Framing of the Fourteenth Amendment* (Urbana, Ill., 1956)
Hans L. Trefousse, *The Radical Republicans: Lincoln's Vanguard for Social Justice* (New York, 1969)
Otis A. Singletary, *Negro Militia and Reconstruction* (Austin, Tex., 1957)

George R. Bentley, *A History of the Freedmen's Bureau* (Philadelphia, 1955)
LaWanda Cox, "The Promise of Land for the Freedmen," *Mississippi Valley Historical Review*, XLV (December 1958)
John and LaWanda Cox, "General O. O. Howard and the 'Misrepresented Bureau,' " *Journal of Southern History*, XIX (November 1953)
William S. McFeeley, *Yankee Stepfather: General O. O. Howard and the Freedmen* (New Haven, 1968)
Richard B. Drake, "Freedmen's Aid Societies and Sectional Compromise," *Journal of Southern History*, XXIX (May 1963)

Martin Abbott, *The Freedmen's Bureau in South Carolina, 1865–1872* (Chapel Hill, 1967)
Joe M. Richardson, "An Evaluation of the Freedmen's Bureau in Florida," *Florida Historical Quarterly*, XLI (January 1963)
Edward K. Eckerdt, "Contract Labor in Florida During Reconstruction," *Florida Historical Quarterly*, XLVII (July 1968)
J. Thomas May, "The Freedmen's Bureau at the Local Level: A Study of a Louisiana Agent," *Louisiana History*, IX (Winter 1968)
Paul David Phillips, "White Reactions to the Freedmen's Bureau in Tennessee," *Tennessee Historical Quarterly*, XXV (Spring 1966)
Joseph E. Holliday, "Freedmen's Aid Societies in Cincinnati, 1862–1870," *Bulletin of the Cincinnati Historical Society*, XXII (July 1964)
Earle H. West, "The Peabody Fund and Negro Education, 1867–1880," *History of Education Quarterly*, VI (Summer 1966)

William Gilette, *The Right To Vote: Politics and the Passage of Fifteenth Amendment* (Baltimore, 1965)
Leslie H. Fishel, Jr., "Northern Prejudice and Negro Suffrage, 1865–1870," *Journal of Negro History*, XXXIX (January 1954)
LaWanda and John H. Cox, "Negro Suffrage and Republican Politics: The Problem of Motivation in Reconstruction Historiography," *Journal of Southern History*, XXXIII (August 1967)
Forrest G. Wood, "On Revising Reconstruction History: Negro Suffrage, White Disfranchisement, and Common Sense," *Journal of Negro History*, LI (April 1966)
Robert R. Dykstra and Harlan Hahn, "Northern Voters and Negro Suffrage: The Case of Iowa, 1868," *Public Opinion Quarterly*, XXXII (Summer 1968)

G. Galin Berrier, "The Negro Suffrage Issue in Iowa—1865–1868," *Annals of Iowa*, XXXIX (Summer 1968)
Everette Swinney, "Enforcing the Fifteenth Amendment, 1870–1877," *Journal of Southern History*, XXVIII (May 1962)

Samuel D. Smith, *The Negro in Congress, 1870–1901* (Chapel Hill, 1940)
Melvin I. Urofsky, "Blanche K. Bruce: United States Senator, 1875–1881," *Journal of Mississippi History*, XXIX (May 1967)
Edward F. Sweat, "Francis L. Cardozo: Profile of Integrity in Reconstruction Politics," *Journal of Negro History*, XLVI (October 1961)
E. Merton Coulter, *Negro Legislators in Georgia During the Reconstruction Period* (Athens, Ga., 1968)
Robert A. Fischer, "A Pioneer Protest: The New Orleans Street-Car Controversy of 1867," *Journal of Negro History*, LIII (July 1968)
Marjorie M. Norris, "An Early Instance of Nonviolence: The Louisville Demonstrations of 1870–1871," *Journal of Southern History*, XXXII (November 1966)

Stanley F. Horn, *Invisible Empire: The Story of the Ku Klux Klan, 1866–1871* (rev. edition, Cos Cob, Conn., 1969)
Francis B. Simpkins, "The Ku Klux Klan in South Carolina, 1868–1871," *Journal of Negro History*, XII (October 1927)
Herbert Shapiro, "The Ku Klux Klan During Reconstruction: The South Carolina Episode," *Journal of Negro History*, XLIX (January 1964)
Ralph L. Peek, "Aftermath of Military Reconstruction, 1868–1869," *Florida Historical Quarterly*, XLIII (October 1964)
Ralph L. Peek, "Military Reconstruction and the Growth of Anti-Negro Sentiment in Florida," *Florida Historical Quarterly*, XLVII (April 1969)
Paul C. Palmer, "Miscegenation as an Issue in the Arkansas Constitutional Convention of 1868," *Arkansas Historical Quarterly*, XXIV (Summer 1965)
Eli Seifman, "Education or Emigration: The Schism Within the African Colonization Movement, 1865–1875," *History of Education Quarterly*, VII (Spring 1967)

John S. Ezell, "The Civil Rights Act of 1875," *Mid-America*, L (October 1968)
T. B. Tunnell, Jr., "The Negro, the Republican Party, and the Election of 1876 in Louisiana," *Louisiana History*, VII (Spring 1966)
C. Vann Woodward, "Seeds of Failure in Radical Race Policy," *Proceedings of the American Philosophical Society*, CX (February 1966)

III: DECLINE AND FALL, 1877–1900

C. Vann Woodward, *Origins of the New South, 1877–1913* (Baton Rouge, 1951)

Vincent P. De Santis, Republicans Face the Southern Question, 1877–1897 (Baltimore, 1959)

Stanley P. Hirshon, Farewell to the Bloody Shirt: Northern Republicans and the Southern Negro, 1877–1893 (Bloomington, Ind., 1962)

George Sinkler, "Race: Principles and Policy of Rutherford B. Hayes," Ohio History, LXXVII (Winter 1968)

Leslie H. Fishel, Jr., "Repercussions of Reconstruction: The Northern Negro, 1870–1883," Civil War History, XIV (December 1968)

Leslie H. Fishel, Jr., "The Negro in Northern Politics, 1870–1900," Mississippi Valley Historical Review, XLII (December 1955)

John G. Van Deusen, "The Exodus of 1879," Journal of Negro History, XXI (April 1936)

Roy Garvin, "Benjamin, or 'Pap' Singleton, and His Followers," Journal of Negro History, XXXIII (January 1948)

Glen Schwendeman, "Nicodemus: Negro Haven on the Solomon," Kansas Historical Quarterly, XXXIV (Spring 1968)

Thomas F. Andrews, "Freedmen in Indian Territory: A Post-Civil War Dilemma," Journal of the West, IV (July 1965)

W. Sherman Savage, "The Role of the Negro Soldiers in Protecting the Indian Frontier from Intruders," Journal of Negro History, XXXVI (January 1951)

William H. Leckie, The Buffalo Soldiers: A Narrative of the Negro Cavalry in the West (Norman, Okla., 1967)

Philip Durham and Everett Jones, Negro Cowboys (New York, 1965)

Guion G. Johnson, "Southern Paternalism Toward Negroes After Emancipation," Journal of Southern History, XXIII (November 1957)

Charles E. Wynes, "Lewis Harvie Blair, Virginia Reformer: The Uplift of the Negro and Southern Prosperity," Virginia Magazine of History and Biography, LXXII (January 1964)

Hampton M. Jarrell, Wade Hampton and the Negro (Columbia, S. C., 1950)

Louis D. Rubin, Jr., George W. Cable: The Life and Times of a Southern Heretic (New York, 1969)

Margaret Law Callcott, The Negro in Maryland Politics, 1870–1912 (Baltimore, 1968)

Charles E. Wynes, Race Relations in Virginia, 1870–1902 (Charlottesville, Va., 1961)

William F. Cheek, "A Negro Runs for Congress: John Mercer Langston and the Virginia Campaign of 1888," Journal of Negro History, LII (January 1967)

Frenise Logan, The Negro in North Carolina, 1876–1894 (Chapel Hill, 1964)

Helen G. Edmonds, The Negro and Fusion Politics in North Carolina, 1894–1901 (Chapel Hill, 1951)

George B. Tindall, South Carolina Negroes, 1877–1900 (Columbia, S. C., 1952)

Albert D. Kirwan, Revolt of the Rednecks: Mississippi Politics, 1876–1925 (Lexington, Ky., 1951)

Henry C. Dethloff and Robert R. Jones, "Race Relations in Louisiana, 1877–1898," *Louisiana History*, IX (Fall 1968)

Fletcher M. Green, "Some Aspects of the Convict Lease System in the Southern States," in Green (ed.), *Essays in Southern History . . .* (Chapel Hill, 1949)

Mark T. Carleton, "The Politics of the Convict Lease System in Louisiana, 1868–1901," *Louisiana History*, VIII (Winter 1967)

C. Vann Woodward, *The Strange Career of Jim Crow* (rev. edition, New York, 1964)

William P. Vaughan, "Separate and Unequal: The Civil Rights Act of 1875 and Defeat of the School Integration Clause," *Southwestern Social Science Quarterly*, XLVII (September 1967)

Bertram Wyatt-Brown, "The Civil Rights Act of 1875," *Western Political Quarterly*, XVIII (December 1965)

Stanley J. Folmsbee, "The Origin of the First 'Jim Crow' Law," *Journal of Southern History*, XV (May 1949)

Albert N. Sanders, "Jim Crow Comes to South Carolina," *Proceedings of the South Carolina Historical Association* (1966)

John Hope Franklin, "Jim Crow Goes to School: The Genesis of Legal Segregation in Southern Schools," *South Atlantic Quarterly*, LVIII (Spring 1959)

Barton J. Bernstein, "*Plessy* v. *Ferguson*: Conservative Sociological Jurisprudence," *Journal of Negro History*, XLVIII (July 1963)

William A. Mabry, *Studies in the Disfranchisement of the Negro in the South* (Durham, N. C., 1933)

Paul Lewinson, *Race, Class and Party: A History of Negro Suffrage and White Politics in the South* (New York, 1932 and 1959)

Amy M. Hiller, "The Disfranchisement of Delaware Negroes in the Late Nineteenth Century," *Delaware History*, XIII (October 1968)

Robert E. Martin, *Negro Disfranchisement in Virginia* (Washington, 1938)

George B. Tindall, "The Campaign for the Disfranchisement of Negroes in South Carolina," *Journal of Southern History*, XV (May 1949)

Joseph H. Taylor, "Populism and Disfranchisement in Alabama," *Journal of Negro History*, XXXIV (October 1949)

William A. Mabry, "Disfranchisement of the Negro in Mississippi," *Journal of Southern History*, IV (August 1938)

John William Graves, "Negro Disfranchisement in Arkansas," *Arkansas Historical Quarterly*, XXVI (Autumn 1967)

Rayford W. Logan, *The Negro in American Life and Thought: The Nadir, 1877–1901* (New York, 1954)

August Meier, *Negro Thought in America, 1880–1915* (Ann Arbor, Mich., 1963)

Samuel R. Spencer, *Booker T. Washington and the Negro's Place in American Life* (Boston, 1955)

August Meier, "Booker T. Washington and the Negro Press," *Journal of Negro History*, XXXVIII (January 1953)

August Meier, "Toward a Reinterpretation of Booker T. Washington," *Journal of Southern History*, XXIII (May 1957)

Daniel Walden, "Contemporary Opposition to the Political Ideals of Booker T. Washington," *Journal of Negro History*, XLV (April 1960)

Donald J. Calista, "Booker T. Washington: Another Look," *Journal of Negro History*, XLIX (October 1964)

Louis R. Harlan, "Booker T. Washington and the White Man's Burden," *American Historical Review*, LXXI (January 1966)

Emma L. Thornbrough, "Booker T. Washington as Seen by His White Contemporaries," *Journal of Negro History*, LIII (April 1968)

John P. Flynn, "Booker T. Washington: Uncle Tom or Wooden Horse?" *Journal of Negro History*, LIV (July 1969)

Herman D. Block, "Labor and the Negro, 1866–1910," *Journal of Negro History*, L (July 1965)

Bernard Mandel, "Samuel Gompers and the Negro Worker, 1886–1914," *Journal of Negro History*, XL (January 1955)

William M. Tuttle, Jr., "Labor Conflict and Racial Violence: The Worker in Chicago, 1894–1919," *Labor History*, X (Summer 1969)

Paul B. Worthman, "Black Workers and Labor Unions in Birmingham, Alabama, 1897–1904," *Labor History*, X (Summer 1969)

Herbert G. Gutman, "Black Coal Miners and the Greenback Labor Party," *Labor History*, X (Summer 1969)

Kenneth O. Porter, "Negro Labor in the Western Cattle Industry, 1866–1900," *Labor History*, X (Summer 1969)

Jack Abramowitz, "The Negro in the Populist Movement," *Journal of Negro History*, XXXVIII (July 1953)

Robert Saunders, "Southern Populists and the Negro, 1893–1895," *Journal of Negro History*, LIV (July, 1969)

Francis M. Wilhoit, "An Interpretation of Populism's Impact on the Georgia Negro," *Journal of Negro History*, LII (April 1967)

William H. Chafe, "The Negro and Populism: A Kansas Case Study," *Journal of Southern History*, XXXIV (August 1968)

Perry E. Gianakos, "The Spanish-American War and the Double Paradox of the Negro American," *Phylon*, XXVI (Spring 1965)

Philip W. Kennedy, "The Racial Overtones of Imperialism as a Campaign Issue, 1900," *Mid-America*, XLVIII (July 1966)

IV: The Progressive Failure, 1901–1919

I. A. Newby, *Jim Crow's Defense: Anti-Negro Thought in America, 1900–1930* (Baton Rouge, 1965)

Guion G. Johnson, "The Ideology of White Supremacy, 1876–1910," in Fletcher M. Green (ed.), *Essays in Southern History* . . . (Chapel Hill, 1949)

Claude H. Nolen, *The Negro's Image in the South: The Anatomy of White Supremacy* (Lexington, Ky., 1967)

Maxwell Bloomfield, "Dixon's *The Leopard's Spots*: A Study in Popular Racism," *American Quarterly*, XVI (Fall 1964)

Louis R. Harlan, *Separate and Unequal: Public School Campaigns and Racism in the Southern Seaboard States, 1901–1915* (Chapel Hill, 1958)

Roger L. Rice, "Residential Segregation by Law, 1910–1917," *Journal of Southern History*, XXXIV (May 1968)

Andrew Buni, *The Negro in Virginia Politics, 1902–1965* (Charlottesville, Va., 1967)

Charles E. Wynes, "The Evolution of Jim Crow Laws in Twentieth Century Virginia," *Phylon*, XXVIII (Winter 1967)

Francis B. Simkins, *Pitchfork Ben Tillman: South Carolinian* (Baton Rouge, 1944)

Claire S. Lopez, "James K. Vardaman and the Negro: The Foundation of Mississippi's Racial Policy," *Southern Quarterly*, III (January 1965)

William F. Holmes, "Whitecapping: Agrarian Violence in Mississippi, 1902–1906," *Journal of Southern History*, XXXV (May 1969)

Dewey W. Grantham, Jr., "The Progressive Movement and the Negro," *South Atlantic Quarterly*, LIV (October 1955)

Harvey Wish, "Negro Education and the Progressive Movement," *Journal of Negro History*, XLIX (July 1964)

Seth Scheiner, "President Theodore Roosevelt and the Negro," *Journal of Negro History*, XLVII (July 1962)

James A. Tinsley, "Roosevelt, Foraker, and the Brownsville Affray," *Journal of Negro History*, XLI (January 1956)

Emma L. Thornbrough, "The Brownsville Episode and the Negro Vote," *Mississippi Valley Historical Review*, XLIV (December 1957)

John B. Wiseman, "Racism in Democratic Politics, 1904–1912," *Mid-America*, LI (January 1969)

August Meier, "The Negro and the Democratic Party, 1875–1915," *Phylon*, XVII (Summer 1956)

Aruthur S. Link, "The Negro as a Factor in the Campaign of 1912," *Journal of Negro History*, XXXII (January 1947)

George E. Mowry, "The South and the Progressive Lily White Party of 1912," *Journal of Southern History*, VI (May 1940)

G. N. Green, "Republicans, Bull Moose, and Negroes in Florida, 1912," *Florida Historical Quarterly*, XLIII (October 1964)

Willard H. Smith, "William Jennings Bryan and Racism," *Journal of Negro History*, LIV (April 1969)

Kathleen L. Woglemuth, "Woodrow Wilson's Appointment Policy and the Negro," *Journal of Southern History*, XXIV (February 1958)

Kathleen L. Woglemuth, "Woodrow Wilson and Federal Segregation," *Journal of Negro History*, XLIV (April 1959)

George C. Osborn, "The Problem of the Negro in Government: 1913," *The Historian*, XXIII (May 1961)

Henry Blumenthal, "Woodrow Wilson and the Race Question," *Journal of Negro History*, XLVIII (January 1963)

William Toll, "A Study of the Institutional and Psychological Consequences of Segregation Under Woodrow Wilson," *Journal of Negro History*, LIII (January 1968)

Nancy J. Weiss, "The Negro and the New Freedom: Fighting Wilsonian Segregation," *Political Science Quarterly*, LXXXIV (March 1969)

August Meier and Elliott Rudwick, "The Rise of the Segregation in the Federal Bureaucracy, 1900–1930," *Phylon*, XXVIII (Summer 1967)

Richard M. Abrams, "Woodrow Wilson and the Southern Congressmen, 1913–1916," *Journal of Southern History*, XXII (November 1956)

Jane Lang and Harry N. Scheiber, "The Wilson Administration and the Wartime Mobilization of Black Americans," *Labor History*, X (Summer 1969)

Walter White, *Rope and Faggot: A Biography of Judge Lynch* (New York, 1929)

Charles Crowe, "Racial Violence and Social Reform—Origins of the Atlanta Riot of 1906," *Journal of Negro History*, LIII (July 1968)

Charles Crowe, "Racial Massacre in Atlanta, September 22, 1906," *Journal of Negro History*, LIV (April 1969)

James L. Crouthemal, "The Springfield Race Riot of 1908," *Journal of Negro History*, XLV (July 1960)

Edgar A. Schuler, "The Houston Race Riot, 1917," *Journal of Negro History*, XXIX (July 1944)

Elliott M. Rudwick, *Race Riot at East St. Louis, July 2, 1917* (Carbondale, Ill., 1964)

Lloyd M. Abernethy, "The Washington Race War of July 1919," *Maryland Historical Magazine*, LVIII (December 1963)

Carl Sandburg, *The Chicago Race Riots* (New York, 1919)

Elliott M. Rudwick, "The Niagara Movement," *Journal of Negro History*, XLII (July 1957)

Mary White Ovington, *The Walls Came Tumbling Down* (New York, 1947)

Charles Flint Kellogg, *NAACP: A History of the National Association for the Advancement of Colored People*, Vol. I, 1909–1920 (Baltimore, 1967)

August Meier and Elliott M. Rudwick, "Early Boycotts of Segregated Schools: The East Orange, New Jersey, Experience, 1899–1906, *History of Education Quarterly*, VII (Spring 1967)

Edgar Allan Toppin, "Walter White and the Atlanta NAACP's Fight for Equal Schools, 1916–1917," *History of Education Quarterly*, VII (Spring 1967)

Ruth Worthy, "William Monroe Trotter, 1872–1934," *Journal of Negro History*, XLIII (July 1958)

W. E. B. Du Bois, *The Souls of Black Folk* (Chicago, 1903)

W. E. B. Du Bois, *Dusk of Dawn: An Essay Toward an Autobiography of a Race Concept* (New York, 1940)

W. E. B. Du Bois, *The Autobiography of W. E. B. Du Bois: A Soliloquy on Viewing My Life from the Last Decade of Its First Century* (New York, 1968)

Francis L. Broderick, *W. E. B. Du Bois: Negro Leader in a Time of Crisis* (Stanford, 1959)

Elliott M. Rudwick, *W. E. B. Du Bois: A Study in Minority Group Leadership* (Philadelphia, 1960)

Mary L. Chaffee, "William E. B. Du Bois' Concept of the Racial Problem in the United States," *Journal of Negro History*, XLI (July 1956)

V: The Need for Identity, 1919–1929

T. Lynn Smith, "The Redistribution of the Negro Population of the United States, 1910–1960," *Journal of Negro History*, LI (July 1966)

Emmett J. Scott, *Negro Migration During the War* (New York, 1920)

Louise Kennedy, *The Negro Peasant Turns Cityward* (New York, 1930)

Dewey H. Palmer, "Moving North: Negro Migration During World War I," *Phylon*, XXVIII (Spring 1967)

James Weldon Johnson, *Black Manhattan* (New York, 1930)

Herman D. Bloch, *Circle of Discrimination: An Economic and Social History of the Black Man in New York* (New York, 1969)

Seth M. Scheiner, *Negro Mecca: A History of the Negro in New York City, 1865–1920* (New York, 1965)

Gilbert Osofsky, *Harlem: The Making of a Ghetto: Negro New York, 1890–1930* (New York, 1966)

Allan H. Spear, *Black Chicago: The Making of a Negro Ghetto, 1890–1920* (Chicago, 1967)

Abram L. Harris, *The Negro as Capitalist: A Study of Banking and Business Among American Negroes* (Philadelphia, 1936)

Charles H. Wesley, *Negro Labor in the United States, 1850–1925* . . . (New York, 1927)

Sterling D. Spero and Abram L. Harris, *The Black Worker: The Negro and the Labor Movement* (New York, 1931)

Richard B. Sherman, "Republicans and Negroes: The Lessons of Normalcy," *Phylon*, XXVII (Spring 1966)

Richard B. Sherman, "The Harding Administration and the Negro: An Opportunity Lost," *Journal of Negro History*, XLIX (July 1964)

Hugh D. Reagan, "Race as a Factor in the Presidential Election of 1928 in Alabama," *Alabama Review*, XIX (January 1966)

David M. Chalmers, *Hooded Americanism: The History of the Ku Klux Klan* (New York, 1965)

Arnold S. Rice, *The Ku Klux Klan in American Politics* (Washington, 1962)

Kenneth T. Jackson, *The Ku Klux Klan in the City, 1915–1930* (New York, 1967)

Robert Moats Miller, "A Note on the Relationship Between the Protestant Churches and the Revived Ku Klux Klan," *Journal of Southern History* XXII (August 1956)

Emerson Loucks, *The Ku Klux Klan in Pennsylvania* (Harrisburg, 1936)

Emma Lou Thornbrough, "Segregation in Indiana During the Klan Era of the 1920's," *Mississippi Valley Historical Review*, XLVII (March 1961)

David M. Chalmers, "The Ku Klux Klan in the Sunshine State: The 1920's," *Florida Historical Quarterly*, XLII (January 1964)

Charles C. Alexander, *The Ku Klux Klan in the Southwest* (Lexington, Ky., 1965)

Sheldon, Neuringer, "Governor Walton's War on the Ku Klux Klan . . ."
　　Chronicles of Oklahoma, XLV (Summer 1967)
Harold F. Gosnell, Negro Politicians: The Rise of Negro Politics in Chicago
　　(Chicago, 1935)
Edwin S. Redkey, Black Exodus: Black Nationalist and Back-to-Africa Move-
　　ments, 1890–1910 (New Haven, 1969)
Bernard Eisenberg, "Kelly Miller: The Negro Leader as a Marginal Man,"
　　Journal of Negro History, XLV (July 1960)
Ben F. Rogers, "William E. B. Du Bois, Marcus Garvey, and Pan Africa,"
　　Journal of Negro History, XL (April 1955)
E. David Cronon, Black Moses: The Story of Marcus Garvey and the Universal
　　Negro Improvement Association (Madison, Wisc., 1955)
Robert H. Brisbane, "Some New Light on the Garvey Movement," Journal of
　　Negro History, XXXVI (January 1951)
Alain Locke (ed.), The New Negro (New York, 1925)
Gilbert Osofsky, "Symbols of the Jazz Age: The New Negro and Harlem Dis-
　　covered," American Quarterly, XVII (Summer 1965)

Harold Cruse, The Crisis of the Negro Intellectual (New York, 1967)
Rebecca Barton, Race Consciousness and the American Negro . . . [in fiction]
　　(Copenhagen, 1934)
Hugh M. Gloster, Negro Voices in American Fiction (Chapel Hill, 1948)
Samuel W. Allen, The American Negro Writer and His Roots (New York,
　　1959)
Herbert Hill, Anger and Beyond: The Negro Writer in the United States (New
　　York, 1966)
John Henrik Clarke, "The Origin and Growth of Afro-American Literature,"
　　Journal of Human Relations, XVI (3d Quarter, 1968)
Edward Margolies, Native Sons: A Critical Study of Twentieth Century Negro
　　American Authors (Philadelphia, 1968)
Robert A. Bone, The Negro Novel in America (rev. edition, New Haven,
　　1965)
Stephen Bronz, Roots of Negro Racial Consciousness: The 1920's, Three Har-
　　lem Renaissance Authors (New York, 1964)
Langston Hughes, The Big Sea (New York, 1940)
Wayne Cooper, "Claude McKay and the New Negro of the 1920's," Phylon,
　　XXV (Fall 1964)
L. P. Fullinwider, "Jean Toomer: Lost Generation or Negro Renaissance?"
　　Phylon, XXVII (Winter 1966)

VI: Hunger—Depression and New Deal, 1929–1941

Gunnar Myrdal, An American Dilemma: The Negro Problem and Modern
　　Democracy, 2 vols. (New York, 1944)
Leslie H. Fishel, Jr., "The Negro in the New Deal," Wisconsin Magazine of
　　History, XLVIII (Winter 1964–65)
Frank Freidel, F. D. R. and the South (Baton Rouge, 1965)
James A. Harrell, "Negro Leadership in the Election Year 1936," Journal of
　　Southern History, XXXIV (November 1968)

David Eugene Conrad, *The Forgotten Farmers: The Story of Sharecroppers in the New Deal* (Urbana, Ill., 1956)

Donald H. Grubbs, "Gardner Jackson, That 'Socialist' Tenant Farmers' Union, and the New Deal," *Agricultural History*, XLII (April 1968)

Dan T. Carter, *Scottsboro: A Tragedy of the American South* (Baton Rouge, 1969)

Hugh T. Murray, Jr., "The NAACP Versus the Communist Party: The Scottsboro Rape Cases, 1931–1932," *Phylon*, XXVIII (Fall 1967)

Robert M. Miller, "The Protestant Churches and Lynching, 1919–1939," *Journal of Negro History*, XLII (April 1957)

Fred Greenbaum, "The Anti-Lynching Bill of 1935: The Irony of 'Equal Justice—Under Law,' " *Journal of Human Relations*, XV (3rd Quarter, 1967)

Robert W. Du Bay, "Mississippi and the Proposed Federal Anti-Lynching Bills of 1937–1938," *Southern Quarterly*, VI (October 1968)

Robert L. Zangrando, "The NAACP and a Federal Anti-Lynching Bill, 1934–1940," *Journal of Negro History*, L (April 1965)

Walter White, *A Man Called White: The Autobiography of Walter White* (New York, 1948)

Catherine O. Peare, *Mary McLeod Bethune* (New York, 1951)

Horace R. Cayton and George S. Mitchell, *Black Workers and the New Unions* (Chapel Hill, 1939)

Raymond Wolters, "Section 7a and the Black Worker," *Labor History*, X (Summer 1969)

James S. Olson, "Organized Black Leadership and Industrial Unionism: The Racial Response, 1936–1945," *Labor History*, X (Summer 1969)

Wilson Record, *The Negro and the Communist Party* (Chapel Hill, 1951)

Wilson Record, *Race and Radicalism: The NAACP and the Communist Party in Conflict* (Ithaca, 1964)

John W. Van Zanten, "Communist Theory and the Negro Question," *Review of Politics*, XXIX (October 1967)

Constance Webb, *Richard Wright: A Biography* (New York, 1968

Vaughn D. Bornet, "Historical Scholarship, Communism, and the Negro," *Journal of Negro History*, XXXVII (July 1952)

VII: HOPE—THE FOUR FREEDOMS AND THE BLACK MAN, 1941–1954

Ulysses Lee, *The U. S. Army in World War II: The Employment of Negro Troops* (Washington, 1966)

Lee Nichols, *Breakthrough on the Color Front* (New York, 1954)

Lawrence D. Reddick, "The Negro in the Navy in World War II," *Journal of Negro History*, XXXII (April 1947)

Dennis D. Nelson, *The Integration of the Negro into the United States Navy* (New York, 1951)

Lawrence D. Reddick, "The Negro Policy of the American Army Since World War II," *Journal of Negro History*, XXVIII (April 1953)

Richard M. Dalfiume, "The Fahy Committee and Desegregation of the Armed Forces," *The Historian*, XXXI (November 1968)

Monroe Billington, "Freedom To Serve: The President's Committee on Equality of Treatment and Opportunity in the Armed Forces," *Journal of Negro History*, LI (October 1966)

Richard M. Dalfiume, "The 'Forgotten Years' of the Negro Revolution," *Journal of American History*, LV (June 1968)

Selz C. Mayo and C. Horace Hamilton, "Rural Negro Population of the South in Transition [1940–60]," *Phylon*, XXIV (Summer 1963)

Harvard Sitkoff, "The Detroit Race Riot of 1943," *Michigan History*, LIII (Fall 1969)

Kenneth B. Clark, "Group Violence . . . : A Study of the 1943 Harlem Riot," *Journal of Social Psychology*, XX (July 1944)

Louis C. Kesselman, *The Social Politics of FEPC* (Chapel Hill, 1948)

Louis Ruchames, *Race, Jobs and Politics: The Story of the FEPC* (New York, 1953)

Samuel Krislow, *The Negro in Federal Employment: The Quest for Equal Opportunity* (Minneapolis, 1967)

Donald Cowgill, "Trends in Residential Segregation of Non-Whites in American Cities, 1940–1950," *American Sociological Review*, XXI (February 1956)

Chester L. Hunt, "Housing: The Northern Conscience and the American Dilemma," *Antioch Review*, XIX (Winter 1959–60)

Henry Lee Moon, *Balance of Power: The Negro Vote* (Garden City, N.Y., 1948)

Oscar Glantz, "The Negro Voter in Northern Industrial Cities," *Western Political Quarterly*, XIII (December 1960)

Harry Holloway, "The Texas Negro as a Voter," *Phylon*, XXIV (Summer 1963)

James Q. Wilson, *Negro Politics* (Chicago, 1960)

Hanes Walton, Jr., *Black Political Parties: A Historical and Political Analysis* (New York, 1969)

Richard Bardolph, *The Negro Vanguard* (New York, 1959)

Arvah E. Strickland, *History of the Chicago Urban League* (Urbana, Ill., 1966)

Loren Miller, *The Petitioners: The Story of the Supreme Court of the United States and the Negro* (New York, 1966)

Clement E. Vose, *Caucasians Only: The Supreme Court, the NAACP, and the Restrictive Covenant Cases* (Berkeley, 1967)

John P. Roche, "Plessy v. Ferguson: Requiescat in Pace?" *University of Pennsylvania Law Review*, CIII (October 1954)

R. Ray McCain, "Reactions to the United States Supreme Court Segregation Decision of 1954," *Georgia Historical Quarterly*, LII (December 1968)

Archibald Cox, *The Warren Court: Constitutional Decision as an Instrument of Reform* (Cambridge, 1968)

M. Lytle Clifford, *The Warren Court and Its Critics* (Tucson, 1968)

Albert P. Blaustein and Clarence Clyde Ferguson, Jr., *Desegregation and the Law: The Meaning and Effect of the School Segregation Cases* (rev. edition, New York, 1962)

Numan V. Bartley, *The Rise of Massive Resistance: Race and Politics in the South During the 1950's* (Baton Rouge, 1969)

DATE DUE

MAR 1 8'		.	
NOV 1 6 '72			
E H			
MAR 1 4 '78			
FEB 22 '78			
FEB 13 '79			
FEB 12 '79			
APR 3 0 '90			
DE 1 2 '92			
DEC 1 4 '9			
APR 2 6 '95			
AP 1 2 '9			
GAYLORD			PRINTED IN U.S.A.